THREE LOVES OF DOSTOEVSKY

Books *by* MARC SLONIM

THE EPIC OF RUSSIAN LITERATURE
MODERN RUSSIAN LITERATURE
THREE LOVES OF DOSTOEVSKY

Anthologies

SOVIET LITERATURE (edited with George Reavey)
MODERN ITALIAN SHORT STORIES
THIS THING CALLED LOVE (edited with Harvey Breit)

THREE LOVES
OF
DOSTOEVSKY

▲

▲

RINEHART & COMPANY, INC.

NEW YORK   TORONTO

Published simultaneously in Canada by
Clarke, Irwin & Company, Ltd., Toronto

25291

To Tania

FOREWORD

THIS BOOK IS A NARRATIVE, BASED ON CAREFULLY CHECKED
material, of the love life of Dostoevsky—who was not only
one of the greatest writers of the nineteenth century but, at
the same time, an extraordinary man and lover.

It is well known that Dostoevsky was a fascinating story-
teller. His novels brought him universal fame during his lifetime, and make him dear to the modern reader because of their
psychological insight and philosophical depth. They are full
of strange plots, fantastic characters, haunting situations and
surprise endings. They explore the dark recesses of the human
soul and deal with perversions of the mind and flesh. Unbridled
instincts, insane drives, pathological twists of spirit and body,
fill his memorable pages with fire and unrest. Yet hardly any
of his works is as startling, romantic or passionate as his own
life—particularly the underground life which he spent with
prostitutes, idealistic married women, women of the world, attractive and independent, and young girls, sensual and self-
sacrificing.

Dostoevsky's widow, as well as his daughter, who together
set the pattern for many later biographers and critics, simply
avoided mentioning certain facts which might throw an unfavorable light on the pure, virtuous, saintlike image of the
great writer they were trying to transmit to posterity. The
widow did not merely conceal many aspects of her husband's
tempestuous life, but blacked out with indelible ink various
passages in his letters and papers that she considered risqué,

indecent or "undesirable." Dostoevsky's own reserve was also responsible for the somewhat falsified picture of his complexes and erotic adventures that has come down to us. In his correspondence, and even in conversation, he jealously guarded his intimate feelings and actions, so that in many instances we are permitted only a casual glimpse of the truth. As far as certain basic aspects of his life are concerned—such as his epilepsy, his presumed rape of a child, other sexual aberrations—we are reduced to conjectures.

However, despite the scarcity of material, and the gaps and evasions in what we have, we do possess a sufficient amount of data to attempt a reconstruction of the principal events of his inner history. We can trace the highly controversial pattern of his affections, and we are well informed about the women he loved, since several of them left revealing diaries or memoirs.

To follow Dostoevsky through his erotic "underground" is in many respects an excellent way to understand his personality, and makes a real contribution to the comprehensive interpretation of his work. But above all, we are offered a story of unusual human significance and depth. One does not need to be a rabid Dostoevskian, or even much of a reader of his tales, to be stirred by the odd and passionate record of his love affairs. It reveals so much about sex, women, man's nature, love, marriage, that it ceases to be merely a footnote to literary history and enters into the category of genuine, firsthand human documents.

The fact that there are very few notes should not mislead the reader or embarrass the scholar. The accuracy of every fact reported in these pages, down to the most trivial details, is vouchsafed for by letters, diaries, recollections of contemporaries and other original source material. The reader will find at the end of the volume a partial list of the many works the author consulted during his three years of research.

CONTENTS

PART ONE
MARIA:
▲

The First Love

EARLY IN THE MORNING OF THE TWENTY-SECOND OF DE-
cember, 1849, Baron Alexander Wrangel, a sixteen-year-old
cadet at the Alexandrovsky Lycée, looked out of his window
and saw, in the dismal murk of a St. Petersburg winter, a string
of sleigh-coaches, each drawn by two horses. Such coaches were
usually favored by the pupils of the Smolny Institute for aristocratic young ladies or by the girls studying ballet at the Imperial Theatrical School. This morning, however, instead of
pretty young girls the coaches were carrying political criminals:
twenty members of the Petrashevsky group were being driven
to their execution.

Their arrest at the beginning of the year had made a great
stir in the society of the northern capital. It was rumored that
the Secret Police had unearthed a plot against the Czar; that
the group believed in socialism, civil rights, emancipation of
the peasants and other outrageous ideas. Michael Petrashev-
sky-Butashevich, leader of the revolutionaries, as well as some
of his friends (N. Speshnev, N. Kashkin, Al. Europeus), were
graduates of the very Lycée in which Wrangel was enrolled,
and consequently the gendarmes had raided its classes in
search of subversive literature.

Wrangel had naturally become interested in the affair of
the Petrashevists, as they were called, but one could hardly
discuss them except among one's closest friends, and even then
only in a lowered voice. It was said that Czar Nicholas I was

angry and disturbed, and wanted the members of the group severely punished as a public example. Karl Egorovich Manderstern (subsequently the Commandant of the Fortress of Sts. Peter and Paul), a relative of Wrangel's, had acted as adjutant general on the military tribunal that sat in judgment on the Petrashevists, and it was from him that the young cadet had learned, while home for the Christmas vacation, that many of them had been sentenced to execution before a firing squad.

Fyodor Mikhailovich Dostoevsky was one of the condemned. Very recently Wrangel had read *Poor Folk*, the novel which had laid the foundation of Dostoevsky's reputation as a writer, and his unfinished tale, *Netochka Nezvanova*. Both had made a strong impression on the boy, and he was very much grieved to learn that the writer he admired was about to die.

On the memorable morning of the twenty-second of December, Wrangel's uncle, an officer in the Horse Guards, had to be present with his company at the execution of the Petrashevists. He agreed to take his nephew along. When they arrived at Semenovsky Place, where the execution was to be carried out, they found a cordon of troops already ranged in a hollow square. Behind the black ranks of the soldiers milled the idle populace—muzhiks, pedlars, rabble in sheepskin jackets and short overcoats. There were practically no spectators of the better sort. Another kinsman of Wrangel's, also an officer wearing full dress, hurried over and begged him to leave without delay—otherwise the curious cadet might be seen, might even through 'some misfortune be suspected of criminal sympathy for the condemned men!

Wrangel became a little scared and promised to go home. He did not leave, however, but lost himself in the crowd. This bold action he kept a secret which he dared not share with anyone.

By standing on tiptoe and craning his neck, he could see a wooden scaffold in the middle of the square and some posts set into the ground. The condemned men (nine on one side of the scaffold and eleven on the other) had been stripped of their outer garments and were standing in the twenty-degree frost only in their shirts. Wrangel heard a clerk reading out the sentence: "Dostoevsky, Fyodor Mikhailovich . . . for participation in criminal designs and for the promulgation of a letter by the littérateur Belinsky, the said letter filled with scurrilities against the Orthodox Church and the reigning Power, and for the attempt, in collusion with others, to disseminate by means of a lithographic process certain writings against the government, is deprived of all property rights . . . condemned to be shot to death."

A priest with a cross replaced the officer on the scaffold and called upon the condemned to make their last confessions. Only one man approached to be shriven. The others merely put their lips to the silver cross when the priest quickly and silently held it up to each one. Then shrouds were put on Petrashevsky, Mombelli and Grigoriev, and these three were blindfolded and tied to posts. Dostoevsky was waiting his turn in the next group. A platoon led by an officer ranged itself before the posts; the soldiers brought up their guns and took aim. But just as the command of "Fire!" was about to be given, one of the higher officers waved a white handkerchief, the execution was halted and the condemned were untied from their posts. Grigoriev was swaying: he had gone insane during these few minutes of waiting for the end. Mombelli's hair had turned white.

The new sentence was read out: commutation through the Czar's grace. Four years at hard labor and another four years of military servitude, both terms to be served in Siberia, was Dostoevsky's punishment. The victims were allowed to put on their jackets and overcoats. Wrangel stole out of the crowd, trembling with excitement and pity, and hastened home without waiting to see them carried off to the Fortress of Sts. Peter and Paul.

Four years later, in 1853, after his graduation from the Lycée, Wrangel served briefly in the Ministry of Justice and, at his own request, was appointed prosecutor in the recently established Semipalatinsk Area, consisting of the southeastern regions of the Kirghiz Steppes and the southwestern Altai District. At that time Siberia had been little explored and Wrangel was drawn to remote parts: he was more interested in travel and hunting than in jurisprudence.

When his appointment became known in St. Petersburg, he was fated to hear the name of Dostoevsky once more: the former Petrashevist had just finished his penal servitude in Omsk, and on the seventh of March, 1854, was enrolled as a private in the Seventh Siberian Battalion of the Line, stationed at Semipalatinsk. Michael Dostoevsky asked the new prosecutor to carry a letter and some money to his brother Fyodor, and the young man promptly agreed.

In November, 1854, Wrangel at last reached Semipalatinsk and, having barely taken up his quarters at the house of a local merchant, sent word to Dostoevsky to call: it seemed to him that they had known each other for a long time and he impatiently awaited his meeting with the ex-writer, ex-convict, and now private of the line. When Dostoevsky came into the room, Wrangel could not take his eyes off this stocky soldier in his baggy uniform of coarse cloth. Everything about his appearance, figure and dress was plebeian: he decidedly did not seem to belong to the gentry or the intelligentsia. His face, too, was the sort one. often finds in Russia among artisans, burghers and godfearing merchants: a wiry, ruddy, spade-shaped beard; a thin and stubborn mouth under a thick mustache; light, closely cropped hair over a broad brow; the eyes, with bluish shadows under them, so deep sunken that they seemed to have fallen through. His face was of an unhealthy color, ashen, freckled, the skin of the cheeks and forehead furrowed with wrinkles. His voice was stifled, somewhat hoarse (the consequence of a throat ailment), and he spoke quietly, sparingly, as though unwilling to talk, choosing simple words. When he grew animated, however, his speech became sonorous and rapid, his words rang with passion, he almost spluttered; his movements, despite their impulsiveness, became lively and easy; he was transformed, and not a trace remained of his former moroseness.

Tears came to Dostoevsky's eyes as he read his brother's letter. Just then mail from Russia was brought to Wrangel and, recalling how remote his own family and St. Petersburg were, and watching his caller's exhausted, suffering face, he could not restrain his own tears. The young bureaucrat and the political criminal exchanged looks and embraced. This moment marked the beginning of their friendship. Wrangel was twenty-one at the time; Dostoevsky was thirty-three.

FYODOR DOSTOEVSKY, BORN IN 1821, HAD BEEN BROUGHT up in a large family of five brothers and two sisters, absolute power over which was wielded by the father. Michael, the elder, a doctor attached to the Marinsky Hospital for the Poor in Moscow, completely controlled the lives of his children. Dr. Dostoevsky was fond of saying that an ancestor of his had been with Prince Kurbsky at the time of the latter's famous correspondence with Czar Ivan the Terrible, and that his line went back to the Tartar Golden Horde. He himself, however, could boast neither of distinction nor wealth. The son of a priest, he belonged to the impoverished and deteriorated gentry and could hardly be regarded as successful. Ambitious and harsh, he considered himself overlooked: his career was a most modest one and he barely managed to make ends meet. Hot-tempered, morose and suspicious, he was given to pathological exaggerations in his fancies. He continually imagined that all sorts of wrongs had been done him. He accused his wife of infidelity (in the seventh month of pregnancy!) and was tortured by his suspicions. His outbursts of wrath also bore the same abnormal character. It is possible that Fyodor's epilepsy was due to an eruption of his father's uncurbed temper. Possibly too there was some act of cruelty to his mother or one of the domestics. Yanovski, who was the family physician, speaks of this in enigmatic terms: "Fyodor Mikhailovich was overtaken precisely during his childhood by that sombre and oppressive Something which never passes without exacting a penalty during mature years."

That the father was "horrible" during such flare-ups we know from the testimony of his son Andrew, but it is also known that he never laid a finger on his children and that corporal punishment, so generally accepted at that time not only in Russia but in England and America, was never resorted to in his family. Was this, perhaps, what Fyodor was thinking of when he wrote enthusiastically to his brother Michael in later years: "Come, our parents were people of advanced views." The relations between father and children, especially the sons, were really friendly. There is no doubt, however, that an iron discipline prevailed in the godfearing and conservative household of Dr. Dostoevsky and that the heavy hand of the father was felt in all the small details of family life. It is difficult to form a judgment concerning Fyodor's subconscious enmity toward his father and his attachment to his mother. The children were brought up to obedience; the father instilled fear and respect into them and they had to toe the line. In the small wing of the Marinsky Hospital where the Dostoevskys lived with their seven domestics, no frivolity of any sort was tolerated. A puritan atmosphere prevailed in the household, and women could be referred to only in poetic terms. The brothers Dostoevsky could not possibly have carried on any flirtations or have been openly infatuated in their youth: they were never allowed to go anywhere by themselves and were never given any pocket money—up to the age of seventeen Fyodor did not have a copper for personal expenses and, in consequence, did not know how to handle money in later life. Michael and Fyodor were taken in the family coach to the Chermak boarding school and brought back home the same way for the weekends. There were few domestic diversions, and all these were of the most innocent nature. In the summer the family went to the Darovoye estate (it became Dostoevsky Kolhoz—or Collective Farm—after 1930) which was bought with great hardship in 1831, after Fyodor's tenth birthday. There the children enjoyed a certain amount of freedom, playing with the village small fry; nevertheless the parents always kept a close watch on them as adolescents. "Our father," Andrew (the youngest son) used to say, "was exceedingly observant and watched after the morality of the children, especially my older brothers when they were already young men. I do not remember a single occasion when they went out alone."

The sisters, who were younger than Fyodor, and the little country girls during the summer, were all the feminine society the boy knew up to the age of sixteen. His first erotic sensations were, of course, bound up with these recollections of childhood, and this was reflected in several ways in his later life and work. As a writer Dostoevsky revealed a heightened interest in little girls, while corruption of the morals of a minor was a theme of unfailing fascination for him: it was not merely by chance that he devoted to it staggering pages in *The Humiliated and Wronged, Crime and Punishment* and *The Possessed.*

The relations between the parents created another unconscious source for first impulses of love and hatred.

Dr. Dostoevsky had, it seems clear, those traits of duality and even neurosis, which proved so sharply contradictory in his great son. The father loved his children very much, yet ruled them with an iron hand, so that they did not dare to sit down in his presence whenever he tutored them. He willingly spent money on their education, yet was pettily calculating and miserly in everything else. It is true he was poor; money did not come to him easily, and he had to pinch and scrape to meet his obligations in buying Darovoye. The estate did not do well: there were several dry spells and a fire, disasters which seemed to the owner too catastrophic to get over and which deepened his natural melancholy. Fyodor, like his father, lived in constant dread of being left without a kopeck, but the father's tightfistedness was in the son's case transformed into reckless generosity, into financial anarchy. Fyodor's gloom, his reserve, his lack of manners and amiability were wholly inherited from his father. Both father and son had marked characteristics of pettiness, despotism and irritability. Dr. Dostoevsky was envious and embittered by nature, but he concealed his ambition and selfishness, just as his son did after him. The father led a lonely life: he had no relations of his own; it was his wife's people who came to the house, and the head of the family felt himself isolated. Also, certain of his wife's relations (the merchants Kumanin, for instance) were rich, and this helped to form a complex of discontent and inferiority which in its turn led to injured pride and pathological touchiness.

Maria Dostoyevskaya (nee Nechayeva) came from a family of well-to-do Moscow merchants. As a matter of fact, she was not a cowed and uncomplaining victim of a tyrannical husband, as certain biographers have gone out of their way to prove, but was innately cheerful, intelligent and energetic. Naturally, she fully acknowledged the authority of the head of the family, yet was not at all passive and without a voice. She genuinely loved her husband with a deep and ardent love. Her letters to him evince both a naïve devotion and a considerable poetic strain: for a woman of the 1830's, with only a modest education, she wrote exceptionally well and showed a certain literary gift which she transmitted to two of her children. She not only did not live in fear and trembling of her fiery-tempered husband, but was his constant prop and helpmate, encouraging him in times of emotional stress and trying to overcome his testiness and melancholy. She always told him and wrote him the "harsh truth" (to use an expression of hers) about how she felt. Gentle and kindly, she was at the same time noted for both practicality and shrewd-ness, and whether in town or country, ran the household with a firm hand, like so many active, typically Russian women. And that was the image of her which Fyodor retained in his memory. In appearance she was exceptionally feminine and fragile; her health, weakened by frequent childbirth, was deli-cate. She was unable to nurse her children and had to hire country wet nurses. While Fyodor was still a child, it was discovered that she had tuberculosis; she was ailing much of the time, and whenever the children wanted to kiss her wasted, blue-veined hand, they had to approach the sickbed where she spent so many of her days. This formed another ineradica-ble memory: Fyodor was to remember his mother's illness throughout his life, and in his consciousness love and pity, femininity and blight, blended into an indivisible and touch-ing whole. She died comparatively young, in 1837, before Fyodor had reached sixteen.

After their mother's death the father took Michael and Fyodor to St. Petersburg and placed them in the School for Military Engineering. From the monastic seclusion of a clan-nish family, Fyodor was catapulted into the bureaucratic at-mosphere of an inbred military school: the novices (or *trouts* as they were called) were snubbed and hazed by their seniors. This institution was admittedly of higher scholastic standing than mere military academies and, as the novelist Leskov noted later on, not a few excellent men emerged from it. How-ever, the spirit of deadening discipline and goose-stepping was there just the same. The other students met Fyodor with jeers: he had neither manners, nor money nor an illustrious name. At home his family had considered him lively—if any-thing, he was reproached for his liveliness. Both his father and his mother agreed that Fyodor was what would now be called a ball of fire. He was the leader in all games and showed an unusually high spirit and imagination. Among strangers, however, he kept to himself. Konstantin Trutovsky, a school-mate of his who later became known as artist and academician, tells us that in 1838 Dostoevsky was lean and gawky, that his clothes hung on him like a sack, and that although one could sense his kindliness, he was morose and constrained in ap-pearance and manners. He was unsociable, even ridiculous at times and must have looked like an unfledged nestling to all those aristocratic youths who at seventeen had already been initiated into the mysteries of love by serf girls or St. Peters-burg prostitutes. Fyodor, however, was far better at discussing Pushkin, whom he deified (after the poet's death he asked Dr. Dostoevsky for permission to wear mourning), or Schiller, or historical personalities—anybody, in short, but women. Only two or three of his friends knew that, despite his outward list-lessness and aloofness, he was an ardent and impulsive youth who could be sharp-tongued on occasion. Even at that time he was known for his ecstatic idealism and a hypersensitive im-pressionability. He avoided social calls, did not know how to behave in company and became dreadfully embarrassed in the society of women. There is a story to the effect that, at the be-ginning of 1840, he fainted away at a soirée given by the Viel-gorskys when he was presented to Seniavina, a celebrated beauty of that period. It is possible that this fainting spell was of an epileptic nature.

All this does not mean that Dostoevsky was a scarecrow, a simpleton, or altogether ignorant of the facts of life. At any rate, they were brought sharply to his attention in 1839, when he received the staggering news of his father's death. After his wife died, Dr. Dostoevsky had retired to settle down in the country, where he took for his mistress Katherine Alexandrova, who had been his servant in Moscow. He drank hard, and flogged his serfs and domestics at the slightest pretext, while his apprehensiveness, suspiciousness and outbursts of rage be-came practically hysterical. When Fyodor wrote him in 1838 about flunking an examination, he had a nervous seizure. This, however, did not prevent Dr. Dostoevsky from writing back to his son in gentle and restrained terms.

The peasants hated him and had evidently formed a plot against him in 1839, with the active participation of Ephim Maximov, uncle of the doctor's mistress. One day that summer, when he was cursing them furiously, a group of peasants fell upon the demented landowner and killed him. They must have given a considerable bribe to the authorities who came to make an investigation: the conclusion of the official report stated that the death of Staff Physician Dostoevsky, whose mutilated body was found in a grove, had been brought about by an "apoplectic stroke." But although the affair was hushed up, it was impossible to conceal the truth from relatives and neighbors.

His father's end shocked Fyodor. He was overwhelmed by the particulars of the horrible death, with its combination of drunkenness, lechery, violence, a certain element of mystery and a succession of prosaic yet enigmatic details. All these facts, together with his own feelings about them, made such a deep impression on his memory that he was able to utilize them forty years later in *The Brothers Karamazov*, although it is hard to say to what extent the portrait of Karamazov *père* coincided with Dostoevsky's recollections of his own father. But even without such literary evidence, it can surely be taken for granted that the eighteen-year-old youth was deeply shaken by the tragedy at Darovoye.

Freud maintains that up to that point Fyodor's illness had been of a comparatively innocuous nature; the traumatic shock transformed it into epilepsy. In the opinion of the Viennese analyst the young man was subconsciously wishing for the death of his father, of whom he was jealous on his mother's account, and when this wish came to pass the son experienced horror and an insuperable feeling of guilt and remorse: he was ready to accept any punishment to expiate his secret sin. Freud and his disciples utilize the Oedipus complex to explain not only Dostoevsky's masochism and acceptance of suffering but his rebellion against all forms of authority or paternalism. He (or at any rate, the heroes he created) warred against both the Father in Heaven and the Little Father Czar—and Dostoevsky always felt that this conflict was criminal, even though it held an unwholesomely strong fascination for him. All his contradictions, all his oscillations between socialism and conservatism, between disbelief and ecclesiasticism, are likewise seen as rooted in a basic psychological defect. Dostoevsky, a subconscious parricide, became a faithful son of church and throne because he was unconsciously impelled to overcome his criminal inclinations. "Reconcile yourself, proud man," "I believe, I accept, I submit"—these words formed his magic exorcism, through which he hoped to be rid of the evil demons of rebelliousness. And is it not remarkable that his most profound and complex novel, *The Brothers Karamazov*, is built around the theme of parricide, and that all his creativity is dedicated to the problems of crime and punishment in their most varied aspects?

No matter what one's attitude may be toward the application of psychoanalytical theories to explain Dostoevsky's personality, it is perfectly obvious that it would be risky to hold the Oedipus complex alone responsible for all his rebelliousness and all the contradictions of his faith and lack of faith, his revolutionism and servile monarchism, his Slavophilism and Westernism, religious anarchism and ecclesiasticism, intuition versus logic. Dostoevsky's intellectual, ideological and psychological complexity cannot be exhausted by any schematic Freudian interpretation—and this despite the aptness and justice of many observations made by Freud and his disciples concerning the inner conflicts of Dostoevsky as man and writer.

Freud holds that because Dostoevsky could not resolve his Oedipus complex, could not rid himself of it, he endured the pathological manifestations of a neurosis usual in such cases and became an epileptic. During the seizures he experienced (according to his own admission) an oppressive sense of guilt, just as if he really was a great sinner; this was followed by an instant of lucidity, of complete blissfulness, and then by loss of consciousness and a deep faint. It is precisely this admission which enabled Freud to connect his epilepsy with his secret wishes to kill his father and to be punished for his sinful obsession. Dostoevsky's daughter, one of the most unreliable witnesses as to his life, writes: "According to our family traditions, Dostoevsky's first epileptical seizure occurred when he learned about the death of his father." The recollections of those who had known him in his youth (one of them a physician who had attended him for several years) do not confirm this.

Orestes Miller, his friend and biographer, placed its first appearance in the writer's early childhood; Liubov, Fyodor's daughter, claimed it coincided with his father's murder, while Dostoevsky himself referred the beginning of this affliction to his imprisonment in the Fortress of Sts. Peter and Paul, to his penal servitude, and even to his stay in Semipalatinsk. At any rate, the legend that the epilepsy was apparently the consequence of corporal punishment to which Dostoevsky was supposedly subjected during his penal servitude should be rejected, as utterly unsubstantiated.

Most of the data indicate that the aggravation of Dostoevsky's nervous spells came a number of years after his father's murder, and in all probability was a consequence of his arrest and transportation. There are no indications anywhere that the young Dostoevsky reacted to the event in Darovoye by falling down in epileptic convulsions. And it would be altogether fantastic to accept the assertion of his friend Grigorovich (as related by Zinaida Hippius) that "the muzhiks mangled Michael Fyodorovich before his son's eyes." At the time of the murder Fyodor was hundreds of miles away from Darovoye. Curiously, there is almost no reference to his father's death in Dostoevsky's correspondence; according to his daughter the murder was considered a horrible and disgraceful affair by the family and for that reason they hardly mentioned it.

It is difficult to judge the correctness of Freud's thesis as to the rôle played by the Oedipus complex in the life of Dostoevsky. The father-image is ambivalent both in his letters to Michael and in his novels. It is possible that to some extent the father's conduct in Darovoye, and his relations to women, supplied the psychological basis for the lecherous Karamazov *père*. The problem of paternal and filial relations is one of the main themes in *A Raw Youth*, while the interrelations of parents and children contribute to the plots of *Netochka Nezvanova*, *The Humiliated and Wronged*, *The Idiot* (in part) and several other works. It is clear that Dostoevsky always found these problems of the greatest interest. But it is utterly impossible to tell with any assurance, upon the basis of the facts available, to what degree this interest was due to an unresolved, deeply rooted complex of enmity toward his father and of love for his mother. This also applies to the origin of his affliction, which Freud called an affective and not an organic form of epilepsy. In other words, he was stressing the psychosomatic nature of the disease, and spoke of Dostoevsky as a neuropathic subject and not a psychopath. We do not even know whether the frequent spells of poor health in the writer's youth were the manifestations of an acute neurosis or actual seizures of epilepsy.

One thing only is known with certainty: the formation of his personality during his teens must have been a difficult and painful process, at times excruciatingly so. A number of factors contributed to the nervousness, susceptibility to impressions and the pathological sensitivity of the youth. The restraints instilled in him by his bringing up, the habits of a pent-up and sober way of life created by the pious staff physician and his bustling wife (a way of life not at all idyllic, but well-ordered and definite) disintegrated upon contact with the new reality of St. Petersburg. A flood of passions abruptly swept away family custom, leaving nothing to take its place. His mother's death, his father's drinking, mistresses, hatred of the peasants and their craftiness, the murder of his father, the venality of the officials, the hypocrisy of the people about him—all these were break-throughs into a sort of primordial chaos, the alarming warnings of a frightening and delirious universe. And in addition to all that, he had to live in a military school in a predominantly bureaucratic capital, to struggle from day to day and to endure the injustices and contradictions of a completely unsympathetic society. Left an orphan at eighteen without any help of support, lonely and self-conscious, he suffered cruelly because of the contrast between the honest and spartan atmosphere of his childhood and his new environment, official and soulless. The things which interested and stirred him left the other young cadets in the Engineers' Castle unmoved.

He dreamt of the creative life, of poetry and freedom: life confronted him with geometry, the malicious haughtiness of his fellow students and the stupidity and stolidity of those in charge of him. Occasionally the ecstasy of awakening thought, the keenness of new sensations and the sweep of his dreams so engrossed him that the career he was facing turned into a nightmare. "I have a project: to become a madman," he confided in secret to Michael. To become a madman: *i.e.*, to protect himself against people who annoyed him with their practical demands, their rules of life, their conventions and standards—to remain free and independent behind the bulwark of a feigned madness. At eighteen he wrote the prophetic words: "Man is a mystery. It must be unriddled; even if you have to spend all your life in unriddling it, do not say you have wasted your time. I occupy myself with this mystery, since I want to be a man."

IN THE YEAR 1841, WHEN HE WAS ABOUT TO GRADUATE, life seemed particularly hard to Dostoevsky. At night he was planning his dramas and novels, but the officer in charge was harshly ordering him to bed. He might be standing at attention during a school inspection or review, but his mind was taken up with *Hamlet* and the poems of Pushkin. He was sent as an orderly officer to Grand Duke Michael Pavlovich, brother to the Emperor and, absorbed in thoughts of his own, forgot to salute properly. "They will send me fools like that!" commented the Grand Duke.

Fyodor's unusually intensive inner life burst forth at rare intervals: during certain disputes with his classmates he would unexpectedly become gay, witty and animated; his words, according to one of his comrades, were just like the "spindrift of a whirlpool." But ordinarily he was morose, sad, and given to pondering on the vanity of all things under the sun.

In 1841, Dostoevsky was made a junior second lieutenant and had to round out his education by attending an officer's class. This meant that he had the right to live outside the school and could enjoy comparative freedom. He rented a four-room flat with some of his friends (only one of the rooms was furnished, however), and spent days and nights poring over his books and writing. Dreams seethed within him; he was making the most fantastic literary plans. When Michael came

from Reval to visit him, the young author read him fragments
of his dramas, *Maria Stuart* and *Boris Godunov*, the manuscripts of which have disappeared without a trace. In the
evenings, especially during the summer, when St. Petersburg
lay shimmering and changing color under the milky white
mirage of the northern twilight, he loved to roam the quais
of the Neva. He became friendly with Shidlovsky, who was
much the same sort of dreamer as himself, and held many
talks with him, quietly yet with so much feeling and conviction that they willy-nilly infected his friend with his own
hatred of injustice and his hopes for a better future for humanity. The destinies of mankind stirred him very much
at the time, and he began to take an interest in social utopias.

In 1843, Dostoevsky graduated as a second lieutenant and
was assigned to the drafting room of the Department of Engineering. His career as an officer proved brief, however. In
fact the young lieutenant was far more taken up with the
hazy contours of *Poor Folk* and *The Double* than the exact
lines of the departmental plans. There is a legend that he
resigned in September, 1844, a year after his appointment,
because a plan he had drawn unfortunately came to the eyes
of the Emperor; Nicholas I is supposed to have written on
it: "What idiot drew this?" The regal dictum was, according to custom, covered with a fixative so that it might not be
lost to posterity. Dostoevsky, offended at the idea that so
uncomplimentary a comment would go down through the
ages, immediately handed in his resignation. No plan with
such a remark in the Czar's hand was ever found in the administrative archives of the School of Engineering; this does
not exclude the possibility, however, of its having been ab-
stracted when Dostoevsky became famous as a writer.

One thing is beyond doubt. It was no chance affront that
made Dostoevsky resign his post; he simply found the work
unendurable and wanted to be a writer rather than a petty

official. Once resigned, without a copper to his name, he wrote Michael: "Why lose one's best years? I'll find some way of earning a crust of bread. I'm going to work like the devil. I am free now."

He was interested in the novels of Eugene Sue and Frederic Soulié, was translating the works of Balzac and was deep in his own literary experiments. He was organically repelled by the routine and monotony of a bureaucratic job and its red-tape rituals. He himself was very careless about details and remained so to his death; he did not know how to manage either his time or his money. Chaos reigned in his quarters and he could pass from plenty to penury within four and twenty hours. He was liable to pay a usurer one hundred rubles (the ruble was then worth approximately fifty cents) interest on a four-month loan of three hundred. The description of Raskolnikov's hatred of the old pawnbroker was based upon the author's personal experience. He was capable of sending down the drain in a single night the monthly remittance from his guardian and then subsisting on tea, bread and sausage for weeks at a stretch.

The decision of Dr. Riesenkampf, a friend of Michael's, to share quarters with him proved vain: the prudent German failed to bring the lackadaisical young writer to his senses. On one occasion Fyodor received a thousand rubles from his guardian, but the very next morning tackled the amazed doctor for a loan of five rubles. On the first of February, 1844, a new remittance (likewise for a thousand rubles) arrived, but toward evening Dostoevsky had only a hundred left: he had contrived to lose the rest at billiards and dominoes. He "lent" money to the doctor's poorer patients, paid fantastic sums to scalpers for tickets to Liszt's concerts or for performances of *Russlan and Liudmila*, and when Riesenkampf caught a cold, he cured him by a method all his own: bringing the doctor to Lerch's well-known restaurant he treated him to such a dinner of game, wine and champagne that the patient recovered overnight. After the concerts and champagne dinners, however, it was necessary to subsist on crackers and milk—and even for these he had to run up a bill at his grocer's. During the winter he was subject to colds: his rooms were unheated, since there was no money for firewood.

To keep warm he used to frequent taverns and sit for hours on end with "lost souls"—cashiered government clerks, rumpots, cardsharps and suspicious persons of both sexes. One of these fugitives from the St. Petersburg underworld, a pickpocket and toady by the name of Keller, became Dostoevsky's constant bottle companion. However, it was Keller who drank the vodka: Fyodor was not at all drawn to alcohol and actually could not take it. He avoided strong drink: at taverns and during friendly gatherings he drank wine or beer, and even these in small quantities. As for eating, his attitude to it was rather indifferent. But he did have a sweet tooth and was very fond of candy and pastries. He was at that time markedly thin and sickly—he was susceptible not only to colds but to stomachaches and nervous spasms. He astonished his friends by his oddities; he was superstitious, attributed great significance to signs, symbols, omens and prophecies, patronized female fortunetellers and was haunted by an inordinate fear of falling into a lethargy and being buried alive. This phobia attained such proportions that whenever he was unwell he would leave a note on his desk, requesting that in the event of his death he was not to be buried until five days afterward. Once, on coming across a funeral procession, he fainted away.

Despite the outward disorderliness of his existence, Dostoevsky was working persistently and systematically on *Poor Folk*. He had staked everything on this short novel. "If my undertaking does not succeed," he wrote Michael, "I may hang myself." In 1845, wretchedly poor, sickly and weary, lonely and utterly unknown, he was constantly reworking and correcting this first outstanding work of his, yet did not know what to do with it: whether he should send it to some periodical or try publishing it himself. Troubled and unable to come to any decision, he lost weight and could not sleep at night. Yet his torments held a peculiar pleasure for him. "No, if ever I was happy," he wrote in *The Humiliated and Wronged,* "it was at that time . . . when I had not yet read, or even shown, my manuscript to anyone; during those long nights spent in rapturous hopes and dreams and a passionate love of hard work, when I had grown used to living with my fantasy, with the characters I myself had created, as if they were my kindred, as if they had an actual existence—loving them, rejoicing and grieving with them, and now and then shedding the most sincere tears over my unpretentious hero."

However, in May, 1845, Dmitri Grigorovich, the future author of *Anton Goremyka* and friend of many Russian and French littérateurs of the nineteenth century, who was sharing Dostoevsky's quarters, showed the manuscript of *Poor Folk* to the poet Nekrassov, at that time editing an annual of prose and verse. After reading the novel, Nekrassov became so enthusiastic that he decided to visit the young author immediately. In vain did Grigorovich suggest postponing the visit, pointing out that, at four in the morning, Dostoevsky was probably asleep. "What does it matter if he is?" Nekrassov flared up. "We'll awaken him. *This* is more important than sleep."

The impression made on Dostoevsky by this night visit, by the excited praises and hugs bestowed upon him by Nekrassov, was unforgettable. Fame had come to him with the dawning of a spring day in St. Petersburg; the dream of his youth had been fulfilled. "That was the most rapturous day of my whole life," he confessed many years later. A meeting with Belinsky, who also appraised the novel highly, did much to strengthen his joyous mood; the great critic described *Poor Folk* as "hor-

ror and tragedy." Many of those who read the novel in manuscript could not help shedding tears of pity.

Love was the theme of this story—but a love meek,
dreamy and unhappy. Makar Devushkin, a petty government
clerk, elderly and homely, who had fallen in love with a much
younger woman, Barbara, a next-door neighbor of his, did
not at all resemble a romantic hero. He labored under every
imaginable handicap—timidity, awkwardness, poverty, naïveté
—and he himself despaired of winning the girl. He merely
pitied her, wanted to help her, to make her life of toil and
need easier, and self-denial was all the joy he derived from his
love. To sacrifice himself, to spend his beggarly savings upon
her, to endure privations for her sake—to the extent of giving
up smoking, of going around in ragged clothes so that he might
send her dainties and flowers—to sacrifice himself with resignation, in secret, without expecting any reward: there you
have the love of a little man living in the backlots of life. This
"oppressed and, if you like, rather simple-minded government
clerk, who had lost even the buttons of his uniform," spoke
in the simplest language, yet it became evident from his unpretentious story that "the most oppressed man, the last of the
least, is a man nevertheless and to be called my brother."
Barbara, at long last, sees though his white lies, his neediness
and his sacrifices, and decides to go away in order to make his
lot easier and to save herself from poverty by marrying a
"decent" man with money, though she does not love her
wooer and even fears him, being doubtful of his feelings toward her. Thus ends Makar's dream, and he is left crushed and
lonely, in the darkness and drabness of that underground
existence which was the lot of the St. Petersburg poor.

EVEN THOUGH DOSTOEVSKY BORE NO RESEMBLANCE TO
Devushkin, his life, too, held nothing beside a dream of love.
In *White Nights,* an autobiographical short novel written soon
after *Poor Folk,* and issued in 1848, he portrayed a young man
who roams the streets of the capital and dreams of a requited
love. But all his affairs are played out only in his imagination;
in real life he is timorous and lonely: "True enough, I am
timid with women, I have grown altogether unused to them
—that is, I never did get used to them, for I am all alone. . . .
I don't know how to talk to them, even." One day he meets
Nastenka on a street corner; he confides his dreams to this
pretty and endearing girl, while she tells him of her love for
another. And although this St. Petersburg dreamer comes to
love his chance friend passionately, the help he extends to her
is disinterested and entails self-sacrifice. He goes away so as
to leave her free when his fortunate rival appears.

Thus in all his outstanding works Dostoevsky dealt with
the failures of a love bound down by sacrifices and sufferings:
he was unable to describe a love triumphant, joyous, shining
with masculine faith.

In *White Nights* the author was obviously retelling his
own experiences. He became confused and timid where
women were concerned. "I don't know whether Mme. Belins-
kaya has given birth to a boy or a girl," he wrote Michael. "I

heard a baby bawling two rooms away, but it was somehow embarrassing and odd to ask."

He could dream for hours on end about love and fair incognitas nestling their heads against his bosom, but when he had to meet living women he became awkward and ridiculous, and his attempts at intimacy invariably ended in catastrophe.

The success of *Poor Folk* opened the doors of St. Petersburg salons to him, and at the home of Ivan Panaev he was introduced to the writer's wife, Avdotia (Eudoxia). "Yesterday I was at the Panaev home for the first time," he wrote Michael on November 16, 1845, "and I think I fell in love with his wife. She is clever and a pretty little thing and, to boot, amiable and impossibly straightforward. I am having a gay time."

Avdotia was twenty-two. A small, coquettish brunette, with flawless features set in a lively face, she seemed to be all asparkle: the gleam of her teeth, the glitter of her brown eyes, the sheen of her fair skin, the flashing of the large diamonds in her necklace and earrings, all blended into some sort of dazzling radiance. Her dark, lace-trimmed dress emphasized her lithe grace. Thus did Dostoevsky see her, and she vanquished him at first sight. But she was always surrounded by people, and in the throng of her admirers Nekrassov was the least secretive about his feelings: within two years she became his mistress.

Dostoevsky himself told Michael of his infatuation in a letter dated February 1, 1846, less than three months after he had first met Avdotia: "I was quite seriously in love with Panaeva; I'm getting over it now, but I'm still uncertain. My health is frightfully upset; my nerves are affected and I am afraid of a brain fever or a nervous attack." This first infatuation was both agonizing and humiliating. It became clear to him from the very beginning that he could not hope for love in return, and that his passion could not possibly bear any sort of fruit. And to the failure of his love there was added a social debacle as well: the interest the society of St. Petersburg had taken in him rapidly declined, and besides, he was behaving in the most preposterous and foolish manner.

"From the first glance at Dostoevsky," Panaeva tells us in her *Recollections*, "it was evident that he was a frightfully nervous and impressionable young man. He was rather thin, rather small, with hair like flax, his face of an unwholesome color; his small gray eyes kept shifting somehow uneasily from object to object, while his lips twiched nervously. . . . Because of his youth and nervousness he had no self-possession and betrayed too clearly his artistic vanity and his high opinion of his talent as a writer. Being an impressionable individual, stunned by his unexpected and brilliant first step in the literary arena and swamped by the praises of competent critics, he could not conceal his pride before other young littérateurs. When these appeared in our circle, one had to be wary about falling prey to their keen wit, yet Dostoevsky, as if on purpose, left himself wide open through his irascibility and a haughty attitude of being incomparably superior to them because of his talent. And so they went to work on him, needling him in their talk to irritate his self-pride. Turgenev in particular was a master at this sort of thing; he deliberately drew Dostoevsky into controversy and brought him to the highest pitch of exasperation. Dostoevsky went to extravagant lengths, vehemently defending absurd opinions which he had let slip in the heat of the debate, but Turgenev seized upon them and made sport of him. Dostoevsky revealed a frightful suspiciousness. . . . He eventually suspected everybody of envying him his talent and found an intent to minimize a work of his, to affront him, in almost every word which was uttered, however innocent. He used to come to us already seething with rancor, pick out a few words and then pour all the bile that was

suffocating him upon those who envied him. Instead of looking on him tolerantly as an ailing, nervous man, they nettled
him still further by their sneers." His irritation was intensified
because this took place in the presence of the woman he loved
but who showed nothing but a humiliating condescension
toward him.

Dostoevsky was living through his love for Panaeva all
the more excruciatingly since she was probably the only woman
who had aroused him to such an extent. In his extensive correspondence during the 1840's there are no references to his
being in love except with Panaeva; also, the reminiscences of
his contemporaries do not mention a single woman's name in
connection with Dostoevsky at this period. However, it would
not do to make the erroneous deduction that Dostoevsky, at
the age of twenty-five, was virginal, as some of his biographers
seem to think. Riesenkampf, who shared his quarters, tells
us that in 1842 women did not interest Dostoevsky, that he
apparently felt antipathy for them, while Dostoevsky's daughter maintains that his emotions had not yet been awakened.
It is difficult to believe these assertions. Riesenkampf himself
adds that "it is possible he was concealing something in regard
to this," and then recalls Dostoevsky's great curiosity concerning the love affairs of his companions. And he continues, "it
is well known that misogyny frequently conceals not indifference but an acute sexuality."

This sexuality bore, probably, a dual character—and it
is here that we must look for an explanation of Dostoevsky's
peculiarities of behavior and his emotional contradictions.
Like most epileptics, he evidently had heightened sexual excitability and, at the same time, was an idealistic visionary.
That "illumination of the flesh" mentioned by some of his
biographers came to him not in the guise of the enraptured
first love of youth but took the form of shameful encounters
with prostitutes and other women of easy virtue. It is very

difficult to judge to what extent these hired embraces led him to experience the "somber premonition of feminine charms and elemental passion:" but it is clear that young Dostoevsky began to differentiate between love and physical pleasure. They had come to him as two unconnected aspects of some elusive unity and, although he understood that the highest attainment lay in some sort of fusion, he could not seem to achieve it. For the dreamer of *White Nights*, Panaeva remained in the sphere where lofty passion reigned without physical possession, while the women he found in the slums on the outskirts of St. Petersburg offered him the stark satisfaction of sexual desire. The same letter in which he told Michael of his hopeless love for Panaeva contains an addendum: "I am so depraved that I cannot live normally; I am afraid of typhus or fever, and my nerves are deranged." Thus did the double image of Eros-Asmodeous haunt Dostoevsky's youth. This is all the more comprehensible if we recall the theme of duality in his creative work of this period. In *The Double*, his second novel published in 1846, the hero Golyadkin has tendencies toward paranoia and erotic fantasies. Of course, through his creativity Dostoevsky freed himself from many of his own complexes and contradictions, but the catharsis could not exhaust completely the agitations of his flesh and imagination.

In the society in which he moved at this time (and, according to his own admission, he took part in the sprees of his comrades), the noisy evenings usually wound up in brothels, and it is hard to believe that Second Lieutenant Dostoevsky did not go along. It is also hard to believe that during all the evenings he spent in taverns he escaped contact with prostitutes and meretricious love of every sort. He must have had a very good knowledge of it, to judge by all the descriptions of the dregs of humanity that are scattered throughout his works, both of the early period and the late. It is enough to

read *The Landlady*, *Netochka Nezvanova* and *The Double*
to become convinced of the diversity of the author's personal
erotic experiences. *The Humiliated and Wronged*, which came
later, provides further confirmation.

Besides everything else, he was by temperament an individual of great passions and excessive sensuality. At the
sunset of his life he told Opochinin what a great sway sex
exercised over man and mentioned the subordination of the
will to sexual impulse, and also commented that the mental
stimulation of desire, of the flesh, is worse than the sin itself.
Evidently he had known in his youth both this mental stimulation, this play of the erotic imagination, and the direct
gratification of the sexual urge, to which he subsequently referred as sin. There is proof after proof on this point.

"The little Minnas, Claras, Mariannae *et al* have grown
unbelievably pretty, but they come fearfully high. The other
day Turgenev and Belinski hauled me over the coals for my
disorderly life," he wrote Michael in November, 1845. Even
if we consider as a joke this roll call, so typical of St. Petersburg's professional women of the time (Germans or natives
of the Baltic provinces, for the most part), it is not without
a grain of truth. This is confirmed by other passages from his
correspondence: "I am incapable of leading a decent life, that's
how worthless I am," he wrote in 1846. And in 1849, after his
arrest, he wrote from the prison-fortress: "Cell-life has by now
rather killed my carnal demands, not altogether pure; I've
taken little care of myself hitherto." There is no need to doubt
the tempestuous character of these demands: "My nature
cannot help but break out in extreme cases, and break out
precisely in excesses, hyperbolically." He could not bear, as
he wrote in February, 1844, pharisees and scribes, who
preached smugness and condemned "a strong, ardent soul
unable to endure their vulgar daily timetable and their worldly
calendar," and he bestowed unprintable names on his im-

aginary adversaries: "the C . . . . good-for-nothings." He at any rate, did not hold to established rules of morality and polite behavior.

Those who knew Dostoevsky well speak of his lust, of the dark and secret recesses of his sexual personality. His erotic life was constantly complicated by ill health, self-consciousness and melancholy. It is possible that the attacks of his disease (nervous seizures or epilepsy, if we are to consider the latter as having begun in 1839) made him hypersensitive and vacillating: he did not believe in the possibility of being successful with women and drove all thoughts of marriage from him. What was the use of that for a poor and sick man like himself? Or else, like Prince Myshkin, the hero of *The Idiot,* he was afraid of impotence because of the state of his nerves. Potency in individuals of his physical condition is always extremely variable, and is not subject to conscious control of will power. And the sequence of events in his life could not possibly have strengthened his self-confidence.

TWO EVENTS MADE DOSTOEVSKY'S SITUATION CRITICAL IN 1847–48. The first blow was his fiasco with Panaeva: he had not as much as dared to confess his love, so incongruous and impossible did it seem to him. He had to steel his heart and watch others paying court to her, rivals who went out of their way to make him look ridiculous. It is probable that his hatred for Turgenev dates from this time.

The second blow was what used to be called a turn of the Wheel of Fortune. The intoxication of the unexpected success of *Poor Folk* passed quickly. *The Double*, that prose-poem of St. Petersburg, which he had hoped and believed was to surpass his first novel, pleased neither the public nor the critics. The reviews considered it a weak imitation of Gogol and overlooked all the concepts which the author had tried to put into it. A similar fate befell other short works which appeared in periodicals. The only ones considered comparable to his first brilliant experiment were *White Nights* (1848) and *Netochka Nezvanova* (1849). But by the time they appeared their author was already immured in the Fortress of Sts. Peter and Paul.

He had a very hard time of it during his literary debacle. Envy, righteous self-esteem and outbursts of egotism alternated with depression and despair. Either he was comparing himself to Gogol and promising "to show all of them" that "supremacy in literature" would be his at last, or he was confessing with bitterness: "I have horrible vices—boundless self-pride and ambition." To his feelings of injury, disenchantment and self-doubt were now added material insecurity, debts, continual poverty, the need to find new ways of earning even a subsistence. The nagging work of a literary hack—translations, writing stories against advances, proofreading—paid off only in coppers. He was living in ill-concealed distress, he was lonely and neglected. Because of his nervous tension, physical exhaustion, disorderly way of life and intensified work, Dostoevsky developed something in the nature of a psychopathological condition, which he subsequently referred to more than once, even though in a rather guarded way. He described it in *The Humiliated and Wronged:* "Little by little, with the coming of twilight, I began to fall into that spiritual state which I called mystic horror. This is a most serious, most excruciating fear of something I cannot define, something inconceivable and non-existent in the order of things, but which may inevitably become reality at any moment, as if to mock all the arguments of reason."

The onslaughts of this mystic horror, so similar to the "illumination" preceding the convulsions of epilepsy, were followed by hypochondria and lethargy, accompanied by weakness and impotence. At times, however, he felt an irresistible need to forget himself at any cost. Since Dostoevsky did not drink, he could sink into oblivion only through gambling or women. Both in his psyche and his experience these two were closely intertwined.

In 1847–49 he was leading a fantastic life, filled with mystic alarms, soaring flights of ecstasy and spasmodic falls into the abysses of the flesh. He was, of course, sublimating his inner conflicts by putting them into creative forms: *The Landlady,* *Netochka Nezvanova* and some short stories of this period supply extensive psychoanalytical material. But his hidden impulses found escape in life as well: there were certain real outlets for his passions. The taverns, gambling and women: he tried them all during these painful years—and tried them with shame, with remorse for his lack of restraint, with self-flagellation for his dissoluteness.

Many years later the hero of *Notes from the Underground* (published in 1864 and translated here by B. G. Guerney) described his youth as follows: "I was twenty-four at the time. My life was grim, disorderly and lonely to the verge of savagery even then. I kept away from everybody and even avoided speaking with others burrowing further and further into my cubby-hole. . . . At home I read most of the time. . . . Reading helped a great deal, of course; it agitated, delighted and tormented me. But at times it became a frightful bore. After all, one wanted to be up and stirring, and I would suddenly plunge into dark, subterranean, vile depravity—no, not depravity but 'depravitishness.' My passionlets were acute, searing, because of my constant, sickly irritability. . . . The impulses were hysterical, accompanied by tears and convulsions. . . . To top everything off, my melancholy would come to a boil; a hysterical avidity for incongruities, for contrasts arose, and so I went in for depravity. . . . I indulged in it of nights, furtively, timorously, feeling a shame which did not desert me even at the most loathsome moments and which at such moments actually made me curse myself. . . . I was frightfully apprehensive of being seen by some chance, of coming across somebody, of being recognized. . . . And the haunts I frequented were quite shady. . . . After all, it was a bore to sit twiddling one's thumbs, and so I went in for all sorts of dodges. . . . I conjured up my own adventures and invented a life for myself, so that I might at least have a taste of life, somehow. . . . But my streak of 'depravitishness' would come to an end and I would feel dreadfully queasy. . . . However, I had a device to reconcile all things: this was to flee into everything that was 'beautiful and lofty'—in my dreams, of course. I was an awful dreamer; I dreamt for three months at a time, huddling there in my nook. But how much love—Lord, how much love!—I used to dream through in these dreams of mine. . . ."

Nicholas Strakhov, Dostoevsky's biographer and his friend, maintains that "the personages who resemble him most are the hero of *Notes from the Underground*, Svidrigailov in *Crime and Punishment*, and Stavrogin in *The Possessed*." The same critic speaks of Dostoevsky's "animal lust" and of how "dissolute" he was. "In addition he was sentimental, disposed to sweet sentimentality and lofty and humane reveries, and these reveries are his literary muse and his main direction. Essentially, however, all his novels constitute self-justification, proving that all sorts of abominations can contrive to exist side by side with nobility of character." (This is part of a letter to Leo Tolstoy dated November 28, 1883—two years after Dostoevsky's death.) Strakhov added that in the biography which he was then preparing for the press he could not, of course, refer to such traits in the personality of the great writer: "Let truth perish, then; we shall show off only the right side of [his] life."

Dostoevsky's humane dreams brought him face to face with all those problems which he later explored in his novels. It was precisely during those painful years—when he was a literary proletarian, working for none-too-generous employers, when he was straining under oppressive conditions and torn between "beautiful and lofty" impulses and suffocating "abominations" (as Strakhov put it)—that he began to be haunted by the problem of the "daring personality" and its right to freedom of action and even to crime. The questions of evil in this world, of the religious reconstruction of humanity, of God, who had created all the torments and sufferings of our existence, and of the contradiction between moral ideals and the terrible political and social reality of Russia in 1848 and 1849, he found particularly agitating.

Nevertheless, during this period when the historian sees but dead wood—bureaucracy, serfdom and reaction—significant changes were secretly taking place in Russian society. Slavophiles and Westernizers argued about the destinies of the people and the mission of national culture, while the philosophers were helping the liberal intellectuals to form a system of general ideas. Public opinion, oppressed by censorship and police interdicts, was more and more insistently turning to problems of the social and economic organization of the country and of political freedom.

Dostoevsky, yielding to the mood of the intellectuals he was intimate with, was greatly taken up with humanitarian ideas and utopian socialism, especially as interpreted by the French. The plans of the Russian Socialists blended in his imagination with hazy hopes for that particular *logos* which Russia had been preordained to utter to the world. These hopes made him feel with particular shame and pain the hideousness of everything around him. The arbitrariness of the authorities, the sufferings of the poor, the crushed and degraded condition of the common people and the cruel injustice of legalized serfdom moved him deeply. It was these very impulses that led him to join the Petrashevsky circle, where the works of Saint-Simon, Fourier and Owen were read aloud and discussed —to say nothing of Belinsky's famous *Letter to Gogol*, in which the great critic reproached the author of *Dead Souls* with obscurantism, submission to the Church and the support of autocracy and slavery.

At one of their gatherings Dostoevsky delivered a speech on Lamennais, the Christian Socialist whose Biblical and prophetic style was close to his own mystical strain, and his inspired words filled his listeners' eyes with tears. He did not know that an agent of the Secret Police was among those present and that he himself was soon to pay dearly for his call to *Liberté, Egalité, Fraternité*.

On April 23, 1849, Dostoevsky was arrested and placed in a cell of the Fortress of Sts. Peter and Paul. He spent eight months there and his health became much worse: he could not eat because of the pains in his stomach, he was tortured by hemorrhoids, at night he was seized by onslaughts of the familiar mystic horror, and if he did manage to doze off, he had nightmares. As he himself put it, at that time "I was living only on my own means—my head alone, and nothing more. . . . Everything has gone into my head, and from the head into thought—everything, absolutely everything."

On the twenty-second of December, of the same year, after the horrifying ordeal of the mock-execution, where he had waited for the end to come at any moment, he wrote Michael: "I did not whine and did not lose heart. Life is life everywhere, life is within ourselves and not in externals. . . . There will be people near me, and to be a *man* among men and to remain a man for all time . . . that is what life consists of, that is its problem. I am aware of this. This idea has become part of my flesh and my blood. Yes, true enough: that head which used to be creative, which lived the higher life of art and has become accustomed to the higher demands of the spirit—that head is already lopped off my shoulders. . . . Can it be that I shall never pick up a pen? I think there is a chance of my doing so four years from now. My God! How many images lived through, created by me will perish anew, will become extinguished in my head or spread through my blood as bane. Yes, if it will prove impossible for me to write I shall perish. Better fifteen years of solitary confinement but with a pen in one's hand. . . . Farewell! Now I tear myself away from everything that was dear. It hurts to leave this behind! It hurts to break one's self in two, to tear the heart into halves."

Two days later, on Christmas Eve, after he had said farewell to Michael, eight-pound irons were welded onto Dostoevsky's legs and he was placed in the sleigh which was to transport him as a political criminal, for two thousand miles, by way of Yaroslavl and Nizhni Novgorod, to penal servitude in Siberia.

FROM 1849 TO 1854 DOSTOEVSKY SERVED FOUR YEARS
of penal servitude in the penitentiary of Omsk where, as he
himself put it, the coffin lid was clamped on him and he was
buried alive. The supposition of certain biographers that his
term was not a bad thing after all is patently arbitrary. Dostoevsky himself has given a perfect description of it in a letter dated
November 6, 1854: "It was inexpressible, interminable suffering." To say nothing of physical deprivations, nervous seizures, rheumatism in his legs, stomach ailments, insults and
degradations (Major Krivtzov birched any convict who slept
on his left side and not the right, as the regulations demanded),
he had to undergo the spiritual torment of compulsory and
constant association with his prison-mates. He was surrounded
by a rabble of murderers, thieves, violent and insane criminals;
their attitude toward him was one of suspicion and animosity,
since he was the only man of gentle birth among them. Nor
was he on friendly terms with S. Durov, another Petrashevist,
or with the transported Polish noblemen. Consequently he
lived all four years in complete loneliness, yet without the
least opportunity of being alone.

In a letter to his brother Michael, dated February 23,
1854, he wrote: "Life was very hard for us. I passed all the
four years in prison without ever leaving it, except to do hard
labor. At work I strained myself beyond my strength, in in-
clement weather, in the wet, in the mire, or in the unbearable

frost of winter. We lived piled up on one another, all of us together in a single barrack. In summer, unbearable stuffiness; in winter, insufferable cold. All the floors were rotted through. The dirt on the floor was an inch thick; you could slip and fall. We slept on bare wooden ledges, with nothing but a pillow allowed. Fleas, lice and cockroaches by the bushel. For food they gave us bread and sauerkraut soup—at Lent, just boiled cabbage. My stomach became unbearably upset and I was sick several times. Owing to the derangement of my nerves I had epilepsy. I still have rheumatism in my legs."

In February, 1854, Dostoevsky was "set free" and was sent to Semipalatinsk to serve as a private in a Siberian infantry regiment.

Military life was certainly not easy for him since it meant early morning drill, marching, dress parades, felling timber more than twenty miles from town, harsh discipline maintained with bludgeons, birch rods and blows that knocked the teeth out. In the filthy wooden barracks the soldiers slept two to each narrow ledge of bare boards, with hungry rats scurrying between the ledges. The men ate mostly thick soups, dipped out of an iron trough with wooden spoons which they had to carve themselves. But to Dostoevsky this seemed a comfortable change after all those years in Omsk's jail.

To get out of the rat race, the bondage and stifling atmosphere of the convict quarters, to go without the convict's brand of a yellow ace of diamonds on the back of his coat and eight-pound irons on his legs, not to strain any longer with every fiber of his being in the mines and brick-making yard, to regain the status of a man, even though a drill-broken private in a battalion of the line—all these practically amounted to happiness. Several weeks after his transfer to Semipalatinsk he wrote Michael: "For the time being I am taken up with military service, drilling, and memories of old times. My health is quite good and has improved considerably during these two months." He had grown stronger physically, and his nervous spells (which he defined as "resembling epilepsy, and yet not epilepsy") had become less frequent: up to then they had been recurring every three months.

The feeling of freedom, even though that freedom was limited, was so strong that he did not mind his poverty (he had no money and could count on only small and casual remittances from Michael), nor the disagreeable things entailed by his status as a private and an ex-convict. When Dostoevsky first reported to his company, Captain Vedenyaev, who was nicknamed Blizzard, told the sergeant, "This fellow comes to us from penal servitude. Keep your eyes peeled and don't give him any leeway." A few days later Dostoevsky was not quick enough about leaving the barracks and the sergeant struck him very hard on the head. When he was visiting his friends, officers took him for an orderly and expected him to help them on with their greatcoats. But the most excruciating experience was standing in line with a stick and having to bring it down on the bare back of some victim being led through "Green Street," as running the gauntlet was called. Vedenyaev used to stroll behind the rows of soldiers and put a chalk mark on the back of anyone who seemed reluctant with his blows or did not deal them out heartily enough. These marked backs were later beaten in their turn. Dostoevsky had to pay dearly for his part in the punishment: after one of them, he fell down in convulsions.

Semipalatinsk in the 1850's was a wilderness in the Kirghiz steppes, not far from the borders of China. It derived its name, "Seven Halls," from the ruins of seven strongholds on the high right bank of the Irtysh River; these ruins were still in evidence at the time. The site had once been an important Mongolian center, a fact attested to by inscriptions on rams' shoulder bones (the usual memorial tablets of nomads) dug up by archeologists. About the middle of the last century it was transformed into one of the outposts of the Russian Empire, a garrison fortress of stone with wooden barracks huddled around it. The whole population of the town, counting the military, did not exceed six thousand. A stone church, a government pharmacy and a drygoods shop were the chief points of interest. Merchants from Tashkent, Bokhara and Kazan did business in tents or stalls or in the stockaded trading post, a meeting ground for caravans of camels or pack-horses. Prices for everything were so high that for people of the humbler sort, like soldiers, they were altogether out of reach. The only luxury Fyodor could permit himself at the market place was an occasional loaf of white bread or a cracknel.

The streets were unpaved; there was nothing but sand which turned into a quagmire in the fall and, in summer, into dust. No vegetation anywhere—not even a sapling or a scraggly shrub before the small houses which were one-storied and mostly built of logs. Everything was bare and discouraging, as if in a desert. But not far from the small town began a forest—of firs, pines and willows rooted in the sandy soil—which stretched away for hundreds of miles. At night the streets were plunged in impenetrable darkness; there were no street lamps, and only the barking of innumerable watchdogs betrayed the presence of a single house. The house furnishings were scanty and semi-Asiatic: *koshmi* (felt mats) on the floor and walls, with here and there crude woodcuts of the heroes of 1812 on prancing chargers.

Mail came only once a week; newspapers and periodicals were subscribed to by some fifteen persons, and those who were educated took turns in having gatherings to share the news and find out what was going on in the two capitals. Lieutenant Colonel Belikov, Dostoevsky's commanding officer, did not happen to like reading to himself, regarding the fatigue it entailed as detrimental to his health. He preferred to listen. Therefore, when he heard of the "mighty learned" soldier in his ranks, who had once been a gentleman, he called the man in to read his newspapers aloud. This marked Dostoevsky's introduction into the society of Semipalatinsk. The chief occupation here, even as in all provincial social circles, consisted of drinking, cards and gossip.

At first Dostoevsky did not leave the barracks often. His bunkmate was a seventeen-year-old converted Jew by the name of Nicholas F. Katz, the son of a soldier and himself a soldier from his cradle up, through the *canton* system of military servitude. Katz owned a samovar and used to treat the taciturn "gentleman" to tea, wondering at the fortitude with which he endured the hardships and mishaps of a soldier's life. Dostoevsky, in his turn, did favors for the young man and helped him whenever he could. Eventually the writer was permitted to take up private quarters in a lopsided log hut on a wasteland at the edge of town. He was paying five rubles ($2.50) a month for his room and board, which consisted of cabbage soup, buckwheat gruel and black bread. The low-ceiled, half-dark room— with a bed, a table and a chair as its only furnishings—contained a startling number of fleas and cockroaches. His landlady, a soldier's widow, had a bad reputation: she was carrying on an open trade in the beauty and youth of her two daughters, one sixteen years old, the other twenty. The younger was exceptionally good-looking, and Dostoevsky became friendly with her—perhaps even more than friendly. After four years of penal servitude and enforced abstinence, he was irresistibly drawn to women, and every new encounter made a strong impression on him. He also formed a friendship with Lizanka (Elizabeth) Nevorotova, a seventeen-year-old beauty who sold white loaves from a stall in the market place; her whole life consisted of nothing but hard work and she supported her entire family. The soldier Dostoevsky she found appealing because of his kindness and consideration. It is not known just how intimate their relations were, but she never married, and she treasured to the day of her death the tender letters Dostoevsky wrote her, refusing to show them to anybody.

However, the casual feminine companions of his first months in Semipalatinsk did not affect him deeply, either physically or emotionally, and he forgot them on the appearance of the one woman to whom he became attached with all the exaltation of his nature and all the ardor of a belated first love.

WHEN, IN 1854, DOSTOEVSKY FOUND HIMSELF IN SEMI-palatinsk he was a mature man of thirty-three. During his penal servitude he had attained mastery over his moods—or at least, over their outward manifestations. His former traits of reserve and secretiveness had intensified, while what he called his "absence of form" (or of manners) had taken on the character of harshness and even eccentricity. He had also undergone an inward upheaval: he had rejected the former social theories that had brought about his arrest, had accepted his punishment, and having come in contact with actual representatives of Dark Russia, had changed his opinions about the common people. He felt more strongly than ever the necessity of a faith in God, while Christ, who suffered on the cross and redeemed the sins of mankind through His death, became for him the closest and most comprehensible image of man and a symbol of the religion of all-forgiveness and compassion. "Believe this, that there is nothing more splendidly beautiful, more profound, more sympathetic, wiser, manlier and of greater perfection than Christ—there is not and there cannot be. Nor is that all: if anyone were to prove to me that Christ is outside of truth, and if it were *actually* to turn out that truth is outside of Christ, I would want to remain with Christ rather than with truth," he wrote Mrs. N. Von Visina upon his release from penal servitude. Yet almost at the same time, in February, 1854, he wrote to Michael: "I am a child of the age, a child of unbelief and doubt to this very day and (this I know) until the coffin-lid comes down on me. What fearful torments this thirst to believe has cost me, and is still costing me."

His former tendency to daydream remained, yet even that had changed greatly. Now, much more than in his youth, he knew the difference between the earthly Aphrodite and the celestial. He had witnessed and lived through a great deal during the stages of his transportation and his stretch at hard labor in the prison at Omsk, where his comrades in misfortune went in either for sodomy or making love to market women, the mere sight of whom was enough to make one's blood run cold.

He had grown so unused to feminine society that he dreamt of it as the highest happiness and arrived in Semipalatinsk with secret longings which he himself feared to admit. He was very much in the position of a convalescent after a mortal illness, who feels with redoubled force all the splendor and seductiveness of being. He himself wrote: "I had a great deal of hope. I wanted to live." And he wanted to love as well.

A few months after coming to Semipalatinsk he met Alexander Isaev and his wife, Maria, at the home of Lieutenant Colonel Belikov.

Isaev, who at one time had been an instructor at a *gymnasia* directed by his father-in-law, had come to Semipalatinsk as controller of the distillation and sale of liquor. His position was a sinecure, but liquor itself held an unfailing attraction for him. He lost his post, and finding himself without a job and without means, took to drinking harder than ever. Poor in health, weak in will-power, he fell into the company of drunkards and scoundrels, of whom there were a good many in the little town, and in a short while was altogether down and out. When in his cups, he like to orate about the loftiness and fineness of his feelings, and assured Dostoevsky that he loved him both as man and writer. Dostoevsky had these words to say about Isaev two years later, in a letter to Michael: "He led a most irregular life, and besides was quite disorderly by nature, passionate, obstinate and grown a little coarse. He had sunk very low in the opinion of the town and had many unpleasant experiences; at the same time he has suffered many undeserved persecutions from the society here. He was as carefree as a gypsy, full of self-esteem, proud, did not know how to control himself and (as I've said already) was slipping horribly. Yet, with all that, his was a greatly developed nature, of the utmost kindness. He was educated, and understood everything one might broach to him in conversation. He was, despite all the mire, exceedingly noble."

Undoubtedly Dostoevsky the novelist was very much interested in the "noble drunkard with ambition." Probably that image came to life again in his memory when, several years later, he was creating the characters of Marmeladov in *Crime and Punishment* and Lebedev in *The Idiot*.

When his acquaintance with Dostoevsky began, Isaev was already ill and wretched. The society of Semipalatinsk, made up of officials and army officers and their wives, disliked and despised him. The local authorities were indignant over his drunken speeches and impudent sorties; his sprees and shiftless life had reduced his family to poverty and debt. Dostoevsky often pled with him and lectured him, but all that did not help and everything went on as before.

Maria, Isaev's wife and the mother of his seven-year-old boy, Pasha, suffered very much from the situation her husband had brought about. Her father, Dmitri Constant, Chief of Quarantine at Astrakhan, was in all probability the son of a French aristocrat who had fled to Russia from the Reign of Terror, like so many of his compatriots. One should not attach much significance to the testimony of Dostoevsky's daughter Liubov who, among other stories and fantasies of hers, informs us that Maria's father was (supposedly) one of "Napoleon's mamelukes," who, taken prisoner in 1812, was sent to Astrakhan, where he had captivated the heart of some merchant's young daughter; she married him and made him an officer in the army. Although Liubov admits that "Maria's appearance did not betray her African extraction," she could not refrain from commenting, "Like all Negresses, she was crafty." This fairytale about Maria's extraction, like so many other details at her expense, had one definite purpose: to vilify her, to prove that she was given to intrigues and deception and that Dostoevsky had not loved her. We know that Anna, the author's second wife, painstakingly crossed out of his letters all the passages wherein he spoke of his love for Isaeva or praised her. This jealousy toward his past was evidently transmitted to her daughter as well, and she also tried to blacken Maria.

Actually, Colonel Constant's daughter had received an education that was good by the standards of the time. In 1854, she was twenty-eight or twenty-nine—"a rather handsome blonde of medium height, very thin, of a passionate and highly strung nature" is Wrangel's description of her. "She was widely read, sufficiently educated, fond of knowledge and unusually animated and impressionable." In a contemporary daguerreotype which has come down to us her wavy light hair is parted in the middle; the mouth is somewhat wide with the lower lip prominent and just a little puffy, giving a capricious expression to the entire face; the eyes are dark, deep but not large. Strakhov tells us that her features were small but attractive, while her cheeks had a hectic flush. Her appearance was, on the whole, frail and sickly, and in this respect she at times must have reminded Fyodor of his mother. The gentleness of her face, her physical weakness and a certain defenceless-ness aroused his desire to help her, to guard her as one would a child. That fusion of the infantile and the feminine, which always appealed so strongly to the susceptible Dostoevsky, on this occasion also aroused within him complex emotions he neither could nor would clarify. Maria had instantly cast a spell over him by her maternal solicitude, while her fragility attracted him physically. Besides that, he was enraptured by her exquisite and unusual nature—or so it seemed to him.

Maria was nervous, almost hysterical, but Dostoevsky (especially at the beginning of their relationship) perceived in the inconstancy of her moods, the breaks in her voice and her ready tears, signs of deep and exalted feelings. When he began calling on the Isaevs, Maria took pity on her eccentric guest and was kind to him, although she hardly took his exceptional nature into account. Simply, as a woman, she sensed that this clumsy private—who could sit for hours almost without a word and then, suddenly taking fire, deliver long tirades which were not always comprehensible—had endured more than any of the people she knew. And she found it pleasant to be his good angel, to feel his lightning-quick and grateful reaction to every kind word, to every concerned glance: it flattered her over-developed vanity. Besides that, she herself was in need of support at that time. Her life was tedious and lonely; she could not keep up her friendships because of her husband's drunkenness and outrageous actions, to say nothing of there being no money for entertaining anybody. And although she bore her cross proudly and conscientiously, fulfilled "the duties of a servant and tended her husband and son," she often wanted to complain, to unload the painful burdens of her heart. And Dostoevsky was a superb listener. He was always at hand, had an excellent understanding of her wrongs, helped her to bear all her misfortunes with dignity. And above all, he diverted her from the morass of provincial tedium.

"I never left their house. What happy evenings I passed in her company. Rarely have I met such a woman," he wrote later on. The husband preferred a grogshop to his home, or else sprawled half-drunk on the divan, and Maria found herself alone with Fyodor, who shortly ceased to conceal his adoration of her. Never, during his whole life, had he experienced any such intimacy with a woman—and a woman from society, at that, and cultured, with whom he could talk about all the things that occupied his thoughts. For the first time in many years he was not met with jeers. He did not have to contend with rivals, as in Panaeva's salon; he did not feel himself humiliated but could be on an equal footing with the woman he loved.

It is quite possible that Isaeva became attached to Dostoevsky, but she was not at all in love with him, at least not in the beginning, even though she may have rested her head on his shoulder and responded to his kisses. He, however, fell hopelessly in love with her, accepted as reciprocated feeling what was on her part no more than amiability, interest, and a light flirtation out of boredom. He was going on thirty-four, and he had never yet had an inamorata, someone to care for both idealistically and passionately. He was seeking love, he was in need of love, and the crystallization of his emotions found an excellent object in Maria. She was the first intelligent young woman he had met after four years at hard labor, and he wreathed her with all the flowers of his unsatisfied desire, his erotic fantasies and romantic illusions. All the joy of life became incarnate for him in this emaciated blonde woman. She seemed charming, graceful and clever, kindhearted and desirable. And to round it all off, she was unhappy, she was suffering—and suffering not only attracted him as a writer but overwhelmed his imagination and aroused an immediate, impulsive response in him as a man. Sensitivity to the grief of others heightened, in a strange manner, his erotic excitability. Sadistic and masochistic inclinations were interwoven in him in a most peculiar fashion: to love meant to sacrifice one's self and to respond with all one's soul and all one's body to the suffering of another, even at the cost of torments. But on occasion, to love meant to torture in one's own turn, to cause suffering, to wound and hurt the person loved. Then the highest delight lay in eventual sacrifice, in relieving the suffering just inflicted—to jump into the flames after kindling them, to brave everything for her sake.

Maria was not easy to get along with; she was quick to take offence, she had frequent attacks of migraine due to her worries and troubles, she had a way of pressing her fingers to her temples in a gesture of despair. She was subject to constant irritation, and was forever saying that the "vile society" in the little town did not appreciate her. She called herself a martyr, while Dostoevsky agreed and was quick to sympathize with her. She did not love her husband—or she had ceased to love him; at any rate, the remnants of whatever feelings she may have had for him were destroyed by his preposterous behavior and his drinking, which aroused her anger and aversion. She had shifted all her hopes to her son Pasha who, in her opinion, was bound to become a remarkable man—although so far, the seven-year-old boy evinced no outstanding qualities.

Although Maria might keep saying endlessly that her life was over and done with, the fact remained that she was not yet thirty and, of course, she longed not only for life but love, and happiness and good fortune. That Dostoevsky had come to love her ardently with a genuine, deep passion she understood very well—women usually have little trouble in recognizing these things—but she accepted his "courting," as she called it, without attaching any great significance to it. After all, he had been deprived of civil rights, he was a transported convict and, to use another phrase of hers, "had no future." But despite his numerous and at times frightening peculiarities, one could depend on him, and she was in no position to overlook even a feeble prop.

After the intoxicating fog of first love had disappeared, Dostoevsky made out rather clearly those special circumstances in which his feeling toward Maria had been born: "The mere fact that a woman held out her hand to me marked a veritable epoch in my life," he admitted later on. He began to see still more clearly all the difficulties of his relations with a married woman and a mother when he had the opportunity of discussing them in endless talks with his new friend, Wrangel.

WRANGEL'S COMING TO SEMIPALATINSK IN THE WINTER of 1854 seemed a gift of fate to Dostoevsky. Despite an air of coldness and aloofness, which he found quite helpful in his administrative career, the young prosecutor was an exceedingly kind and responsive individual, and of a romantic disposition. A year after making Wrangel's acquaintance, which turned into a close friendship, perhaps the only one in Dostoevsky's life— he was more frank with Wrangel in speech and correspondence than with anybody else and this for many years—Fyodor characterized him in a letter to Michael: "A very young, very mild man, with a strongly developed *point d'honneur*, unbelievably kind, a little proud (but that's just put on: I like that), a little given to the shortcomings of youth; educated, but neither brilliantly nor profoundly; likes to study; his character very weak, femininely impressionable, hypochondrial and rather apprehensive; things which would move another man to rancor and fury make him feel hurt—the sign of a splendid heart." To this it must be added that he had become sincerely attached to Dostoevsky, and immediately after his coming he began to help the writer with all the ardor of youthful idealism.

He introduced Fyodor to the military governor, Spiridonov, and from that time on the exiled former convict began to be received in the homes of the town notables. This raised Dostoevsky's social prestige a great deal; he was shortly promoted to the rank of noncommissioned officer and his living conditions improved considerably. He now had more leisure and the opportunity to use it in his own way. He could talk to Wrangel with perfect frankness, and when the baron in his turn fell in love with a married woman in Barnaul, who had several children and was mercilessly flirting with him, the talk of the two friends turned into a frank meeting of hearts. The young prosecutor listened patiently as Dostoevsky extolled Maria: "She is kind, charming, graceful, superbly magnanimous. She is a pretty little thing, educated, very clever." Wrangel was not only the friend and confidant but was active in assisting Dostoevsky as well. He liked to play a part in all the involvements of this love affair, where new complications were an almost daily occurrence.

Early in 1855 Maria at last responded to Dostoevsky's love. Whether this was simply a moment of casual intimacy or whether their relations had turned into a real attachment, it is hard to say. They had, at any rate, drawn nearer to each other. But hardly had he come to believe that Maria returned his feelings and, as he wrote, had given him "proofs of love," when Isaev was appointed assessor to Kuznetsk, some five hundred miles from Semipalatinsk. To top it all off, it was Dostoevsky who had to get the money so that they could leave: Isaev did not have a kopeck and, naturally, turned to the best friend of the family. Dostoevsky, of course, had no money of his own; he borrowed some from the never-failing Wrangel and handed it over to Maria.

In the spring of 1855, Wrangel rented a summer residence in the neighborhood of Semipalatinsk, and since Dostoevsky's battalion had been transferred to summer quarters nearby, the noncommissioned officer managed to live for weeks on end at the house of his hospitable friend. When the Isaevs finally set out for Kuznetsk in June of the same year, they made a stop at Wrangel's place to say goodbye. The host served champagne and did not find it particularly hard to make Isaev drunk and

put him in the tarantass, peacefully asleep. In the meantime
Fyodor and Maria made their way to the garden. According to
the baron's testimony, at the moment of departure the lady
herself was overcome by her feelings for Dostoevsky. The lovers
embraced, murmured a few words and held hands as they
sat on a bench under the shady trees. The driver, however,
was insistent that his fares should start at once; it was imperative to leave. Fyodor, his eyes brimming with tears, saw
Maria to the tarantass in which Isaev was snoring. A last kiss,
the driver swung his whip, the horses dashed away. When the
tarantass had disappeared in a cloud of white dust, Fyodor
still stood and watched the road that disappeared among the
pines.

Seeing the painful emotions of his friend, Wrangel tried
his best to divert him. The country house had an enormous
garden, the care of which was entrusted to the two pretty
daughters of Dostoevsky's landlady. These lively girls brought
not a little laughter and gaiety—and perhaps even something
more—into the menage of the two young men. News of the
flowers cultivated in the villa garden spread through Semipalatinsk, and the local young ladies of fashion, for whom
Wrangel had no particular liking, took to calling. Dostoevsky
helped his host to discourage them. He was very downhearted,
was forever mooning like a schoolboy about the bench where
Maria and he had parted and kept muttering something—he
had a habit of talking to himself. He was, to quote Wrangel,
"in ecstasies" over Maria and was constantly repeating how
remarkable she was and expressed astonishment that such a
woman had been able to respond to his love.

He considered himself hardly worthy of her notice but
was always writing to her, although he had to restrain himself
because of her husband. "Taking into account how badly I
feel without you," he wrote her shortly after her departure, "I
judge thereby the strength of my devotion. You wrote that

you are upset and even ill. My God! Come, do you deserve such a lot, all these cares and annoyances—you, who might serve as an ornament to any society? You are an amazing woman, with an amazing heart, a child's goodness, like one's own sister. A woman's heart, a woman's sympathy, infinite goodness . . . I have found all these in you. . . . I now live all alone; I have absolutely nowhere to go." He actually was in a tragic mood and paid no attention to the flirtatiousness of the young and pretty Marina O., the daughter of a transported Pole, whom he was tutoring. The pupil, lively, energetic and somewhat harum-scarum, was not indifferent to her teacher, especially when she found out that he had had a *love affair* with another woman! Maria was duly informed about Marina and was very jealous of her.

Whenever Dostoevsky's mood improved, he declaimed—he liked to read aloud, especially the poems of Pushkin—or walked the girls about the garden, or held endless conversations with Wrangel. By now a number of people in his circle had learned about his love, and they decided to help by arranging for him to meet Maria in secret somewhere between Semipalatinsk and Kuznetsk. Since a noncommissioned petty officer ran great risks in leaving town without official permission (besides, he was still under police surveillance, letters to him were censored, and his own letters were forwarded to the addresses in Russia through Section III, the Russian Secret Police of the period), a near-conspiracy was formed. Dostoevsky claimed to be ill, a friendly doctor certified that he had to spend a few days in bed, but meanwhile the supposed patient was racing to Zmiev, about one hundred and ten miles from Semipalatinsk, on horses furnished by his friends. It can hardly be doubted that Wrangel took part in this plot.

At Zmiev, however, a frightful disappointment awaited him: instead of Maria herself he found a letter from her informing him that, owing to changed circumstances, she had been unable to leave Kuznetsk. Without even pausing to rest, he at once started back for Semipalatinsk.

The "changed circumstances" turned out to be the last illness of Isaev. Toward the end of July his condition became hopeless; he died in a fortnight. Dostoevsky learned of this on the fourteenth of August 1855, from a letter of Maria's telling him how her husband had blessed her and their son before dying as a Christian should, and describing everything that had happened, as well as the state of her own spirits, in rather trite and rhetorical phrases. She had been left without any means and did not know what to do. Dostoevsky immediately sent her twenty-five rubles (all he had) and turned to Wrangel, who was at that time in Barnaul on official business. Fyodor begged his friend in the name of all the saints to come to the aid of the poor widow. Her situation really was critical. She found herself alone in a strange town, without means, without relatives and friends, and burdened by a young son. Isaev's death, on the other hand, changed Dostoevsky's position a great deal. He no longer had to keep his love a secret and at once asked Maria to marry him. He was guided not only by the desire to help her, to regulate their relations, and by a consciousness of his passionate love ("My God, what a woman this is; it is a pity you know her so little," he had written Wrangel); he was also strongly drawn to married life.

"There is nothing in the world superior to domestic happiness," he had written Michael on being released from penal servitude. The family life of his parents appeared to him unsullied and happy, while his own childhood was his best and purest recollection. To have a family of his own, it seemed to him, would be a return to that golden time which, after all his tribulations and misfortunes, he willingly idealized. Also, from his seventeenth year, he had not had a corner he could call his own; he dreamt of marriage as of a serene haven, he had visions of domestic comfort, of feminine solicitude. Marriage with Maria—a marriage of warm, genuine love—promised to resolve all his problems and to arrange not only the material but the sentimental and sexual aspects of his life.

Maria, naturally, had different views on all this. In answer to the ardent letters of her lover, who insisted on a definite and immediate decision, she wrote that she was sad, despairing, and did not know what action to take. Dostoevsky understood that the chief obstacle to the "disposition of our fate," as she called their proposed marriage, was his personal insecurity.

His social position was unenviable: he was a noncommissioned petty officer in a battalion of the line, an ex-convict deprived of his status as one of the gentry, under surveillance of the police and under suspicion of the authorities. Ahead of him were three more years of military service, and after that he was faced with absolute uncertainty. Maria could form no judgment concerning his talent as a writer: she had seen no new works of his, while the success of *Poor Folk* had been scored ten years before. No one could say with assurance whether he would ever be granted permission to publish his writings, and access to European Russia was for the time being barred to him. He had no means; he had to exist on the small sums his relatives sent him. How, then, could he start a family?

True, prospects for the Petrashevists seemed brighter after the death of Nicholas I and the ascent to the throne of Alexander II, in March, 1855. Dostoevsky was now writing letter after letter to his relatives and friends, pleading with them to exert themselves toward getting him promoted in the army and securing permission for him to publish his works. At times, when he informed her of his attempts to "conquer destiny," Maria took heart and was ready to give her consent to the marriage, only to lose faith again in a short while. Her temperament was not remarkable for constancy. Her father was sending her money from Astrakhan, and she could get along somehow while waiting for the modest pension coming to her as the widow of a government official. But she was frequently ailing; her ill health—a forerunner of consumption—made her irritable; in turn she made life miserable for Dostoevsky by her suspicions and jealousy. Why did she have to believe him after ten months of separation? For all she knew he was carrying on with Marina, or was sleeping with one of his landlady's daughters! As for all those girls from merchant families whom he was tutoring in mathematics—surely they must have tried to turn his head.

And Maria decided to "test" his love. Toward the very end of 1855, Dostoevsky received an odd letter from her. She asked an impartial answer from him as a friend: "Suppose somebody, elderly but kind and financially secure, were to appear and propose to her . . ."

On reading this Dostoevsky staggered and fainted away. When he recovered he told himself in despair that Maria was getting ready to marry somebody else. There was nothing impossible about this. He had learned in roundabout ways that certain old busybodies in Kuznetsk were doing their utmost to find some "reliable person who would make a good husband" for the poor widow. True, in the same letter Maria assured him of her love, but he took her words as evidence of her kindness, of a desire to console him.

His nerves were so strained by the long separation and all the uncertainty that the thought of possibly losing Maria overwhelmed him altogether. After passing a night in sobs and torments, he wrote Maria in the morning that he would die if she left him. "Great is the joy of love," he wrote Wrangel about this episode, "but its pangs are so horrible that it would be better not to love. I swear to you I am thrown into despair. I hardly understand what people are saying to me and how I am living. I have a fixed idea in my head." Shortly before he had begun a "comic" novel, *The Hamlet of Stepanchikovo*, but the work was not making any headway. "One circumstance, one incident which had been slow about coming into my life and which at last has befallen me, has carried me off and swallowed me whole," he wrote to Maikov in January, 1856. "I was happy and could not work. Then sorrow and woe came upon me. I have lost everything that constituted everything for me. I was separated by hundreds of miles. I could not write."

Maria's hesitation, which was driving Dostoevsky mad and feeding his most monstrous doubts, was due to a variety of reasons: she was not sure herself whether to marry, she hesitated out of practical considerations and, besides, it afforded her pleasure to feel her power over a man who was in love with her—and so genuine feelings were here combined with a game.

Playing a game of any sort was, however, out of the question for Dostoevsky. He loved with all the force of a belated first love, with all the ardor of novelty, all the passion and excitement of a gambler who has staked everything on one card. His sleep was haunted by nightmares and tears choked him. Waiting for a letter from Kuznetsk was an ordeal; when it did come at last, it was either disappointment or an outburst of new doubts and suspicions. He knew that Maria was weak and trusting, and he was apprehensive of the influence of others upon her: "One can make her believe anything on earth." He knew also that she was "irritable and big-hearted"—meaning that she was likely to yield to anybody's blandishments. Everybody perceived her weakness and gentleness, but he knew her as others who saw her never did. It was she of whom he wrote subsequently in *The Humiliated and Wronged:* "Melancholy gripped my heart when I made out those gaunt, wan cheeks, the lips parched and in a fever, and the eyes glinting from under their long dark lashes with a febrile glow and a certain passionate resolve." But perhaps it was someone else who had been able to kindle this febrile glow? He was jealous and, even while she had been in Semipalatinsk, had annoyed her by scolding her for every glance she cast at some other man.

But Maria, who was sickly and suspicious, was even more jealous of her lover. She suspected him of having an affair with every woman he met. In 1856, during Shrovetide, Dostoevsky had many invitations to parties and danced with the ladies; despite a certain unwieldiness he was an excellent dancer and loved to dance. He himself wrote to Maria about these innocent diversions, but she imagined the worst and decided to make him suffer in return. Hints about suitors for her hand and secret aspirants for her favors again appeared in her letters. This tragi-comedy of errors went on until April, when Maria had to admit that she had been playing a game. The Kuznetsk matrons had suggested a prospective husband to her and she had let them know that she already had someone in mind. Word of this reached Dostoevsky and once more he was thrown into despair: it turned out, however, that the man she had in mind was none other than himself. Nevertheless she did not discard the myth of marrying some elderly and wealthy suitor, and whenever she wrote to Dostoevsky about her ardent love for him she did not fail to mention: "As for marrying anybody —it would be only out of practical considerations."

Dostoevsky in the end came to the conclusion that Maria, because of her weak character, was in the same situation as Barbara, the heroine of *Poor Folk*, who had decided to marry the "steppe landowner," Bykov, to escape poverty and not to ruin Makar. "I certainly have been a prophet of doom for myself," Dostoevsky complained in one of his letters. But Barbara had no family, whereas Maria did have to think about her son. Doubtlessly things were not easy for her, but Dostoevsky had exaggerated her straitened circumstances when he had written Wrangel that she did not have a kopeck and borrowed right and left to send her money. Immediately after Isaev's death her father sent her three hundred rubles, a by no means small sum in those days, and he helped her regularly later on; Dostoevsky had to admit subsequently that she "did not lack for anything."

His personal affairs were in a far worse state: he was chronically in debt, his living quarters were beggarly, he was still a subordinate in the army. Most excruciating of all, although he was living chiefly on hopes, he was in constant dread of some catastrophe that would deprive him of Maria. In his letters to Wrangel, who at this time had gone to St. Petersburg and in his turn was in torments over Katherine Herrngross, the lady of his heart whom he had left in Barnaul, he exclaimed: "I will perish if I lose my angel: either I'll go out of my mind or will drown myself in the Irtysh." Yet to win her once and for all, he had to make sure of enough "external security" to armor himself against any well-to-do rivals in Kuznetsk. Security occupied his thoughts and was the theme of all the letters he wrote at the time: at the minimum his program called for his transfer from military service to some salaried post in the civil service, as well as a certain sum to tide him over until his appointment. Dostoevsky was now dreaming of becoming a government clerk of the fourteenth grade, that is, one of those wretched quill-drivers he had drawn in *Poor Folk* and *The Double*.

The best solution, of course, would be to receive permission to publish his writings: "Everything would work out then; for the main point is that no one knows either my powers or the extent of my talent, yet these are what I am mainly relying upon." This phrase gives him away: he could have wished for a clerkship only during his hours of utter despair. Actually, he had one insuperable longing: to see himself in print, to earn his living through literary work, to pick up his pen once more—that pen which had been taken away from him when he was first imprisoned in 1849, which had been withheld from him through the years of his penal servitude, and which was finally restored to him after a great deal of trouble, since he was still a soldier in a godforsaken Siberian garrison.

"After all, I'm not going to marry right off but shall wait for something that offers security; as for her, she'll gladly wait awhile, as long as she has hopes that my future will be securely arranged." And, one after another, the letters go winging from Semipalatinsk to St. Petersburg: to General Totleben, to Wrangel, to important people in the government, to his friends, his relatives. As always, he forms the most fantastic projects: Should he write to Maria's father to make him shoo his daughter's suitors away? Or address a petition to the Czar? Or turn to the generals who knew him in his School of Engineering days? He twists and turns and, according to his nature, becomes excited and exaggerates things. The petty details of daily life assume frightening aspects in his imagination; obstacles turn into nightmares. His writing also worries him a good deal; it is very hard to get on with it.

By the time he was released from penal servitude, Dostoevsky had practically forgotten how to write. *On the Events of the Year 1854* (the verses which he composed in May of that year) had an obvious intent: to prove his patriotic and loyal feelings. In the poem he rumbles along against the French and English who are coming forward to defend the Turks against Christ, and glorifies the Czar of All the Russias, God's Anointed and Defender of the Faith. The literary value of this work is negligible. Later, after the Isaevs had left Semipalatinsk, Dostoevsky at last buckled down to prose, and for a long stretch had to overcome that stiffness, amounting almost to petrifaction, so familiar to painters, writers and other artists after a period of inactivity. He was making a laborious comeback to the point where he had been overtaken by the catastrophe seven years before.

Maria's letters during May, 1856, again sounded disquieting notes. She either wrote that she was sad and pining, or suddenly announced, "We have suffered too much, have been too unfortunate, to dream of marriage." She was not the one to make him happy—it would be best to forget, to renounce everything. The only thing she asked of him was to do something for Pasha; the boy was going on nine, he must be placed in some private institution of learning.

Exhausted by all this correspondence, with its alternations of hot and cold, Dostoevsky decided on an extreme measure: he must see Maria personally; he had to talk things over with her and clear up everything. And that meant he had to go to Kuznetsk.

After a great deal of trouble and all sorts of dodges, he managed to enlist the aid of his battalion commander, who was well aware of the unhappy course of his love. Dostoevsky, as a noncommissioned officer, was assigned to deliver a wagonload of ropes to Barnaul—and Kuznetsk was not so far away. He set out on his long trip, hoping to see and embrace Maria in a few days.

IN JUNE, 1856, DOSTOEVSKY LEFT BARNAUL SECRETLY FOR
Kuznetsk, dreaming that the meeting with the woman who,
to use his own expression, was "rightfully his" would resolve
all his doubts and difficulties. But instead of a joyful reunion,
Kuznetsk set the stage for a terrible fiasco. When he came
into Maria's room, she did not throw herself on his neck; instead she broke into sobs and began kissing his hands, scream-
ing that all was lost, that the marriage could not take place.
She had to make a clean breast of everything: she had fallen
in love with another. This successful rival, Nicholas Vergunov,
a native of Irkutsk, who taught at a primary school, was a
rather good-looking fellow of twenty-four; Maria had become
physically infatuated with him and was even thinking of marrying him.

Fyodor clutched his head as he listened to her. When she
had finished, he remarked that the time would come when
Vergunov would reproach her for having been moved only by
passion and ruining him. At first she was sure he was jealous,
but then she grew thoughtful and started crying again. Now
she no longer believed in any man's love. Vainly he tried during
their long talk to get to the bottom of her real feelings and
find out what her relations and Vergunov's were; this disjointed
conversation most probably resembled the one he later gave in
The Humiliated and Wronged to Vanya and Natasha: " 'You
don't respect him, don't even believe in his love, yet you're

going to him irretrievably and are ruining everyone for his sake. What is this, then? He will harass you all life long, and you will do the same to him.'—'Yes, I love him like a madwoman,' she answered, paling, as though from pain. 'I have never loved you so, Vanya. For I myself know I've gone out of my mind and that I don't love him as one should. I love him in an evil way. . . . Why, I knew this before, and even during our happiest moments had a premonition that he would give me nothing but torments.' "

Instead of the "solid" suitor he had dreaded and whom Maria was ready to marry "out of practical considerations," Dostoevsky found in Kuznetsk a rival far more fortunate in love but hardly any better off financially than himself. He had been apprehensive about a re-enactment of the situation in *Poor Folk*, but in reality he was threatened by a situation out of *White Nights*—or even worse. Maria insisted on his meeting Vergunov. "I met him; he cried in my room; however, that is all he can do—cry," Dostoevsky wrote bitterly to Wrangel. Perhaps his feeling toward his rival was the same as that of the hero of *The Humiliated and Wronged* toward Natasha's lover: "He was weak, trusting, and timid of heart; he had no will power whatsoever. To injure, to deceive him would have been a sin and a pity."

To spare Vergunov's feelings Dostoevsky concealed what he himself was going through and calmly discussed the chances of Maria's marriage to the young teacher. He had to weigh his words and resort to small wiles. "I know the false position I was in," he wrote Wrangel, "for if I were to begin advising them against it (the marriage), to represent the future to them, both would have said: 'He's looking out for himself; he's purposely inventing future horrors.' " But no matter what he might say to Maria, he understood very well that she felt she had unlimited power over Vergunov, while he himself was no more than her victim. "She anticipated the delight of loving

madly and of torturing excruciatingly the one she loved, and
that precisely because she loved, and for that reason, perhaps,
hastened to give herself as a victim to him first"—this description of Natasha in *The Humiliated and Wronged* is fully ap-
plicable to Maria and her attitude toward Vergunov and, no
matter how strange it may seem, toward Dostoevsky as well.
She was torturing both her lovers and, at the same time, undergoing torture on their account and finding a peculiar delight
in this mixture of moral and erotic sadism and masochism.
And this unwholesome and complex sensation called to and
found a response in precisely the same tendencies in Dostoevsky. He felt crushed, racked—and the very keenness of his
sufferings brought on a chilly rapture. The strain he was under,
the strangeness of the circumstances, the tears and passion,
the humiliation and desire—all these were blended into exhausting and vital sensation of the intensity of existence. At
moments it seemed to him that he now loved her more than
ever, because of her own betrayal, because she had tortured and
wronged him.

He had an insuperable urge to give everything up for
Maria's sake, to sacrifice his love to her new passion, to go
away and not hinder her in arranging her life in whatever way
she wanted. But when Maria saw that, instead of reproaching
her, Dostoevsky was merely concerned about her future, she
was as overwhelmed as Natasha, who tells Vanya, "You're a
kind, honest man! And you don't say a word about yourself!
Why, I was the first to leave you, yet you have forgiven everything; my happiness is the only thing you're thinking of."

Perhaps because of this Dostoevsky was not compelled to
suffer long in the role of a martyr, for Maria refused to accept
his voluntary sacrifice. "Don't cry, don't grieve," he quoted her
as saying later. "All is not lost yet. There are just the two of us
—and no one else." At the most crucial moment pity for
Fyodor and a tender feeling for him flared up in her once more.

"She recalled the past, and her heart turned to me anew," was how he described the shift in her emotions. When he was least expecting it, she threw herself into his arms and recompensed him for everything he had gone through. "I don't know what the two days I passed through were like," he wrote Wrangel. "They were bliss and unbearable torture."

Whether Dostoevsky transmitted his passion to her, whether she was swept away by a return of her old emotion, whether she was caught in the trap of her own intricate game or simply did not want to give up her control of either man— no matter what the cost—the fact remains that she yielded to Fyodor and he was able to inform Wrangel: "I left toward the end of the second day *completely* hopeful." He stressed the word himself. But despite her "proof of love," as he put it, he realized the difficulty of his position. His former illusions had crashed; Maria appeared before him in a new light and, instead of the former clarity, utter chaos now reigned in his soul. When, on his way back from Kuznetsk, his head cleared from the intoxication of his recent intimacy, he reflected that according to the French proverb, the absent are always in the wrong: "I am far away while he is with her." No matter how ardent Maria's recent kisses had been, he could not rely on her being faithful to him. For who could guarantee that after his departure she would not begin to vacillate and go back to the younger lover?

Hardly had he returned to Semipalatinsk and recovered to some extent after his physical and spiritual shock, when a letter came from Maria: she was despondent, lachrymose, and repeated that she loved Vergunov more than Fyodor. Worn out and thoroughly humiliated, he forgot all diplomacy and wrote urging both her and Vergunov to look at everything coolly and with common sense. Why, for them to live together—and to marry of all things!—would be sheer madness. Maria let this pass in silence, but the teacher took offence and answered with

coarse insinuations. This did not keep Dostoevsky from trying
to help Vergunov to better his condition for, after all, his
rival might shortly marry Maria, and her welfare was the dearest
thing on earth to him. He overcame his jealousy and resentment and, quixotically, offered himself as a sacrifice.

He was, however, suffering unbearably because of his own
magnanimity. The idea of a marriage of convenience for Maria
had offended his moral sensibility, arousing his indignation
against injustice, against the "evil lot of the poor"; but the
idea that she was about to marry a pauper wounded his pride as
a man, since he and Vergunov were equally able—or unable
—to support a family at present. Besides, the twenty-four-
year-old teacher could not expect anything but a miserly salary
in the future—he had little education, and only a most insignificant career lay ahead of him, still in the same primary
schools, whereas Dostoevsky was a writer, he had once attained recognition and even now, during his lonely nights, had
faith in his great calling. Therefore Maria must have preferred
Vergunov solely out of love. The matter had to do with
sentiment, pure and simple. Why did the woman he had
chosen, to whom he had given his heart, refuse to share his
faith? Why could she not see that fame awaited him? Why had
she not gambled on him? For there is no greater humiliation
to a man than to realize that he is merely one of the herd to
the woman he loves and that she has read nothing prophetic on
his brow. A very great deal in Dostoevsky's later life is explained by his resentment of this affront: it is rarely forgiven
by anybody even of modest talent.

But for the time being it was necessary to swallow his
pride: he had no other choice.

"It is simply impossible for me to let her go, under any
circumstances," he explained to Wrangel. "Love at my age is
no whim; it has lasted for two years—you hear?—for two
years; during the ten months of separation it not only has not

weakened but has reached preposterousness." He no longer had the strength to master this preposterousness. Recollections of their intimacy, even though momentary, baited both his flesh and imagination: he was forever citing the "proofs" of her love, as well as his "rights" to it.

These searing recollections did not make things easier, of course; everybody noticed that Dostoevsky had reached the end of his tether. In the early fall of 1856 he looked like a ghost during military drills and parades; those who knew him best feared he would collapse. His nervous tension found release in an attack of epilepsy, after which he was ill for a whole week. Material cares were added to his physical and spiritual torments: his assistance to Maria (he was constantly sending her money) and the trip to see her had put him in debt to the tune of more than a thousand rubles. There was no way of paying this off. Whichever way he turned he ran into a high, inexorable wall; there was no way out, and all life seemed to him either a journey through the circles of a Dantean inferno or the unreal vision of a sick brain.

AT THE VERY MOMENT WHEN IT APPEARED TO DOSTOEV-
sky that he had touched bottom and reached the very limits
of degradation and grief, his existence took a turn for the better.
The dark streak of ill luck had come to an end and he could see
gleams of light ahead. After the first of October, 1856, he was
made a "praporshchik" (the first officer rank) and this meant
restoration to the privileged class, outside of which it was so
hard to live in Russia. Also, hopes increased for his pardon
and, consequently, for his return to Russia proper. Owing either
to these circumstances or to the changeability of her character,
Maria grew perceptibly cooler toward Vergunov. The question
of marrying him vanished of itself, somehow, and she wrote
Fyodor that the teacher was "impossible in a material way"
—he was earning only three hundred rubles a year. She began
to use tender phrases in her letters to Dostoevsky: she called
him her brother and said she was pining for him. And in November, 1856, he wrote to Wrangel: "She is, as before, *everything* in my life; I love her to the verge of madness. . . .
Separation from her would bring me to suicide. I am a miserable madman. Love of that sort is a sickness." He attempted
to give a sensible explanation of his state: "She came to me
during the most grievous time in my destiny and resurrected
my soul, my whole existence."

On learning that Vergunov was out of favor, his spirits
rose and he again brought up the question of marriage. When

another opportunity of going to Barnaul presented itself, this time under better conditions, since he was now an officer, he dashed off to Kuznetsk—but on this occasion he stayed there not two days but five. A reception far different from the one given him five months before awaited him. Maria assured him that she no longer trusted Vergunov and did not really love anyone but Fyodor. Before leaving her, he won her formal consent to their marriage in the very near future. On December 21, 1856, he wrote Wrangel: "If a certain circumstance does not interfere, I will be married before Lent." What was this circumstance? And to whom did it refer? To Vergunov, who had unwillingly renounced his beloved; to Dostoevsky, who feared new complications; or to Maria, who was liable to change her mind once more?

At any rate, Dostoevsky now considered himself formally engaged to Maria. He had attained his long-cherished purpose —his dream was about to be realized at last. Yet at that moment he was experiencing not ecstasy but weariness and apathy. Each hour is a law unto itself, and only what comes at the proper hour is good. Whatever is delayed too long loses its value, and the gift which might have made one drunk with joy yesterday no longer touches the heart today. Like a runner in a strenuous race, Dostoevsky found himself at the tape so exhausted by his effort that he received his victory almost with indifference.

At any rate there is neither enthusiasm nor triumph in his correspondence concerning his approaching marriage: there are only sober words about money and arrangements. At least six hundred rubles were needed for the wedding, and he had to borrow the sum from one of his friends in Semipalatinsk.

What had moved Maria to consent to the marriage at long last? Dostoevsky's daughter affirms (and certain biographers follow in her light steps, even though not quite so categorically), that Maria married Fyodor not for love but out of practical considerations. She is portrayed as a clever schemer, who not only provided for herself and her boy and led her naïve suitor around by the nose, but at the same time was slyly keeping up her affair with Vergunov, who was supposed to be tagging after her from town to town. All these accusations do not jibe with the image of Maria as seen by Dostoevsky or by his close friends. Stratagems and mine-laying were simply not the part of her character. On the contrary, she was incapable of any prolonged effort or concentrated action toward a set goal and always acted through intuition, at the caprice of some chance mood. It is, of course, quite possible that she may have considered marriage with Dostoevsky as the best way out of a serious situation. After the wedding she wrote both to her relatives and his that she had married for the sake of her son. But why should she have intrigued, or lured Dostoevsky into her snare when he himself was rapturously breaking his neck to get into it, constantly talking about his passionate and tender love and begging her to be his forever?

He, at any rate, thought that she was marrying him for love, and did not doubt her devotion and attachment. "She loves me, and has given me proof of it," he had written Wrangel. Marriage seemed to him the natural consummation of everything that had passed between them: "I was all taken up with my relations with Maria Dmitrievna during the last two years. At least I was living—suffering, but living." He understood, however, that to live under such tension all the time was impossible, and he pictured marriage as a relief, as the beginning of that domestic happiness of which he had dreamt so long.

By the New Year everything had been agreed upon. He borrowed the needed sum, rented living quarters, obtained permission from the authorities and a leave of absence, and at the beginning of January, 1857, left for Kuznetsk. There all was in readiness for a "quiet" wedding and, on the sixth of

February, Maria and Fyodor were married in a church at Kuznetsk: the record of the marriage has been preserved in the church register.

Immediately after the wedding ceremony the couple took their places in a tarantass and set out for Barnaul, where they were to spend their first night together. But when they reached the house of their friends, Dostoevsky had a frightful attack of epilepsy. Moaning, his face deadly pale, he crashed to the floor in appalling convulsions and lost consciousness. When he came to, he was so weak that he could hardly talk or move. Maria was so frightened that she almost fainted in her turn. Dostoevsky's seizure had a staggering effect on her. Doctors were called in, but their diagnosis not only did not reassure her but actually increased her panic: they declared that Dostoevsky had epilepsy and warned that there was a possibility of his dying during a seizure from a constriction of the throat. Maria burst into sobs and began to reproach Dostoevsky because he had concealed his malady from her.

He tried to justify himself, assuring her that he himself had not known the exact nature of the disease. Up to then he had really supposed that his attacks, even though they did resemble epilepsy, were nevertheless not actually that. He had written this to Michael on being released from penal servitude, he had said it to his friends and acquaintances. Yanovsky, his physician, had asserted the same thing, even before Dostoevsky's arrest. But now there could be no doubt of any sort, and the verdict of doctors sounded a grim warning. And as a beginning for married life, an epileptic seizure could hardly be considered the happiest omen.

When Fyodor's condition became somewhat better, the pair resumed their trip: she disillusioned, exhausted by all she had gone through; he extremely weak (as always after one of these attacks), crushed and morose. "If I had known for a certainty that I had epilepsy," he wrote his brother shortly afterward, "I would never have married. My wife was ailing when I brought her to Semipalatinsk." What he failed to write about was of considerably greater importance. The seizure in Barnaul had probably occurred at the very moment when the newlyweds first found themselves alone. It had, of course, brought on a succession of shocks and even traumatic consequences of a strictly sexual nature. Possibly it is precisely here that one must seek for the solution of why Fyodor's marriage with Maria proved a failure primarily on physical grounds.

The Dostoevskys arrived in Semipalatinsk on the twentieth of February, 1857, and began making a home in small and poorly furnished quarters. When Fyodor had fully recovered from the blow that had "overwhelmed" him "physically and morally," he tried to straighten out his marital relations. But physical intimacy had not brought him that happiness and forgetfulness he had dreamt of. Both husband and wife were nervous and ailing; Dostoevsky was haunted by a feeling of guilt that alternated with eruptions of passion—tempestuous, convulsive and sickly—to which Maria responded either by fright or frigidity. And since her own emotions were markedly hysterical, their moods and desires hardly ever coincided. If Dostoevsky's mate had been a simple and well-balanced woman, she might have calmed his doubts, built up his confidence in his own powers and provided a normal release for his hypersexuality, lessening his masochistic, sadistic and infantile complexes. Their marital relations might have gradually attained a certain emotional and sensual equilibrium. But in the tense, nervous atmosphere Maria created, the pathological traits of her husband came to the fore even more prominently and painfully. They irritated, tortured and exhausted each other in an incessant struggle. Their attacks on each other were succeeded by mutual contrition and self-flagellation; the assurances of infinite love turned into a barren duel of bodies; the dissatisfaction of the flesh consumed both body and soul. Instead of a honeymoon they spent a month of disillusionment, pain and exhausting attempts to attain a sexual harmony that never materialized. There was no complete union, and the carnal irritation intensified their spiritual melancholy and their discontent. Maria was, probably, incapable of emotional deception and of creating erotic illusions in her mate. It is even possible that she made unflattering comparisons between Vergunov and her epileptic husband, who at times must have repelled and even frightened her.

To Dostoevsky she was the first woman with whom he was intimate not in the brief embrace of a chance encounter but through regular marital relations, and his attitude toward her was exceedingly complex. He shortly came to realize that she could not become his mate in a strictly sexual sense, that she did not share either his passion or his sensuality. And thereupon, with redoubled solicitude, he became her brother, her protector and guardian. He pitied her with a poignant, human pity; he treated her with tenderness and gentleness, as he might have treated a little girl he wanted to protect from possible misfortunes and disasters. "She is poor, weak, she fears everything—she has a proud, noble heart." His comments on his wife bristle with such expressions. Many years later he told Olga Pochinkovskaya, his proofreader, who bore a very slight resemblance to Maria in looks: "She was a woman with a most exalted and enraptured soul. She was an idealist in the full sense of that word—yes! And as pure and naïve as a child."

But if they were unable to become one physically, why was he unhappy with this noble and exalted nature in everything else? Why did not their life together succeed on any plane, on even one level? And that this was precisely the case is attested to by a host of direct and indirect indications and admissions of Dostoevsky himself. There is also the exact testimony of those who knew both of them during the first years of their difficult and strange union.

The letters Maria wrote very shortly after the wedding

are devoid of any gushing references to her married life (and she was very much the gusher), or any assurances of happiness, such as one might naturally expect from such an emotional and lively nature. To one of her sisters she wrote that she was "loved, pampered" by her "clever husband, who is deeply in love with me." Never a word, however, about her love for him. To her father she wrote in the same vein: "I am happy over my fate and Pasha's." Her expressions are dry and cold; the style is restrained and rational. Still more curious is the tone of Dostoevsky's letters. They show a sharp difference from his effusions of several months prior to his marriage. There is not a trace left of his former raptures and romantic exaggerations. "I love her very much, and so far everything is going quite well," he had written to Michael. Yet in the very next letter he cannot keep back a phrase like "We're living so-so."

This lack of enthusiasm, which clearly indicates disillusionment and incompatibility, stemmed of course from the characters of both husband and wife. Dostoevsky was a strange man and very difficult to get along with. And his love—what with its contradictions of tenderness, compassion, eagerness for physical domination, the fear of causing pain and an unrestrainable yearning to inflict torture—was no light thing. He was a stranger to simple emotions (he confessed later on that he feared and did not understand so-called "simple natures") and Berdyaev described his love as "Dionysian," meaning that it rent apart both body and soul. Then, too, this writer, who could unriddle and explore all the dark corners of mind and heart in his complex heroes, found no word when it came to speaking of the things he himself was living through.

"In certain natures," he wrote in *The Humiliated and Wronged*, "there at times occurs some sort of obstinacy, some sort of chaste unwillingness to evince tenderness even to the person you love, and this not only in the presence of others but even when the two of you are alone—even more so when you are alone; only infrequently does a caress escape them, and it escapes all the more ardently, all the more impetuously, the longer it has been kept in check." This confession is clearly autobiographical: Dostoevsky used the very same terms in writing to Michael and his friends about his own inability to express emotions through a gesture, to show tenderness, to overcome his "woodenness." Maria, probably, took for coldness what was no more than a habit due to a lonely life, to timidity and a certain inner shyness.

Concerning Maria after their marriage he wrote in muted terms: "She is a kind and tender being, somewhat precipitate, quick, strongly impressionable; her past life has left painful traces on her soul. Her emotional transitions are almost impossibly quick." At the very beginning of their friendship he had mentioned that she had a gay and lively character, even though he did remark on her irritable and impressionable nature. Now he was stressing her nervous instability and her leaps from gaiety to hypochondria. In our day such women as Maria are considered hysterical, with clearly defined tendencies toward melancholy and a persecution mania—that is, as having symptoms of paranoia. She was lightning quick to take offense, perceived evil intentions at every turn, screamed and sobbed during her attacks of rage until she collapsed. Then, having calmed down, she resignedly asked forgiveness and showed such an understanding of herself and others, such meekness and kindness, that Dostoevsky's heart was rent by compassion and he would kneel before her and kiss her hands. Of course, her nervousness and touchiness, her fantastic flare-ups of malice or equally fantastic fits of magnanimity, were to a considerable extent explainable by her general physical weakness; her pulmonary complaint was becoming climactic, while her neurasthenia, as well as her sterility, had deep biologic roots. It was not only difficult but at times actually excruciating to live with her day in and day out. Of course, life with such a genius as Dostoevsky, so complex and prone to suffering and so worn out by life, was also quite an ordeal.

Dostoevsky's daughter, as well as certain students of his life who have followed her lead, are apt to ascribe the failure of his first marriage to a coarser and more obvious cause: Maria is supposed to have gone on loving Vergunov. According to this theory, she was unable to conceal her passion for her former lover, and consequently Fyodor, confronted by her frigidity and even infidelity, turned against her and suffered deeply, even though he could not leave her. He found himself bound hand and foot (it was common knowledge that the church marriage could be dissolved only through difficult and complicated negotiations, entailing much expense), while the further development of his wife's disease kept him from deserting her, since by nature he was exceptionally honest and noble.

Actually, it is curious that immediately after his marriage Dostoevsky, despite his own material difficulties and cares, resumed his efforts in Vergunov's behalf and stated that the teacher was now "dearer than a brother" to him. He had that odd, almost physical feeling of curiosity and predisposition toward him which both men and women very often experience toward those who have been sexually intimate with their mates. This feeling exists side by side with jealousy and despite it. It is a peculiar sort of erotic trait, and in certain individuals it is present to an unwholesome degree. Rosanov, Dostoevsky's self-designated disciple, would probably have explained it as a sexual-carnal sensation of shared possession, approaching incest ("All the lovers of the very same woman are related"), and would have said it is typical for persons of profound sexuality. And Dostoevsky's was a nature given to vividly pronounced and very strong eroticism.

SETTLING DOWN, ATTEMPTS AT GETTING MONEY AND ALL
sorts of cares and worries occupied Dostoevsky's time and mind
right up to the fall of 1857. His duties as an officer took up
almost the whole day. Awaiting him at home was the seamy
side of married life—a shrewish mate, the tedium of provincial
existence. There was only one encouraging sign: he was becoming more absorbed in his writing. Whatever the outcome
of his own personal drama, it liberated his energy as a writer,
and his emotions and thoughts, no longer taken up with the
problem of winning Maria, were now concentrated on new
works.

Almost two years were to pass before Dostoevsky regained
that literary facility he thought he had lost forever during his
penal servitude and his first year in the Seventh Siberian Battalion of the Line. Toward the end of 1857 he could say with
assurance that he again felt he was a writer. He was possessed
anew by that concentration which had formerly amazed his
friends so much. He was truly living in a world of his own in-
vention and creation, forgetting food and drink as he planned
his stories and novels. So absorbed was he in his characters
that he could not reply to his wife coherently, was always
dropping things, and, in general, created the impression of an
absolutely abnormal person. Maria could hardly understand
such an obsession; she found her husband's literary absorption
somewhat frightening and felt bewildered whenever Fyodor,

as he paced up and down the room, talked enthusiastically about some "remarkable" subject. (All subjects, always, were remarkable to him.)

During 1857 and 1858 he completed *Uncle's Dream*, a comic canvas of provincial life, and *The Hamlet of Stepanchikovo*, the hero of which, Thomas Opiskin, is a Russian reincarnation of Tartuffe. *Uncle's Dream* ran to over thirty thousand words and *The Hamlet of Stepanchikovo* to about fifty thousand, but Dostoevsky was cherishing the idea of a larger, full-length work of two hundred thousand words or thereabouts, in a Dickensian vein. This, most probably, was the first outline of *The Humiliated and Wronged*, a novel he completed only three years later and into which he put extensive autobiographical material.

As he continued to write, he was persistently seeking official permission to publish his works. Singlemindedness in the attainment of his goals—like his obsession with hard work when writing—was a characteristic of his that went back to youth: he was fond of speaking about an *"idée fixe,"* of the necessity of "hammering away at one point." His *idée fixe* just then was to stage a comeback in literature.

In August, 1857, eight years after he had vanished from the literary scene, he made his reappearance in print with *Little Hero*, a short story published in *Notes of the Fatherland*. He had begun it as far back as 1849, before his arrest. But two more years were to elapse before *The Russian Word* could bring out *Uncle's Dream* (February, 1859), and *Notes of the Fatherland* was enabled to serialize, in the same year, *The Hamlet of Stepanchikovo*.

The liberal measures of the new regime revived Dostoevsky's hopes, and he held to a strong belief that Alexander II would loosen the tight knots tied by his father. The writer found his duties as an officer most onerous, but handing in his resignation depended on permission to reside in Russia proper.

He could not depend on civilian employment in Semipalatinsk, while his cherished plans of resuming his literary career and thus earning an income were faced with purely physical obstacles: letters to the northern capital took from twenty to twenty-five days. The negotiations with publishers and magazine editors had to be carried on through Michael, who was married and had a business of his own (a cigarette factory) to attend to; despite all the love and devotion he felt for Fyodor he could not become his literary agent. In order to earn a livelihood by writing one had to be at the "sources"—*i.e.*, either in Moscow or St. Petersburg, and this was not even to be thought of until the term of military service in Siberia was at an end. One encouraging sign, however, was the restoration in May, 1857, of Dostoevsky's hereditary status as a member of the gentry. This meant the complete reinstatement of his civil rights. As an officer and a gentleman he no longer felt like a political criminal and a recent convict.

The intercessions of Michael, of Wrangel (who was now in St. Petersburg) and of a number of Fyodor's other friends were, however, moving ahead very slowly. Instead of the realization of his hopes he was confronted by loathsome military drilling, a beggarly salary, the reproaches of his wife. Maria, too, saw that her dreams had not materialized. She had wanted to come back into Semipalatinsk society as victor and to prove to all those stodgy and scornful women that they had made a mistake in looking down their noses at her. But her revenge had not come off: there actually was no money for even the modest entertainment of guests or to buy clothes with, and once more she had to sit at home and sulk. She had succeeded (again through Fyodor's efforts) in placing her son Pasha in the Siberian Cadet Corps, and since August, 1857, she and her husband had been living by themselves. Both were unwell; Dostoevsky ascribed their childlessness to his wife's ill health. "We're living after a fashion," he wrote Constant, "and there is no cause to complain of our lot, but my health is poor." One curious fact is that, according to the record he kept of the dates of his seizures, he was free from epilepsy during the period from September to December (inclusive), 1857, precisely when he was complaining about his health. Evidently his depressed mood had been brought on by other factors.

At the end of November, in the same year, he wrote to Barbara, Maria's sister, whom he liked very much even before actually meeting her and with whom he became very friendly later on: "Do you know I have a certain superstition, a certain premonition, that I am bound to die soon. Such premonitions are due almost always to hypochondria, and I assure you that in the present instance I am not being hypochondrical, and my certainty of imminent death is quite unemotional. . . . It seems to me that I have already lived through everything in this world and that there will be nothing more for which one may strive." He wrote these lines ten months after his marriage to the woman he loved, to that "angel" he "could not live without," and because of whom he had been ready to drown himself in the Irtysh.

In January, 1858, following the advice his friends had sent him from St. Petersburg, he submitted a formal request for permission to resign and to return to Russia proper. After all, he had finished his term: according to the sentence he had to spend four years in Siberia upon his release from penal servitude, and now his fourth year in Semipalatinsk was drawing to a close. Still another year passed, however, before his request (a fully legitimate one) was granted. And this year proved to be so unbearable that Dostoevsky retained the most somber recollections of it. "I am living in Semipalatinsk, which has become a deadly bore to me," he wrote to Yakushkin in December, 1858. "I don't read any periodicals, and it is half a year by now since I've had even any newspapers in my hands."

His writing was going slowly; the reason for this, however,

was his desire to give the best embodiment possible to each artistic design. In May, 1858, he answered Michael's letter concerning artistic creativity: "But what a theory you have, my friend—that a picture must be dashed off, and so and on and on. Believe me, hard work is required at every point, and an enormous deal of it. You obviously are confusing inspiration—*i.e.*, the instantaneous creation of a picture or a spiritual impulse (this always comes about thus) with work. I, for instance, always write down a scene as it first came to me, and am glad to have it; but then for months, for years on end, I work over it, am inspired by it time after time . . . and time after time add something to it or take something away from it."

But in 1858 and at the beginning of 1859 there was little inspiration and for the most part there was only work left, and even that was not jelling.

Dostoevsky's melancholy and apathy were intensified by a growing awareness of his bankruptcy as a family man. Almost as soon as he arrived home from his duties, the hated bickerings with his wife began, and her tears and her reproaches. She still wanted "to play an important rôle" and sulked at him, as though he alone were to blame for their lack of money and the fact that they could not entertain. He had assured her that everything would come out right very soon, so she considered their stay in Semipalatinsk a temporary one and they lived as if they were camping out. Even though Dostoevsky was exerting himself beyond his strength, tutoring and trying all sorts of things to raise a few rubles, to say nothing of borrowing right and left, they simply could not extricate themselves from their poverty. His illusions concerning her as a housewife had quickly disappeared; like him, she did not know how to handle money. Their affairs were in disorder, they lived in constant fear of their creditors, of unpleasantness and a complete collapse of their meager finances; they dreaded the day when there would be nothing left even to buy bread with.

They had barely enough to pay the rent and buy food; they could not afford even to think of other expenses. Mamontova-Melchikova, one of the students Dostoevsky tutored, recalled "how hoarsely he coughed in winter and how he used his uniform overcoat to hide the shortcomings of his dress." This unfortunate year dragged on and on without a single comforting thought or a glimmer of light; of their love nothing remained but a habit of attachment and pity; the future was dressed in the most discouraging colors.

In the spring of 1859, however, came the long-awaited permission to resign and to choose any city in Russia proper as a place of residence, with the exception of Moscow and St. Petersburg. Dostoevsky's spirits rose immediately. He was busied— this time happily—with his departure. All their friends were outfitting them for the trip: there was little difficulty in borrowing money for their traveling expenses. Pasha was taken from his cadet corps. Official papers concerning Dostoevsky's retirement with the rank of ensign were ready by the thirtieth of June. Two days later Fyodor, Maria, Pasha and a servant left Semipalatinsk in a tarantass bought especially for the journey. Dostoevsky had decided to settle in Tver: the town was not far from Moscow and on a railroad line between the two capitals. Something like three thousand miles had to be covered on horses to their destination.

They traveled for a long time, stopping at various towns. In Ekaterinburg they could not resist splurging on rosaries, cuff links and buttons of semiprecious stones. In Nizhni Novgorod, Maria rested up at the hotel while her husband made the rounds of the famous fair. Maria, on the whole, stood the trip badly and was constantly suffering, and whatever pleasure Dostoevsky had anticipated from the journey did not materialize: no one shared his delight in nature and new faces and scenes, and he felt his loneliness with particular force.

This feeling was sharply intensified when they arrived in

Tver toward the end of August. After much searching they found a furnished flat of three small rooms: Michael had advised this, and besides, they could not afford anything better. Maria remained dissatisfied with the arrangement, however. Everything about Tver displeased her, and she annoyed her husband unmercifully with her reproaches and ridiculous requests. Dostoevsky, too, found Tver unpleasant: it was a tiny provincial town, with grass growing on the streets, but he was excited by its nearness to Moscow and spoke incessantly of his literary plans. Maria complained that she had not a thing to wear and that all her rags reeked too much of the Siberian backwoods. At any rate, here is what he wrote Michael the very day after he returned from penal servitude and exile, after his "resurrection from the dead," as he put it, and an absence of eight years from Russia: "I wrote you yesterday about a hat (for Maria). Don't forget it my friend, for God's sake. A swatch of the ribbon-trim for the hat is enclosed. (These ribbons come from Wichman, in St. Petersburg: so a woman clerk in a shop here told me.) As for the color of the hat: it's the same as that of the small grayish stripe on the ribbons."

Maria's chief concern was not to fall flat on her face before the local fashion plates, but she immediately notified her husband that she would not make any calls, since she had nowhere to receive guests in her turn. She was ashamed of her quarters, took her poverty as an undeserved insult and, in general, behaved like a martyr who was being hurt and misunderstood by an evil tyrant of a husband not worthy of her exalted soul. In *The Humiliated and Wronged*, Dostoevsky described this mood: "It occurs at times with people of the utmost kindness but with weak nerves. . . . Women, for instance, occasionally experience a need of feeling themselves miserable, wronged, even though there may be neither wrongs nor miseries."

Two months after settling in Tver he wrote to a correspondent in Siberia: "I keep up our friendships by myself; Maria doesn't want to do so, since we have no place to entertain. . . . Maria cries at times, remembering all of you." (The last phrase referred to their friends in Semipalatinsk.) If the recent past seemed enviable to her now, and the recollection of it made her shed tears of regret, it meant that the move to Russia proper had brought new disappointments and a new failure. She found everything oppressive; she simply could not reconcile herself to her position, or her husband's work, or his relatives. Michael, whom Fyodor had not seen for nine years, came to visit him. This meeting overjoyed Fyodor, but Maria spoiled everything. She and Michael did not get along well, disliking each other at first sight. Michael concealed his unfriendliness, but Maria flaunted hers: she knew that at one time the elder brother had tried to discourage Fyodor from marrying her. She also knew that Michael was happily married, that his wife, a simple and pretty little German whom he had found in Reval, had borne him children, made a comfortable home for him, and that they were one in heart and soul; in short, she had done everything for Michael and was to him all that Maria could not be to Fyodor.

At any rate, Maria immediately became jealous of Michael's relations with her husband, suspected Michael's family of intrigues against herself, and by all her actions and speeches caused Fyodor unnecessary grief. She was fantastic, touchy, jealous without rhyme or reason, and always of the wrong women; she picked at those Dostoevsky thought nothing of and never suspected those who did interest him. Any and every pretext was enough to bring on tears and scenes. It was impossible to go out with her anywhere. Always some preposterous incident arose; either she had not been served correctly at a restaurant, or the shop clerks had been rude to her, or someone they knew had barely nodded to her in passing. When her husband felt cheerful she was downcast, but no sooner would he become absorbed in thought than she would begin to pester him with jokes and to laugh for no earthly reason. Whenever he sat down to write she reproached him with keeping her practically immured, of not showing his face to their friends, of not sharing any of his feelings or thoughts with her. But he could not share anything with her, since she had no understanding of his religious aspirations or his literary ambitions. Her attitude toward his writings was always somewhat skeptical. She had been brought up on Karamzin, the works of Turgenev were closer to her than her own husband's, and Dostoevsky frowned and became irritated whenever she launched into speeches on contemporary literature, of which she had a very poor grasp. She was also afflicted with an innate provincialism, made unexpected and savage attacks on people she hardly knew, had a tendency to praise somebody at first flush and then demolish him with jeers and insults, and was subject to quick swings from optimistic fantasy to complete frustration. At times, when she gave her suspiciousness full rein and declared that the most inoffensive individuals were her enemies and all but fiends, Dostoevsky could not help feeling anger and resentment rise within him.

12

IT WAS IN TVER THAT DOSTOEVSKY'S MARRIAGE WENT COM-
pletely on the rocks. Was this the result of gradually accumu-
lating misunderstandings and even hatred? Had that physical
intimacy which, for better or worse, nevertheless had existed
between them as far back as Semipalatinsk days, now come to
an end? Or must we believe the improbable story of Dostoevsky's daughter that Vergunov had supposedly followed Maria
to Tver, and that her infidelity had become clear to the husband
who idealized her? Most probably Maria cherished an unrealis-
tic dream that she still loved Vergunov. But even if this were
the case, and Maria had informed her husband that she did
not love him and never had loved him, what value could be put
on her hysterical outbursts? For he knew, if anybody did, that
she was a sick and unhappy woman, who made up things as
some sort of compensation for her torments and bitterness.
He understood only too well that she, too, was suffering. Their
very relations were based on their torment and pity for each
other. These fleeting intervals of woe and tenderness bound
them more than any passion could. A strange emotion, a com-
mingling of pain, compassion (especially on his part), recollections of the past, regret for what had never materialized
between them, drew them together. Then too, a habit had
been created: it was hard to break it. For five years Dostoevsky
had loved Maria, and he was living with her for the third year.
Only after her death did he confess to Wrangel, the one person

who knew the truth about their marriage, "Oh, my friend, she loved me illimitably; I, too, loved her beyond measure, but our life together was not a happy one. . . . Despite the fact that we were absolutely unhappy together (owing to her strange, suspicious and morbidly fantastic character), we could not stop loving each other: actually, the more unhappy we were, the more attached to each other we became. No matter how strange this may have been, yet so it was."

He also wrote Wrangel: "Let us be ever grateful for those days and hours of happiness and tenderness which a beloved woman has given us. It ought not to be demanded from her that she live forever and think only of you; that is unworthy egoism, which one must know how to overcome."

The key to this strange bond must be sought partly in Dostoevsky's childhood: during the years his mother was wasting away from consumption, there had sprung up within him an unconscious association between love and ill health, between tenderness and suffering, attraction and physical deterioration. The fusion of these two similar images, his mother and his wife, into one, that of an ailing and suffering woman, formed at the same time the cause of a physical block in regard to Maria and the basis of a strong emotional attachment.

Maria was conscious that illness had robbed her of her former attractiveness and suffered acutely because she had lost her physical intimacy with her husband, yet shrank from him as soon as he showed his desire. She told him that he was only waiting for her to die so that he could be rid of an unwanted burden, yet when he urged her to have medical treatment, she retorted that he only needed her as a mistress. She accused him of all the mortal sins in the catalogue, of wrongs real or invented, present and past; she enumerated for his benefit all his errors of the last four years. Dostoevsky loved her most of all when he had to be away from her; no sooner did he leave her side than he would begin to miss her and to feel the warmest pity for her. Separation awakened in him a tender longing for her, although he used to flee from her for the sake of a brief respite. Consequently, every parting was followed by touching scenes of reconciliation and by attempts at a new life, and then, after a few days (and occasionally only a few hours) of quiet and harmony, there would be new disputes, quarrels, a domestic hell.

In September, 1859, answering a question of Wrangel's, he wrote: "If you ask about me, what can I tell you? I have taken the cares of a family upon myself and am carrying them. But I believe that my life is not done yet and I don't want to die." The meaning of this admission is clear: nothing was left of the marriage except obligations. His duty was to remain with the woman who could give him neither comfort, nor a family, nor love. He felt the failure of his personal existence very keenly. In October, he wrote Michael: "My situation here is serious, abominable, sad. The heart will wither. Will my misfortune never end?" And then, in various letters, the same motif is sounded: "I am quite alone." This consciousness of his loneliness is the final verdict on his marriage. He had been wrong about Maria: she was a fine and kindly woman, but her character and the circumstances were such that he could expect nothing but sorrow from her.

His sole consolation and salvation lay in writing, but in the autumn of 1859 and at the beginning of 1860 his literary prospects were far from bright. *Uncle's Dream*, which appeared in *The Russian Word*, did not meet with success; with *The Hamlet of Stepanchikovo*, which Dostoevsky called a comic novel, there was a lot of bother before its acceptance, and when *Notes of the Fatherland* did publish it at last, the reviewers did not have a word to say about it. Now Dostoevsky was at work on *The Humiliated and Wronged* and *Notes from the House of the Dead*, and keeping up a correspondence with

Michael about issuing his collected works in two or three volumes—chiefly to bring in some money.

Although he had no epileptic seizures, his health was still
precarious and Maria was obsessed by an *idée fixe* of her own:
she was imagining all the time that Fyodor was going to die
soon and that she and her son would be left worse off than after
the death of her first husband. Consequently, in a letter to
the Czar dealing with a matter most vital to Dostoevsky—
permission to reside in Moscow or St. Petersburg—she made
him include a request to admit Pasha in a *gymnasia* at government expense. He mentioned the "hereditary squire, twelve-
year-old Pasha Isaev" in his other petitions as well, addressed
to various persons in high positions. Both requests were granted:
Pasha was placed in a *gymnasia,* and in December, 1859, Dostoevsky was at last given permission to reside freely in both
capitals. Even before the permission he had made a one-day
trip to Moscow and, on his return, had stirred his wife so with
his rapturous account of life in a capital that she herself began
making plans for moving away from Tver. This was the only
time when she emerged from her usual state of melancholy,
apathy and apprehension about her husband's future. She was
thrown into a panic by the most trifling stomach upset of his,
yet at the same time was hardly aware that she herself was
wasting away from tuberculosis which was gradually but in-
exorably developing in her.

Dostoevsky left for St. Petersburg and, at the beginning
of 1860, was joined by Maria. However, she could not stand
the cold climate and miasmic air there and had to return to
Tver. From this time on their common life was disrupted;
only rarely did they have anything like a home together after
that but, for the most part, they lived not only in different
quarters but in different cities.

In the summer of 1862, Fyodor went abroad by himself,

while Maria settled in St. Petersburg, ostensibly to tutor her son for a school examination. (Pasha proved to be anything but a success as a student.) Dostoevsky explained to certain friends that he did not have enough money to take his wife along. Before departure he gave her power-of-attorney to receive, in the event of his illness or death, all moneys due him. All sorts of evasions and explanations must have been necessary to keep up appearances, but from 1861 on Fyodor and Maria were frequently living apart, not only physically but in every other way. Dostoevsky had a life of his own in which Maria had no share whatever. She was away and dying. He was meeting people, publishing a periodical and writing; he turned out some three hundred thousand words between 1860 and 1862.

He went to Western Europe in the summer of 1862 with an obvious feeling of elation and freedom. For the first time in a long while the letters to his intimates sound gay, even joking: "Ah, if we could be together," he wrote to Strakhov, "we'd see Naples, stroll through Rome, befriend (like as not) some Venetian girl in a gondola (eh, Nicholai Nicholaievich?)." He was passionately longing to visit Italy—and to do so at once, while he still had the strength and ardor and poetry, as he wrote Polonsky, and not to wait until he was bald and would have to set out for the south to treat chronic rheumatism.

He visited Berlin, Paris (which he found very disappointing), traveled through the Rhine country and Switzerland, and then passed a few weeks in Florence and toured almost all of Italy. It was during this trip that he first played roulette and was completely carried away by this new passion.

On his return in September he found Maria sick in bed; her condition was very bad. From then on she was an invalid, and Fyodor became her male nurse. All winter she practically never left her room and kept to her bed for months at a time. In the spring of 1863, her health became so bad that her life was despaired of and she survived only by a miracle. At the first opportunity Dostoevsky transferred her to Vladimir, where the climate was much milder. He enumerated his troubles to Turgenev in June, 1863: "My wife's illness (consumption), my separation from her: having survived the spring—that is, not having died in St. Petersburg—she has left St. Petersburg for the summer, and perhaps for a longer period, and I myself had to acompany her from St. Petersburg, the climate of which she could no longer stand."

But he did not follow her to Vladimir himself. At first he was up to his ears in his publishing and financial affairs, and then took a new trip abroad. Only this time, when he again visited France, Italy and Germany, he was not alone.

PART TWO
APOLLINARIA:
▲
The Eternal Mate

BEGINNING WITH 1860, WHEN HE RETURNED TO ST. PETERS-
burg, Dostoevsky plunged into seething activity. Together with
his brother Michael he had started publishing *Time*, a monthly.
Editorial work and turning out articles taxed his energy a great
deal. At the same time he was writing incessantly. He had an
excellent, almost calligraphic handwriting, preferring a rigid
steel pen and good compact paper, and during his first two years
in St. Petersburg he turned out more than sixteen hundred
pages. *Notes from the House of the Dead* and *The Humiliated
and Wronged*, which ran in his own magazine from January
to July, 1861, had recaptured the attention of public and critics.
In the *Notes* he described all he had seen in Siberian prisons,
and his unassuming story was lit with such an understanding
of criminals and pity for them, it revealed so vividly and con-
vincingly all the contradictions of their nature, capable of
animal violence or sudden bursts of warmth, that these sketches
were before long singled out as an example of the new realistic
school and of the humane tendency. In his murderers and law-
breakers Dostoevsky had discovered a spark of humanity and
a grain of the Divine: hence his faith that the Russian people
cherish a hope for mercy and a dream of Christ even in the
darkest depravity.

The Humiliated and Wronged also expressed, although
on a totally different plane, the humanitarian ideals of its
author. Despite all the melodramatics of the book and its

romantic devices—illegitimate children, a paternal curse, secrets of inheritance and birth, noble-hearted beggars, a prince
as villain, virtuous and splendidly beautiful maidens and pure
magdalens—the book revealed the same compassion for the
poor and disinherited as *Poor Folk*, Dostoevsky's first work,
which made him known fifteen years before. The misfortunes
and sufferings of the chief characters in the new novel drew
sympathy and even tears from its readers. But the autobiographical traits of those characters were, of course, less evident
at the time than they are now.

Ivan Petrovich, a writer, the nominal narrator of the tale,
is in love with Natasha—unselfishly, with all his heart and soul
—yet she prefers Alësha, the son of Prince Vadkovsky, and
goes to live with him—without breaking off her attachment to
Ivan! Their relations are just as exciting and strange as those
of Fyodor and Maria during her infatuation with Vergunov.
However, Ivan is solicitous about his fortunate rival; he helps
the girl to arrange her life with Alësha and consoles her. Two
men in love with the same young woman, who in her turn is
attached to both—this situation is too recurrent in Dostoevsky's
works to be regarded as merely a literary device, outside the
author's personal experiences. The love triangle of *The Humiliated and Wronged* is far too reminiscent, even down to actual
details, of certain events in his first marriage.

The success of these two books helped Dostoevsky to
realize the dreams he had cherished in the depths of Siberia:
he emerged once more among the first ranks of Russian writers,
resuming the place he had lost during his enforced silence of
so many years. True, he was not as popular as Turgenev or one
or two other masters of the 'sixties, but in a comparatively
short time he became one of the outstanding figures in the
literary circles of the capital. He met a host of people, made
the acquaintance of artists, actors and scientists, was introduced
into the homes of Maecenases and journalists and participated

in charity affairs with the stars of stage and literature. All this did not mean that Dostoevsky had become a man of the world. He felt as constrained as ever and preferred staying at home to paying visits, yet he did not reject the way of life demanded by his status as a writer and editor. In fact, he had been so long deprived of the society of people of intelligence that now, having overcome his innate unsociability and love of solitude, he eagerly met the men of letters, the poets and novelists; the whole spirit of the day impelled him toward a lively exchange of ideas.

The government, yielding to the growing pressure of public opinion, had inaugurated an era of great reforms; all of Russia, coming to with a start, was awakening to a new life, seeking new ways. The emancipation of the peasants, the creation of independent and humane courts of law (including the institution of the jury system), innovations in education and commerce, in all the fields of social and economic activity, were transforming the country and preparing the way for a clean break with the past. This passion for freedom and the optimistic hopes of his generation absorbed Dostoevsky, even though he often swam against the current: the intellectuals were veering to the left while he was backing to the right; one-time monarchists were becoming revolutionaries while he was turning into a monarchist; the radical young people were atheistic while he sought God; the nihilists were simplifying everything under the twin banners of utilitarianism and materialism, while he was interested in psychological intricacies and the highest ideals of Christianity.

During the years 1860–62 he was up to his ears in work. It offered him both an emotional and an intellectual outlet and an unconscious recompense for the failure of his personal life. But he also had to toil as hard as any ditch-digger to make ends meet; writing was his only means of livelihood. Dostoevsky is one of the first writing professionals in Russia, and he was proud of the fact, even though he was always complaining about his grinding poverty and the terrible deadlines that kept him from polishing his works. He was in perpetual pawn to the publishers, he had to spend his days and nights working off his advances and turning out the next chapters of a serial novel running in some magazine. He envied such writing aristocrats as Turgenev and Tolstoy, or a writing bureaucrat like Goncharov—they were never under the stress of having to write for money, they certainly did not have to figure how many copies of a new work would take care of the rent or pay off a tailor. However, just as in the cases of both Dickens and Balzac, the critics have greatly exaggerated the influence of Dostoevsky's working conditions on his style. Current opinion blames the lengthiness of his novels and certain faults in their construction on his habit of publishing in periodicals and his acute financial need. But even if Dostoevsky had had more time to polish, he probably would have written in the same fashion, with the same long-drawn-out monologues, dramatic digressions and heaped-up clauses, since that was his manner, his individual and irrepressible stylistic peculiarity, his natural means of expression. He could not have changed it even if material security had permitted him to rewrite each page three times.

Work and his first literary successes decidedly renewed Dostoevsky's courage. As for his married life, he had evidently shrugged it off. Whether or not Maria actually confessed to him in Tver that she had never loved him and had given her heart and body to Vergunov, the breach between husband and wife had now lasted for two years. Maria was ailing; she was practically confined to her room, leaving it only to make hysterical scenes or to go off for a prolonged stay in the country. Yet no matter how difficult such a situation may have been, Dostoevsky had too much energy and desire for enjoyment to consider his sentimental and erotic life at an end. Wrangel, whose love affair with Katherine Herrngross, the wife of the governor of the small Siberian town of Barnaul, was not going any too well, wrote him in a minor key, and he replied: "Both you and I have lived quite a while and have lived through a great deal . . . having survived heart-fever twice you think that you have come to the end of everything. When there is nothing new, why, it seems that one has died for good and all." It may be that a similar mood had actually seized upon Dostoevsky in Tver, but now he declared: "I believe though, that my life is not over yet, and I have no wish to die."

Before his move to St. Petersburg in 1859 his love life was barren; he had remained faithful to Maria and formed no close ties with other women. But after he left Tver, his whole existence underwent an abrupt change. He spent days and evenings away from home, took trips to Moscow and abroad alone, and met interesting young women not only at his editorial office but at his brother Michael's home and the homes of friends. "Studying the characters of women he knew," a contemporary tells us, "was now his favorite occupation." He was completely engrossed in them and did not conceal this fact, much to the astonishment of Michael, who remembered so well how afraid of women Fyodor had been and how he had kept away from them in his youth. But now certain women attracted him very much—Alexandra Shubert, for instance, who was a clever and beautiful actress. It did not take him long to become her close friend: "I am so sure of myself that I am not in love with you," he kept repeating, yet their relationship was most romantic and emotional. Alexandra had settled down in Moscow and whenever Dostoevsky had occasion to go there, he always saw her. Certain of his trips, in fact, were evidently prompted by a strong desire to spend some time with her.

Once more Dostoevsky was longing for the society of women and his affections were free: Maria was no longer in

his heart or on his mind. He also considered himself free in a
strictly physical sense. In this respect the impulses of Dostoevsky and his erotic duality coincided with the tendencies
of his time and the prevailing mood of certain intellectual
circles. When Nicholas Strakhov, his friend and biographer,
became acquainted with the Dostoevsky brothers at the beginning of the 'sixties, he was quite struck by the spirit which
reigned in the editorial office of their periodical: "I noticed
with amazement that here not the least importance was attached to every sort of *physical* excess and deviations from the
norm. Exceedingly sensitive men in a moral respect, cherishing the most exalted modes of thought and for the most part
actual strangers themselves to any sort of libertinage, they
nevertheless regarded with utter calm all irregularities of that
sort, spoke of them as of amusing trivialities, to yield to which
at a leisure moment was fully permissible. Physical indecency
was considered nothing at all. This strange *emancipation of
the flesh* acted as a temptation and in certain cases led to consequences it is painful to recall."

Strakhov's cautious and deliberately hazy expressions refer
to Dostoevsky's environment; but in this case, of course,
genius shared in the general views. Nor was that all: these
views corresponded to his usual differentiation between the
physical and the spiritual aspects of love. Even now, as in his
youth, he considered as perfectly natural encounters that offered him nothing but the gratification of sensual desire. But
what was, to use Strakhov's expression, a simple "emancipation of the flesh" for others assumed in Dostoevsky's case a
more complex character and, at times, even an unwholesome
one. The entire experience of his marriage with Maria had
intensified his realization that sex is secretly associated with
suffering. Other artists of the nineteenth century had also
been aware of the intimate kinship between pain and love, but
probably none had felt it as searingly as Dostoevsky. Baude-

laire perceived this bond in all physical relations between man and woman. He compared the sexual act to punishment—even to an execution—and explained the feeling of possession as the right to violate and to cause pain. It is not without significance, he wrote, that passion evokes moans and outcries in women, as though they were being beaten or tortured. Dostoevsky had an excellent understanding of the indissolubility of physical union and pain, but he expanded (or "sublimated") the inevitable sadistic element of the sexual act, transferring it to the realm of the psychic. In his imagination voluptuousness was inseparable from torture. In all his heroes there emerges in the foreground, as the basic motive of their sexuality, an urge for domination or an eagerness for sacrifice. Even in the case of children Dostoevsky stresses sadism and masochism as the two aspects of the very same emotion. Katie, the little princess, tortures Netochka Nezvanova, yet this is merely a manifestation of her love for her playmate, while Netochka herself experiences a strange delight at being tortured by a little girl whom she adores. Nellie, the beggar-girl in *The Humiliated and Wronged*, is ready to bite the hand of Ivan, her benefactor, and behaves as if she hated him, yet this is but a masquerade of love, half revulsion and half attraction, half rancor and half tenderness. "Love," says the hero of *Notes from the Underground*, "really consists of the right—freely given by the beloved—to tyrannize over her."

This theme sounds with lesser or greater force in all of Dostoevsky's novels. Here, too, there is no question of chance or the repetition of a literary device. His obsessions with certain themes or images, his *idées fixes*, are psychologically rooted in the blocks, complexes and contradictions of his sexual personality, and manifested in his life as well as in his works. This is perfectly clear even to those who do not wish to resort to the methods and terminology of Freudian psychoanalysis. "Being a slave to you is, for me, a delight," the hero

of *The Gambler* tells the girl he loves. "There is delight—
there is!—in the utmost degree of abasement and nonentity.
. . . The devil knows, perhaps it may exist even in the lash,
when the lash falls on your back and tears the flesh to bits.
. . . As for savage, illimitable power—even over a fly—why,
that's a delight of its own kind. Man is a despot by nature
and loves to be a torturer."

"One can't distinguish your love from rancor," Myshkin
informs Rogozhin in *The Idiot*. Rogozhin is the victim of the
passionate, half-insane Nastasia, who plays with him like an
obedient puppet—yet it is he who slays her. Versilov's love
for Ahmakova (in *The Raw Youth*) resembles enmity to such
an extent that his stepson takes it for hatred, thereby pro-
voking the contemptuous laughter of the widely experienced
Tatiana. Nathalia, in *The Eternal Husband*, exerts "an oppressive fascination . . . this woman possessed the gift of at-
tracting, enslaving and dominating. She loved to torture her
lovers—but she also loved to reward them." Stravrogin's love
for Maria (the lame girl in *The Possessed*), whom he marries, is a mixture of mockery, self-abasement and curiosity,
intensified by a desire to overwhelm and domineer. He chooses
a semi-idiot, semi-invalid also because he can count on her
endless feminine gratitude and, therefore, on boundless
mastery. Old Karamazov finds there is something about "Plain
janes and old maids," probably in keeping with the same
principle: a woman to whom no one has paid any attention
is so grateful to the man who has chosen her and found her
desirable that she will repay him with utter devotion, a complete, submissive yielding of herself. This is also well understood by Svidrigailov, who passes from purely physical sadism
(he beats his wife with a lash) to taking delight in his feeling
of power over an inexperienced adolescent girl. Incidentally,
scenes of violence and physical sadism are to be met with in

almost all Dostoevsky's novels, but particularly in *The Pos-sessed*, where Lebiadkin lashes his sister with a riding whip; as for Stavrogin, he watches with bated breath as a twelve-year-old girl is birched on his account: later on she is the very one he rapes.

Pain and suffering as inseparable components of love, phys-ical torture bound up with the sexual act, and spiritual torture combined with all the sentimentalities of intimacy between man and woman—these constituted Dostoevsky's eroticism during the years of his maturity. This is the explanation given by Strakhov in his famous letter to Tolstoy (1883) as to why "together with his (Dostoevsky's) animal sensuality he had no taste, no feeling whatsoever for feminine beauty and charm." It is difficult to agree with this harsh and categorical judgment, especially if we recall heroines like Nastasia, Aglaia or, most particularly, Grushenka, all of whom are enchant-ingly feminine. Evidently what Strakhov wanted to say was that it was neither beauty nor charm which attracted Do-stoevsky in the women he loved or desired—that they aroused and infatuated him through something else. This something else was absolute defencelessness, holding forth the promise of full submission, obedience and passivity on the part of the victim—or on the other hand, it was harsh imperiousness, with its promise of debasement and the delight-in-pain caused by an executioner. It is between these two poles that Dostoev-sky vacillated, self-contradictory in all his relations with lovers and feminine friends, from his wife to the streetwalker and girl in a brothel. Freud remarks justly in his letter to Theodor Reich: "Note Dostoevsky's helplessness when con-fronted with love. He understands either coarse animal de-sire or masochistic submission, or else love out of pity." It is Strakhov again who affirms that Dostoevsky "was drawn to vile-ness and boasted about it. Professor V. A. Viskovatov told

me a story how he (Dostoevsky) had bragged that he had . . .
a little girl while he was taking a bath; the little girl had been
brought to him by a governess."

Dostoevsky himself was embarrassed and even frightened
by a very great deal in his sadistic and masochistic inclinations, despite his conviction that cruelty and torture, as well
as the voluptuousness of self-abasement, are part of man's
nature and therefore natural, just like other human vices and
instincts. But he discovered such twists or exaggerations of
these vices both in himself and in others that he used to flee
into his underground, hiding them from the light of day.
Prince Vadkovsky (the cynic and villain in *The Humiliated
and Wronged*), a demoniacal figure and a precursor both of
Raskolnikov and Stavrogin, says to Ivan: "If it were only possible—however, because of human nature, this can never happen—if it were possible for every one of us to describe his
innermost secrets, but in such a way that none need fear lay-
ing bare not only what one fears telling friends but what one
fears at times to tell even to one's own self—oh, the stench
that would go up in this world would be such that all of us
would have to suffocate. That is why (speaking parentheti-
cally) our worldly conventions and amenities are so good.
There is profound sense in them—not a moral sense, I would
say, but simply a precautionary, a comforting one; which,
naturally, is still better since morality is, essentially, that same
comfort—that is, it has been invented solely for comfort."

These lines were written in 1861. Two years later Dostoevsky created a character who had foregone comfort, had cast
it aside and dared to confess his innermost desires and actions—and what a frightful and intelligent, what a tragic and
repulsive figure he drew in the narration of one of his most
remarkable works, *Notes from the Underground!* This hero is
trying to test his theories on a pitiful prostitute, Lisa, whom
he has found in a brothel; he makes sport of her in a petty

and vile way, at the same time confessing with horror his love for the unfortunate creature. Dostoevsky, however, only fully explored the force and depth of his own instincts when he met a woman who was not his inferior either in complexity of emotions or in will to power. With their meeting began the most tempestuous drama in his life.

WHEN DOSTOEVSKY FIRST SETTLED DOWN IN ST. PETERS-
burg, the radical young people of the day failed to understand the change in his political views and still regarded him
as a victim of the Czarist regime. The man who had been
condemned to death as a member of Petrashevsky's circle
seemed a hero and was surrounded by an aureole of martyrdom. His public readings before student groups in 1861 and
1862 enjoyed great success—particularly the recollections of
his penal servitude, in *Notes from the House of the Dead.*

It was against this background of noisy applause and
ovations that Dostoevsky first met the young woman who was
fated to play such a large part in his life. After one of his appearances he was approached by a graceful girl with big eyes
of grayish blue, an intelligent face with regular features, and
a proudly held head framed in magnificent dark red braids.
Her low, somewhat drawling voice, as well as her sturdy, com-
pactly built body, offered a strange blend of strength and
femininity. Her name was Apollinaria Prokofievna Suslova;
she was twenty-two and was attending lectures at the university. Dostoevsky's daughter maintained that Apollinaria
had written her father a "simple, naïve and poetical letter
—an avowal of love. . . . One could sense it had been written by a timid young woman dazzled by the genius of a great
writer. This letter stirred Dostoevsky: it had come precisely

at the moment when such an avowal was so necessary to him."

There is nothing surprising or improbable about Apollinaria's having taken the initiative in giving her heart to Dostoevsky. In all lands, at all times, young girls have had crushes on noted writers and artists and confessed their love for them —in writing or by word of mouth. At the same time, both because of her age and her personality, Apollinaria can hardly be dismissed as a bobby-soxer, and besides her idol was neither a crooner nor a pensive poet. Even if she had written Dostoevsky a letter (and taking the first step was like her), it signified that she was genuinely attracted by certain traits in his personality or works, which had fired her imagination or which she had intuitively sensed. At any rate, Dostoevsky was impressed, and they began to meet—at first in the editorial rooms of Dostoevsky's periodical, then at the home of his brother Michael, and at last alone. Apollinaria dabbled in literature and in September, 1861, *In the Meantime*, a story of hers, appeared in *Time*. This sketch, feeble and of little originality, was hardly remarkable as a work of art; evidently the editor of *Time* had special reasons for helping along the literary career of his young protégée. (*Before the Wedding*, Suslova's second story, was printed in the third issue of *Time* for 1863.) Apparently Apollinaria had made a strong impression on Dostoevsky, perhaps she had "smitten" him, as Vassily Rosanov expressed it later on, and not through her looks alone: she actually was an extraordinary person.

Of course Dostoevsky was bound to feel the charm of her beauty and youth most of all. He was twenty years her elder, and he had always been drawn toward very young women. In all his novels the heroines are in their twenties and are loved by middle-aged men. This is already apparent in his very first work: in *Poor Folk*, Makar Devushkin is almost twice the age of Barbara. Later on Dostoevsky played every possible varia-

tion on the theme of a mature or elderly man falling in love
with a young girl. Sometimes this is a good and warm-hearted
love (Colonel Rostanov and the governess in *The Hamlet of
Stepanchikovo*), sometimes the belated desire of a libertine
(old Karamazov and Grushenka). From Svidrigailov with his
passion for Dunia to Versilov with his dual love for Katherine,
he constantly reverted to the motif of love relations between
two people of very different age. Maria was only four years
younger than himself and it may have been after his marriage that, by way of contrast, he found youthful women
particularly appealing. Dostoevsky always transferred his sexual
fantasies to young girls, making these fantasies objective. But
whether or not he himself ever gave into such temptations, he
decidedly understood and could describe the physical passion
of a mature man for adolescent and even younger girls—wit-
ness Svidrigailov and Stavrogin.

Apollinaria was exceedingly good-looking; in every move
of hers there was that elusive, exciting force which Americans
call sex appeal and Frenchmen describe as *promesse de
volupté*. Undoubtedly the attraction of the flesh was the basis
for Dostoevsky's interest in Apollinaria. She had aroused instant desire in him—a desire which infallibly increased and
turned into physical passion.

But this erotic aspect of their relations was immediately
enhanced and complicated by emotions of another sort.

Apollinaria was a plebeian; she evinced a muzhik stead-
fastness and tempering; her origin made her unusually typical—Russian—and this meant a great deal to Dostoevsky: his
nationalistic and populistic dreams were constantly on the
increase precisely during these years. Up to this time he had
met—almost exclusively—women who came from the higher
social stratas.

Prokofy Suslov, Apollinaria's father, hailed from the village of Panino in the province of Nizhni Novgorod and had

been a serf of the Counts Sheremetev; he had managed to buy his own freedom and that of his family and then entered the service of his former masters. A clever, energetic native of the Volga region, he had rapidly made his way up in the world and, even before the emancipation of the serfs, had acted as steward and man of business for the Sheremetevs. In the 'sixties he had moved to St. Petersburg, had become a well-to-do merchant and, in due course, the actual owner of a textile factory at Ivanovo-Vosnesensk. He had given an excellent education to his children—two daughters and a son —possibly from funds allotted for the purpose by Count Sheremetev (there are indications of this in the archives of Section III of the Secret Police). The daughters at first studied in Moscow, at the boarding school of Mme. Hennikau, where the main emphasis was placed on languages and deportment. Later both of them decided to get a higher education: Apollinaria entered the University of St. Petersburg, while Nadezhda (Hope), who was three years younger, enrolled in the Academy of Military Surgery.

Apollinaria was typical of the new generation: Dostoevsky was attracted—and at times horrified—by the mentality of the young people who had grown up during his bleak years in Siberia, and he perceived this mentality in her words and conduct. In his meetings with the Suslova sisters and their friends, in 1862, he came in contact with nihilistic young men and women whom he could not accept ideologically. He rejected and criticized their views, called them iconoclasts and atheists, crusaded against them in his novels and articles, yet he could not break with them, and there was something uncanny about the sway they held over his imagination. Here again we find an example of his emotional duality: he loved the very people he should have hated, and nearest of all to him were those same revolutionaries whom he exposed and castigated. They attracted him by the inner fire of their speeches, by the unconscious idealism behind their would-be cynical words and manners. They had the force and ardor of strong, searching and expanding natures. This was what he particularly sensed in Apollinaria. The liberalizing ideas of the age, which stressed personal freedom from all bonds— domestic, moral, social—found a warm response in her, since they corresponded to her individuality. One of Apollinaria's most striking features was that very Maximalism—in views, emotions, demands upon those around her—which Dostoevsky understood so well and described so often in his novels as a basic trait of the Russian character. Will and idealism were blended in her. She could follow to the end whatever she considered right, scorning conventions and conveniences —and at the same time there dwelt in her a naïve dream of perfection, the drives of a passionate, almost exalted nature. Outwardly she was slow-moving, constrained; her gestures were few, almost indolent; she frequently seemed apathetic and listless. Yet inwardly everything was turbulent and seething. She was independent, intelligent and extremely ambitious. Pride and self-reliance, amounting to egomania were the factors which in the end wrecked her love for Dostoevsky.

To judge by various indications in her diary and letters, she had "waited" until she was twenty-three: in other words, Dostoevsky was her first lover. He was also her first strong attachment. Later on, when abroad, she told people she met there that she had not loved anybody up to that time and then had freely given herself to a man of forty: she had paid no attention to appearance or age. Apollinaria, like all those surrounding Dostoevsky (Strakhov has written of that environment), saw nothing to frown on in sexual freedom, and if she had remained a virgin it was due not to moral scruples but to the absence of anyone she could fall in love with. But once she had come to love, no problem of physical intimacy existed for her; in her eyes it was normal and natural, and she yielded, "without questionings, without calculations."

In all probability this final intimacy between her and Dostoevsky took place after his return from abroad, in the fall of 1862. Dostoevsky, of course, was under no illusions as to his purely masculine attractiveness. The graces of a Don Juan were alien to him, and he had merely to take a good look in the mirror to realize he could never conquer the heart of a young girl by his appearance alone. Here is how H. Staken-shneider, a contemporary, describes him: "This was either a very tired or a very sick man, no longer young, very pale with an earthy, sickly pallor, his somber, tortured face covered, as if by a network, by some sort of extraordinarily expressive shadows caused by the exertion of controlling the movements of the muscles. As though every muscle on this face with its sunken cheeks and broad high forehead was inspired with feeling and thought. And these feelings and thoughts pleaded for release, but were held back by the iron will of this emaciated yet at the same time thick-set and broad-shouldered man, quiet and morose. It was just as though he were keeping himself under lock and key: no motions whatsoever, not a single gesture—only the thin bloodless lips nervously twitching as he spoke. And, at first glance, the general impression for some reason reminded me of one of those 'demobilized' soldiers of the sort I more than once had occasion to see during my childhood—on the whole, one was reminded of the prison and the hospital." Whenever he became animated he bit his lips, plucked at his small, scanty fair beard, and a tic ran over his face.

But it was not beauty or physical fascination which Apollinaria was seeking in him. However, she did like certain external peculiarities of his: he had odd eyes—the left was hazel, while the pupil of the right was so distended that the iris was imperceptible. This oddity lent a certain mysteriousness to his gaze. (The apparent asymmetry of Dostoevsky's eyes has engendered a great many misunderstandings. Psychologists and physicians have mentioned it as proof of the psychological deviations, and even perversions, of the writer. In reality, Dostoevsky injured his right eye during an epileptic attack in a collision with some hard object. Occulists persisted in prescribing atropine, as a consequence of which the pupil was constantly distended. All the overingenious theories concerning Dostoevsky's different eyes as a manifestation of his duality are utterly baseless.) He had very strong hands, although they were not big. He was, on the whole, very strong physically when he felt well, but after his epileptic seizures he became as weak as a child.

What Apollinaria saw in him was the writer whose reputation was constantly increasing. She guessed, even though she may not have understood it entirely, the enormous moral and intellectual sweep of his works, and all the pent-up idealism, all the romanticism of a "she-nihilist," who concealed her dreams under the mask of cold practicality and rationalism, drew her irresistibly to this ailing and homely man of forty. She also felt that she had found an unusual lover who was her peer, and she felt flattered at Dostoevsky's being in love with her. Her student friends knew of this. But there were subconscious inclinations as well: she instinctively sensed in him a nature like her own—the mutual fascination of torturer and victim—and the hidden traits of his eroticism corresponded to certain contradictions, as yet unrealized and unexpressed, in her own sexual personality. There was some sort of twist within her: a conjunction of temperament and frigidity, of sexual curiosity and physical squeamishness. She grew indignant at the submission of the female to the male during the gestures of love. She could not forget herself, give herself wholly or, most important of all, accept and acknowledge the force and dominance of the man.

She had gone to Dostoevsky through an instinctual drive and intellectual choice, but it was precisely in the sphere of sex that disenchantment awaited her. Dostoevsky aroused but did not satisfy her sexually. He had revealed bodily love to her, had initiated her into the mysteries of intimacy between man and woman; but it was particularly during the hours of intimacy that she perceived the strange—and, it may be, frightening—aspects of his nature, which repelled or offended her. The two suited each other spiritually, emotionally, but not sexually. Dostoevsky the writer, the thinker, was superior to her and she was enraptured with him, she set him on a pedestal. But this image of a friend and guide became distorted through the experience of intimacy. Dostoevsky the lover was by turns sentimental, weak, or treated her as an inanimate object and offended her by his excesses. She accepted his perversions as the usual demands of lust, but they often inspired her with revulsion. Yet at the same time he isolated the physical side of their love from all the rest; sexual relations were turned into something ordinary and routine. Their embraces were shorn of all romanticism. Too many things about her first affair embittered and degraded the young girl: he made their meetings secondary to his writing, his business, his family, to all the circumstances of his arduous existence. He maintained that he was no longer living with his wife, yet he was constantly thinking of her and taking preposterous, exaggerated measures of precaution not to upset her. As is always the case, Maria, who was jealous of him without any reason where most other women were concerned, did not as much as suspect that he was unfaithful to her with this young student, and Dostoevsky succeeded in keeping his liaison a secret from her.

Solicitous in every way for his wife who was confined to her sickbed, he made no sacrifice whatever for Apollinaria. Nothing changed in his life, at least outwardly: the daily regimen, habits, occupations—all remained as they had been. This irritated Apollinaria. She was deeply jealous of Maria and refused to accept Dostoevsky's explanations as to why he would not divorce an ailing, dying woman. She could not consent to the inequality in the situation: she had given all for this love—he had given nothing. She felt not the least thrill of pleasure or triumph at their meetings; regular and clandestine, painstakingly hidden from the gaze of others. About their regularity and secrecy there was something degrading. "Our relations, as far as you were concerned, were decorous," she wrote him later. "You behaved like a serious, busy person, who understands his obligations after his own fashion and does not forget to enjoy himself either—on the contrary, you may have actually considered it necessary to enjoy yourself, on the basis of some great doctor or philosopher having asserted that it is necessary for hard drinkers to get thoroughly drunk once a month." This orderliness about embraces, this regularity, amounting almost to punctilio, in "sinning," those shameful and dark aspects he had revealed to her, both surprised and crushed her. And besides, love had come to her not as an exuberant life force, not as the rejoicing of free and healthy flesh, not in the image of winged and laughing Eros, but in the contortions of lust inflamed by illness and a somber imagination, in the sardonic and groaning image of a half-insane, wounded Dionysos. Instead of that wise simplicity which all her contemporaries were praising so highly, or those ideals of spirituality which she secretly "bore in her heart," she was confronted with the forbidden and frightening underworld of sex. Again, despite all their speeches on freedom and the individual's right to arrange his life as he wished, despite their preaching of sexual "realism" and contempt for conventions, the young women—and even the young men—of the 'sixties were of a rather puritanic bent, and to depart from this inner puritanism was not easy, especially when one's mentor in the art of love was Dostoevsky. He had awakened the woman in Apollinaria and stirred her profoundly, but had done it in such a way that she both submitted to sensuality and feared it, and saw in the power of sex new chains for every man to fetter her with.

Undoubtedly, in the beginning, Dostoevsky subdued her to himself—both physically, as is the case of a mature man with power over an inexperienced young girl who has never loved before, and morally, as her senior and a wise and educated person. Had he not always affirmed that there is no equality in love? "In the relations between man and woman," he had told Eugene Opochinin in 1879, "one of the parties inevitably suffers, is inevitably wronged." To Olga Pochinkovskaya, his proofreader, he explained: "Marriage, for the woman, is always slavery. Once she has 'yielded' she is, willy-nilly, a slave. The very fact of her having yielded constitutes slavery *per se* and she is dependent on the man for all time." Evidently this is precisely how he felt toward Apollinaria as well; he attempted to deal with her as a lord and master—and at that point ran into the harshest resistance, since she herself was of a lordly rather than the slavish temperament. This was the cause of all their further clashes, and especially of that complex emotion which subsequently overwhelmed Apollinaria and was so very like hatred and vindictiveness. She herself used to tell how, three years later, Dostoevsky once remarked: "If you happen to marry, you will come to hate your husband and will abandon him no later than the third day." An ensuing conversation between them ran as follows: "Recalling Gau [a doctor in Montpellier, who was apparently a gynecologist and a friend of hers], I said that this was one man who did not *try to get somewhere* [*i.e.*, who did not try to sleep with her]. He said, in his usual manner: 'This Gau may have tried.' Then he added: 'Sometime I may tell you a certain thing.' I began to pester him to tell me. 'You can't forgive me because you yielded once and are avenging yourself for that—which is a feminine trait.' This upset me very much."

Of course it was exceedingly tempting for Dostoevsky to subdue a woman like Apollinaria; this was more interesting than having a submissive slave, and every revulsion merely intensified his delight. But as their relationship gradually transformed itself into a tense struggle, Apollinaria's pride was constantly suffering. The situation in which she found herself seemed to her insulting; she was oppressed by a feeling of depravity and by sexual frustration. The basic contradiction between love, as she understood and desired it, and the manifestations of their love made her blush and gasp. Everything about the affair was ugly and vile—the assignations in furnished rooms, the whole background of adultery with her lover's wife gravely ill, all this "illegitimate" affair with its outward details that made one feel hurt and ashamed the day after. She was also offended that he did not admit her into his "laboratory of the spirit," that he hardly shared his literary plans with her; he treated her like an ordinary mistress, he had taken advantage of her freedom, he tormented her, and always displayed his desire to dominate. At times she was irritated by his being "tongue-tied" or by his prolonged silences. Certain eccentric actions of his struck her because of their unexpectedness or aimlessness. He was well aware of these shortcomings: "I am mirth-provoking and repulsive," he had written even in his youth, and, "because of that I am constantly suffering over a misconception about myself. At times my heart may be swimming in love, but there is no getting a kind word out of me." Perhaps this was what Strakhov had in mind when he wrote in 1876: "It is almost incomprehensible why Dostoevsky, who dangled after so many women and has been twice married, cannot express a single trait of passion toward a woman, even though he describes the improbable complications and transports of such passions."

Just how rough the road of Apollinaria's love was is indicated by the first draft of one of the letters she wrote in

1863: "You are angry, you ask me not to write that I blush because of my love for you. Not only will I refrain from writing this; I can (even) assure you that I have never written and have never thought of writing that (since) I never blushed for my love: it was beautiful, even grandiose. I could have written you that I blushed over our former relations. But there should be nothing new in that for you, since I have never concealed it—and how many times did I want to break off those relations before my going abroad." She was, to use her own expression, "no great stickler for forms and observances," and therefore wrote to him frankly and harshly. The sense of what she wrote is perfectly clear: there was no reason for her to be ashamed of her feelings, since she considered them lofty, beautiful, even grandiose; she could not, however, accept the way he treated her as a lover.

Dostoevsky, of course, understood or suspected a great deal. True enough, in some ways Apollinaria was as reticent as he was. A complete explanation was impossible between them. In the beginning he had not evaluated her complexity fully and was constantly praising her character, mind, independence and the high demands she made upon others. In a year or so he had changed this judgment and supplemented it somewhat—he saw his friend in a new light.

It is quite possible that during the first weeks of the affair he did not allow it the significance which it attained later on. The adventure grew into real passion. By the spring of 1863 he was so infatuated with Apollinaria that he could not spend a day without her. She had become a part of his existence; she had grown dear to him not only physically but emotionally and spiritually. He had nothing waiting for him at home except a consumptive wife, the solitude of his study and the complete absence of any living joy or diversion. And Apollinaria was the joy, the excitement, the meaning of his days and nights; she beautified his existence outside his house.

He was leading a double life now, in two worlds that bore no resemblance to each other. How did he manage to exist with a foot in either one, to what extent was he tortured by his position, by his lies and his unfaithfulness to Maria? We have no data as to the inner state of Dostoevsky during the years 1862–63 and can only use our imagination. His love for Apollinaria was no secret from his brothers, at any rate: he both spoke and wrote to them about her, and he met the Suslova sisters at Michael's home. The latter even helped his brother's liaison; he did not like Maria and had always considered Fyodor's marriage to her a mistake. It is possible that he regarded Apollinaria as Fyodor's future wife.

In the spring of 1863, when Maria's illness took a turn for the worse and it became necessary to transfer her to Vladimir, Dostoevsky and Apollinaria came to a definite decision to go abroad during the summer. In Europe it would at least be possible to free themselves from the degradations of a secret affair and to live together freely, without concealment.

But on the twenty-fifth of May, 1863, Dostoevsky's periodical *Time* was suspended on orders from the authorities, who for some reason found one of its Slavophile articles subversive, and Dostoevsky, as the editor-in-chief, had to furnish explanations and carry on negotiations with the censors and other government officials. Apollinaria went off by herself; he was supposed to follow her shortly but could not extricate himself until August. The very fact that she left St. Petersburg without waiting for him seems to indicate a rift, if not an actual crisis, in their relations. Her departure resembled flight. She had a premonition or a hope that in Paris, where the train was carrying her, a new period in her life would begin. Dostoevsky hardly realized this: to him the parting from Apollinaria was merely a temporary interruption.

3

ALL THAT SUMMER OF 1863 DOSTOEVSKY WAS STRAINING
to go abroad, but his affairs were in such a bad state that he
simply could not leave St. Petersburg. Permission for him to
resume publication of *Time* was refused; he had to think of
a new enterprise, under another name. And meanwhile it was
necessary to satisfy creditors, subscribers and contributors, and
to resort to all sorts of dodges. He had to find money for everything—for the support of Maria in Vladimir, for her doctors
and medicines, for his stepson, Pasha, for the apartment in the
city—and for the trip to Paris. But there was no money, and
Dostoevsky went deeper into debt, accepted advances and
signed the most unfortunate commitments. Absence from
Apollinaria only increased his passion; he dreamt of meeting
her, of their trip to Italy together. Apollinaria kept begging
him to come to France and writing that she loved him ardently.
But at the beginning of August she fell silent. Three weeks went
by without a letter from her, and this compelled him to hurry;
it was clear she was angry because he was taking so long with
his preparations.

When he at last was able to quit St. Petersburg, he had
very little money. Yet as always, yielding to another uncon-
querable passion, he decided to stop over at Wiesbaden on
his way to Paris to try his luck at the green-baize tables. Obviously, he should have gone to his mistress at once, without
losing a day. But something held him back: in the clash be-

tween two passions, love and gambling, gambling won out—
if only for a brief while. Perhaps, however, this delay was the
subconscious expression of certain evil premonitions.

From the twenty-first to the twenty-fourth of August
Dostoevsky played roulette. This time he not only succeeded
in winning a large sum but, after losing half of it, managed to
stop playing and leave Wiesbaden. He had five thousand francs
(approximately one thousand dollars) on hand. Part of this
money he earmarked for his wife; the rest he set aside for his
travels with the young woman he loved. Full of radiant hopes
he arrived in Paris and at once dispatched a special-delivery
letter to Apollinaria. He was impatient to see her and, without
waiting for an answer, set out for the *pension* on the Left Bank
where she was staying.

Apollinaria was sitting by the window in her room when
she suddenly caught sight of Dostoevsky striding toward the
house. Within a few minutes the maid informed her that a
visitor was waiting for her in the salon. She went down slowly.
Here is how she describes the interview:

" 'How are you?' I said to him in a voice that trembled.
He kept asking me what was wrong with me, and made me still
more agitated, while at the same time his own uneasiness kept
growing.

" 'I thought you wouldn't come,' I said, 'since I wrote you
a letter.'

" 'What letter?'

" 'A letter telling you not to come——'

" 'Why?'

" 'Because it's too late.'

"He let his head sink.

" 'Polia,' said he after a short silence, 'I must know everything. Let's go somewhere and tell me, or I'll die.'

"I proposed that we ride over to his place.

"We kept silent all the way, except that from time to time

he shouted 'Vite, vite!' to the driver in a desperate and impatient voice, at which the other occasionally turned around with a perplexed look. I tried not to look at Fyodor Mikhailovich. He, too, did not look at me but held my hand all the way, squeezing it now and then and going through some sort of convulsive motions. 'Calm down; after all, I'm with you,' said I.

"When we came into his room he fell at my feet and, clasping my knees, kept saying: 'I've lost you—I knew it.' Having calmed down, he began questioning me: What sort of man was it—was he an Adonis, perhaps young, talkative? For a long while I did not want to answer him.

" 'You have given yourself to him completely?'

" 'Don't question me; it isn't right,' I said.

" 'Polia, I don't know what's right, what's wrong. What is he—a Russian? A Frenchman?'

"I told him that I was very much in love with this man.

" 'Are you happy?'

" 'No.'

" 'But how can that be? You are in love and unhappy. Come, is this possible?'

" 'He doesn't love me.'

" 'He doesn't love you!' he cried out, clutching his head in despair. 'But you don't love him like a slave—tell me that: I must know it. You'd go with him to the ends of the earth—isn't that so?'

" 'No, I'm going to the country,' I said, in a torrent of tears. And at this point I told him what had happened."

Shortly after her arrival in Paris she had become acquainted with a medical student, a Spaniard by the name of Salvador. He had a handsome, masculine face, a proud bearing and excellent manners; she had quickly become fascinated and then actually fallen in love—each day more and more ardently and deeply. This emotion, passionate and abrupt, was probably due to a considerable extent to the contrast between Salvador and Dostoevsky. Instead of an oppressive and somewhat shameful affair with an epileptic of forty, instead of a cerebral and idealized image of love that was far removed from reality, she had come in sudden contact with Latin gaiety, with a healthy sensuality that was completely unmarred. This was like entering a new world. In Salvador's embraces she had found simplicity and ease, qualities which were so enchanting after the recent muddle and complexity. She did not suspect as yet that the simplicity would degenerate into mindlessness, and that the ease concealed frivolity. Her heart and body were deeply touched; to him, however, this was but one fleeting adventure out of many. Following her moral code of freedom and independence, Apollinaria had boldly accepted the love that had overwhelmed her like a wave and, without hesitation, had given herself to Salvador. But once having gained his end or, as Apollinaria put it, *having gotten somewhere*, Salvador began to cool rapidly. It is possible that the vehemence of the "harebrained Russian" frightened him; the fire he had chanced to kindle in her now threatened to become a conflagration, and this was something he did not at all desire.

There arose again tragic contrast between what Apollinaria was seeking and what the handsome student from the Latin Quarter could offer her. To him it was an adventure; to her it was her first passionate love, all the more dangerous because it was her second affair. He took to avoiding her under all sorts of pretexts. Still without thoroughly grasping what was happening but sensing something untoward, she tried to keep her hold on him—with all the tenderness as well as passion, artless or artful, for which she herself afterward felt nausea and revulsion. Autocratic and proud, she found it unbearable to be deceived and to have to pay for her infatuation in pain and repentance. And she refused to admit that the difference between the present and the past was not so great, after all; she had fled from the somber sensuality of an elderly man, only to fall prey to a young animal who had absolutely nothing to him except sensuality.

During the very days when Dostoevsky was on his way to her and then (from the twenty-first to the twenty-fourth of August) had paused to play roulette, she was keeping a detailed record of everything she was going through. On the nineteenth of August Salvador had informed her that he would shortly have to go to America. "Even though I had expected this, he dumbfounded me: the emotion of fright and suffering must have shown clearly on my face. He kissed me. I bit my lip and made an incredible effort not to burst into sobs. . . . I have just now received a letter from Fyodor Mikhailovich. He will arrive in a few days. I wanted to see him so as to tell him everything, but now I have decided to write him." The same day she wrote him a letter and put it in her desk drawer: when Dostoevsky arrived in Paris, she would send him her confession at once.

Up to her meeting with Salvador, Apollinaria had awaited Dostoevsky's arrival with mixed feelings of apprehension and hopefulness. At times she dreaded that the St. Petersburg nights would be repeated in Paris. But whenever she was bored or lonely, she longed for him and wanted him at her side. She was quite ready to travel through Europe, and delighted at the idea of seeing Switzerland and Italy. But no sooner had she fallen in love with Salvador than she ceased to be concerned over Dostoevsky. With all the egotism of youth and her innate cruelty, she had given him no warning of what had happened. She knew very well that her infidelity would be a crushing blow to him. But there was more than a streak of malice in her make-up. She wanted to inflict pain upon her first lover, to demonstrate that she was stronger than he was and that she had no further need of him.

However, when her romantic affair with Salvador became

snarled and troublesome, her thoughts again turned to Dostoevsky. Now she was almost ready to forget all the dark and painful things that had happened in St. Petersburg and saw only the "shining visage" of her friend—his kindness and sensitivity, his intellect and talent. She longed for him to get to Paris; she was in need of his help and counsel, even though she hardly realized this at the surface of her consciousness. But when she learned that he was about to arrive, she suddenly became panicky and, to avoid an unpleasant interview, wrote out the letter which at the proper moment was to inform him of the break.

Three days later, on the twenty-first of August, she reverts to the subject of Salvador: "This time it appeared to me that he is not in love with me, and there arose a strong desire to make him love me. This is possible; one must, however, act cold-bloodedly." On the twenty-fourth of August she did not find him at home and waited a whole hour, without taking her eyes off the hands of the clock, starting at every slight sound and with her heart pounding. At first she wanted to leave him a note, but changed her mind and went away. This is what she said in the outline of that note: "All the people who have loved me made me suffer—even my father and mother. . . . All my friends are good people but poor in spirit and weak, rich in words and poor in deeds. [It would be interesting to know—did she include Dostoevsky in this category?] Among them I have not met one who was not afraid of the truth and did not retreat when confronted with the generally accepted rules of life. They in their turn condemn me. I cannot respect such people; to say one thing and do another I consider a crime. As for me, I fear only my conscience. And if there were ever an occasion when I sinned against it, I would confess this only to my own self. I am not in the least regarding myself with exceptional leniency, but weak and timorous people are detestable to me. I flee from those who unconsciously deceive

themselves, since I do not want to be dependent upon them."
It was just as well that she did not leave these lines for Salvador:
probably the easy-going Spaniard would never have understood
what the Russian Maximalist was talking about.

When she came to their next tryst he was not at home.
She had a premonition of the worst; tears came to her eyes—
nevertheless she refused to believe that he was avoiding her.
Had he not said to her, very recently: "Would I deceive you?"
with such an air of wounded pride that it was perfectly clear
he was above deceit?

But on getting home, she found Dostoevsky's note. He was
here in Paris; he was expecting her. She immediately sent off
her letter to the address he had given: "You have been a trifle
late in coming. . . . Only such a short while ago I was dreaming of going with you to Italy, I even began to learn Italian—
everything has changed within a few days. [She had at first
written 'within a week' but crossed it out.] You once happened
to tell me that I cannot give my heart away quickly. I gave it
at the first call, without struggle, without assurance, almost
without hope that I was loved. I was right in being angry at you
whenever you went into raptures over me. Do not think that I
am condemning you. All I want to say is that you did not know
me—but then, even I did not know myself. Farewell, my dear.
I wanted to see you, but what would it lead to? I very much
wanted to talk with you about Russia."

She had felt sad while she was writing this. She had felt
sorry for Fyodor. She had written in her diary: "How magnanimous, how noble he is! What mind, what heart!" Yet she
had not added one kind word to the letter. There was no
tenderness in it, nor even simple solicitude for the man she
was casting off with decisiveness and harshness.

ACCORDING TO HER NOTES DOSTOEVSKY, SLUMPED IN AN armchair, listened to this story with his head cast down and squeezed between his palms, and did not once interrupt her. When she had finished he straightened up and exclaimed, "Oh, Polia, why are you so unfortunate! It was bound to happen—your falling in love with another—I knew it! . . . After all, you made a mistake in loving me, because you have a big heart. You waited until you were twenty-three; you are the only woman who demands no commitments of any sort. But just think of the cost. Men and women are not the same in this respect; the man takes, the woman gives."

"When I told him what sort of man this [Salvador] was, he said that at that moment he had experienced a vile feeling: that he had felt relieved because this was not anybody who mattered, because this was no Lermontov. We talked a great deal about other matters. He told me he was happy because he had found such a being as myself in this world. He begged me to remain his friend and, in particular, to write him whenever I was especially happy or unhappy. Then he suggested I come along to Italy—he would still be like a brother to me during the trip. When I told him that he would probably be busy writing his novel, he said: 'What do you take me for? You think that everything will blow over without leaving a trace!' I promised to come the next day. I felt relieved after this talk with him. He understands me."

Dostoevsky saw her home and, on his return to the hotel, received her letter. And although he already knew everything and it could not shock him in any way, he found those lines bitter; he was deeply wounded both by the dryness of her tone and the cruelty with which he was being dismissed.

Only now did he fully realize what had happened to him. So this was what he had hurried to Paris for! His ears rang, his head ached as if it were clamped in a vise; he was afraid he would fall down in a fit.

His whole world was tumbling about his ears. He felt stunned by the catastrophe. He simply could not force himself to concentrate, to think anything over. He was tormented by nightmares all night long. His fitful sleep was haunted by visions: he saw Apollinaria nestling next to a man with black eyebrows, he heard the Frenchman who had laughingly and casually remarked to him at Wiesbaden, "He who is favored at cards, M'sieu', isn't favored in love!" No wonder he had been lucky at roulette! At that very moment, perhaps, Apollinaria had been in Salvador's arms. Jealousy and a sense of injury overcame him; he burst into sobs as he tossed in bed and bit his pillow. Toward daybreak he felt better; he had somehow become numbed by fatigue and suffering. He quickly drank several cups of coffee, but this did not help much in clearing his thoughts.

He felt lonely, old, unwanted as he lay on a divan in the chill, ugly, impersonal room of a Paris hotel, with the noise and awakening life of the enormous city bursting in through the open window. Love, upon which he had staked so much, had betrayed him. This time he had lost everything. All his stratagems, hopes, lies, all the torture of his conscience had proved useless. Once more with bitterness and a sense of guilt, he thought of Maria dying in Vladimir. "How sad I feel, and what melancholy is mine," he wrote his brother Michael two days after his arrival in Paris. "It makes my head ache. I keep thinking of all of you; I often think of Maria also. How I would like to receive good news about her. How is her health?"

No doubt Dostoevsky recalled how, seven years before, when he had come to Kuznetsk to see Maria, he had found almost the same situation. Why did the complications he described in his novels not only occur in his life but have to repeat themselves? And how painful was his own particular treadmill. Once more a woman whom he loved had betrayed him, and he had to be her consoler and counselor and listen to her complaints against a younger lover.

Apollinaria came to him next morning and they had a long talk. He spoke to her rather sternly, harshly calling things by their right names.

"I wouldn't want to kill him," Apollinaria said of Salvador, "but I would want to torture him a long time."

"Come," Dostoevsky answered, "it isn't worth while; he wouldn't understand anything; he is simply vermin that ought to be exterminated with insecticide. What's the use of ruining yourself—it's stupid!"

She shifted the conversation to other topics and even wept when Fyodor informed her of Michael's illness. He remarked on this, since she was not particularly inclined to sentimentality and tears did not come easily to her. However, she was in such a nervous state just then that she might well have collapsed in hysterics.

When she came back to her *pension*, Apollinaria found a note from a comrade of Salvador's, saying that he was confined with typhus at the house of some friends, and that she must not see him. Two days later, however, she chanced to meet him in the street, hale and hearty. The whole deception was exposed, and she finally grasped that he simply wanted to get rid of her. Back in her room she became crazed and kept shouting she would kill him—then fell into a coma, out of which she was aroused with a fever. She hoped that she had fallen ill, but

there was nothing the matter with her except a growing desire
to put an end to herself or to kill Salvador. Dostoevsky's daughter tells us that Apollinaria got hold of a long knife somewhere
and came to Dostoevsky with it. Apollinaria's own version is
not so melodramatic. "I had not slept all night," she writes,
"and next day, at seven in the morning, went to see Dostoevsky.
He was asleep. When I came, he let me in and again lay down
and wrapped himself up in a blanket. He was looking at me
with perplexity and fright. I was quite calm. I told him to come
to my place at once. I wanted to tell him everything and to ask
him to be my judge. I did not want to stay with him, since
I was expecting Salvador. When Fyodor Mikhailovich came to
see me, I got up from my breakfast, chewing a piece of bread.

" 'There, you can see that I am calm,' I said, laughing.

" 'Yes,' said he, 'and I'm glad. But then, who can make you
out!' "

She told him everything, without keeping back a single
detail.

"Fyodor Mikhailovich said that I ought to pay no attention to all this; that I had muddled myself, of course, but that
this [affair] was merely an incident; that Salvador, since he
was a young man, needed a mistress—well, I had turned up
and he had helped himself: why shouldn't he, with a rather
pretty little woman whom he found tasteful? Fyodor was right:
I understood this perfectly—but think how I felt!"

From that moment on she took counsel with Dostoevsky
about everything—without thinking, of course, how *he* must
have felt. She asked his advice on how to avenge herself on
Salvador; read him the outlines of a letter intended to wound
the young Spaniard; discussed whether she should send him
money to repay him for what he had spent on her. Incidentally,
in the rough draft of this letter she says of herself: "I am an
uncultured person and a complete barbarian: so keep yourself
as far from me as you can."

It was precisely during these preposterous days, while she was weeping on Dostoevsky's shoulder about her rejected love for someone else, and he was giving her friendly advice on how to soothe her hurt feelings, that they finally decided to take the journey they had dreamt of in St. Petersburg. It could hardly be in the nature of a honeymoon now; it was already overshadowed by pain.

He had become reconciled to re-enacting in real life one of the roles in *The Humiliated and Wronged*—he would arrange the love affairs of the very same woman who had been unfaithful to him, since he still loved and desired her, and undoubtedly hoped to win her back during their trip. For, after all, the affair with Salvador had come to a dramatic close and she had lost him. His rival was no more than a recollection, and even that was obscured by his lies and her own sense of injury. Why, then, could not Apollinaria change toward Dostoevsky just as Maria in Kuznetsk? This seemed all the more probable since his sexual intimacy with Apollinaria was considerably stronger: he had been her lover for several months by now—her first lover besides. In promising to be "like a brother" to her, so that she would agree to travel with him, he was, of course, concealing his real intentions. She apparently understood this thoroughly but was by no means willing to satisfy his desires. She had been so humiliated by her recent experiences, and her romance with Salvador had turned into such a vulgar and ugly intrigue, that she was disgusted with herself and wished above all to get out of Paris, which she had come to hate. As for Dostoevsky, her feelings toward him were compounded of a little gratitude, a little (very little) pity, and a certain malicious joy because she realized that now she had the whip hand. In St. Petersburg he had been master of the situation and had completely dominated her; she had also suspected that he loved her less than she loved him. But now—as she saw very well—her adventure had actually increased his love instead of diminishing it. In the

sideration the situation of the person I am traveling with." As long as that "person" was by his side, he was unabashed either by general poverty or by his losses in gambling. However, in Baden-Baden he met with success neither at roulette nor in another more hazardous game. Here is what Apollinaria wrote about it: "My trip with Fyodor Mikhailovich is quite amusing; while getting the visas for our tickets, he squabbled a bit at the Papal legate's; all the way he kept speaking in rhymes; finally here, where we found two single bedrooms only after some difficulty, he registered as *officier*, at which we laughed very much. He is playing roulette all the time and, in general, is very carefree. On the way he told me he was not without hope, although previously he maintained that he had none. I made no comment on this, but I knew that nothing would come of it. He liked my determination in leaving Paris—he hadn't expected that. But still, one can't build any hopes on that; quite the contrary. Last evening these hopes were particularly obvious. We were drinking tea about ten. When I had finished I lay down in bed, since I had tired during the day, and asked Fyodor Mikhailovich to take a seat closer to me. I was in a good mood. I took his hand and held it in mine. He said he felt fine sitting like that.

"I told him I had been unfair and rude to him in Paris, that apparently I had thought only of myself, but I had had him in mind as well, although I didn't want to say anything to hurt him. Suddenly he got up and wanted to leave, but stumbled against my shoes lying near the bed and just as hastily came back and sat down.

" 'Come, where did you want to go?' I asked.

" 'I wanted to shut the window.'

" 'Shut it then, if you want to.'

" 'No, it's unnecessary. You don't know what came over me just now!' said he with a strange expression.

"I glanced at his face: it was very much agitated.

" 'I wanted to kiss your foot just now.'

" 'Ah, what for!' I said in great embarrassment, almost in fright, and tucked my feet under me.

" 'That's what I felt like, and I decided I would.'

"Then he asked me if I felt sleepy but I told him no; I wanted to sit with him a while. Thinking of undressing and going to sleep, I asked him if the chambermaid would come to clear the tea things away. He felt sure she would not. Then he kept looking at me in such a way that I felt awkward, and I told him so.

" 'I, too, feel awkward,' he said with an odd smile.

"I hid my face in the pillow. Then I asked him again if the chambermaid was coming and he again felt sure she wasn't.

" 'In that case go to your room; I want to sleep,' said I.

" 'Right away,' said he, but stayed on for some time. Then he kept kissing me very ardently, and at last, began lighting his candle. Mine was burning out.

" 'You're going to be left without any light,' said he.

" 'No, I have a whole candle.'

" 'But that's mine.'

" 'I have another.'

" 'You know all the answers,' said he, smiling, and left the room. He did not close his door and soon came into my room under the pretext of shutting my window. He walked up to me and advised me to get undressed.

" 'I'm going to undress,' said I, making believe I was only waiting for him to leave.

"He went out once more and once more came back under some pretext or other, after which he left and shut the door. Today he reminded me about yesterday and said that he had been drunk. Then he told me that probably things were unpleasant for me, because he was tormenting me so. I answered that it didn't matter to me and did not dwell on this subject, consequently he could be neither hopeful nor hopeless. He said that I had a very crafty smile, that he probably struck me as foolish, that he himself was aware of his foolishness, but that it was of the unconscious sort."

This self-justification could deceive nobody, and Apollinaria must indeed have been smiling while he was explaining how he had really been tipsy: up to the crucial point he had been drinking tea with her, and if he was drunk it was not from wine. His head was spinning because he was so close to a beautiful young woman, who had once been his mistress, and one who had now become doubly enticing. As in the case of so many men, the thought that the woman he loved had been untrue to him and had belonged to another not only did not repel him or fill him with hatred but made her still more desirable and attractive, as though her fall had imparted to her some sort of peculiar, secret and shameful erotic charm. Never yet had he been so conscious of Apollinaria as a woman; never yet had he desired her so much as during this journey, when they were like newlyweds—in all things except the most important one.

In *The Gambler*, Alexis Ivanovich, the teacher, describes Polina, with whom he is in love: "She's good-looking, though —she is that; good-looking one would say. For she turns the heads of others too. Tall and graceful. Only too slender. It seems to me you can tie all of her in a knot and bend her in two. Her footprint is rather narrow and long—excruciating. Excruciating, precisely. Hair with a red tinge. Eyes downright feline, yet how proud and haughty she can make them look." The episode of the unrealized kiss on Apollinaria's foot and the lines about Polina's "excruciating" footprint are very characteristic of Dostoevsky; he had indubitable traits of fetishism, and he found the feminine foot, both up to then and afterward, an object of searing erotic excitement.

The daily association with Apollinaria enflamed Dostoevsky physically and he was, actually, being consumed over the slow fire of his unsatisfied passion. At the same time he was ashamed before her, considered his desire a moral weakness, castigated himself because he had not justified her trust, and was perhaps even surprised that he had been unable to remain on the spiritual heights of brotherly tenderness. Also, Apollinaria's behavior confused and disturbed him, since she was not even trying to help him to overcome his evil instincts and curb his impulses. On the contrary, she called them forth, she teased him, testing her power over him and then, with keen delight, refused him physical gratification. This, however, was not in the least difficult for her. The important entry in her diary after their arrival in Baden-Baden declares: "It seems to me I shall not come to love anybody, at any time." She recalls Lermontov's words: " 'But life, when one looks about with cold scrutiny, is such an empty and stupid jest.' " She found all men detestable, and she was taking vengeance upon Dostoevsky for the fiasco she had just gone through. She looked on his naïve attempts to possess her, the onsets of his desire, with a mockery that was gradually turning into chill contempt. She liked to play with him, to bring him to the verge, and then thrust him away—to handle him, in general, the way a woman trainer handles a dangerous beast.

There was a special voluptuousness about all this which Dostoevsky understood only too well. She had always maintained an ambivalent attitude toward him—and now it was out in the open with all its variations of cruelty and despotism. Dostoevsky wrote from personal knowledge when he made the hero of his *Gambler* say: "All this she understands amazingly, and the thought that I quite correctly and clearly realize how perfectly unattainable she is for me, how perfectly impossible my fantasies are—this thought, I am convinced, affords her extraordinary delight, for otherwise could she, so cautious and clever, be on such intimate and frank terms with me?"

Occasionally the tension would pass, there would be peace.

Fyodor would pace the room and sing romantic ballads in a low voice, for the most part echoing whatever some organ-grinder might be playing outside the window. In the evening, if they were staying in and both were in a quiet mood, he would bring fruit (pears, of which he was very fond) and sweets (raisins, nuts and dates) and tell her stories of all sorts. He liked to recall episodes from his childhood in Darovoye—for instance, how his father used to come in to his sisters, Vera and Alexandra, just before bedtime and look under their bed to see if they had hidden anybody there. And, smilingly, he pretended to look under Apollinaria's bed. She smiled in her turn, but she knew very well how insanely jealous he was and that he watched her when she went out alone to a museum or to do some shopping. This both amused and irritated her. There were also moments when Apollinaria experienced something like stings of conscience. She recalled the moral demands which both she and her sister had always insisted on. At present she doubted if they were necessary: "In general, that catechism which I had previously formulated and had been so proud to carry out, seems to me very narrow. . . . Fyodor Mikhailovich has lost a lot at gambling and is somewhat worried because there isn't enough money for our journey. I feel sorry for him —sorry, in part, that I can't repay him in any way for these worries; but there's no help for it—I cannot do it. Is it possible that I am under an obligation to do so?—no, that's nonsense." Occasionally, though very rarely, she would feel a kind of pity for her exhausted traveling companion and cease to torment him: "Tenderness toward Fyodor Mikhailovich has overcome me again," she wrote in Turin, ten days after Baden-Baden. "I happened to reproach him, but afterward felt I had been in the wrong; I wanted to smooth things over and was gentle toward him. He responded with such joy that it touched me, and I became doubly tender. While I was sitting close to him and looking at him caressingly, he told me, 'There, that's a familiar look

—it's a long time since I've seen it.' I sank on his breast and began to cry.

"While we were at dinner he said, as he watched a little girl taking a lesson, 'There, just imagine a little girl like that with an old man, and suddenly some Napoleon or other says, 'Raze the whole town!' That's the way things have always been in this world.' "

But her spurts of tenderness did not last long, and Dostoevsky had plenty of other opportunities to find out how little compassion there is not only in a Napoleon but in a young woman with feline eyes. At Rome another scene was played out, which she records in her diary: "Yesterday Fyodor Mikhailovich was importuning me again. He said that I regarded too seriously and strictly things which weren't worth while. I said that I had a certain reason for this, which I had no occasion to give before. Next he said that I was being eaten up by utilitarianism. I said utilitarianism was out of the question in my case, despite a certain tendency toward it. He disagreed, saying that he had proofs. He evidently wanted to know the reason for my obstinacy. He was trying to guess that reason.

" 'You know that's not it,' I said in answer to his various suppositions.

"He had an idea that this was a caprice, a desire to torture.

" 'You know that it won't do to torture a man so long,' he was saying, 'he will at last stop trying.'

"I couldn't help smiling and almost asked him his reason for saying this.

" 'There is one main cause for all this,' he began with positiveness (later I found out he felt certain of what he was saying). 'This cause, which inspires me with disgust, is the Peninsula (Salvador).'

"This unexpected reminder upset me very much.

" 'You are hoping.'

and poets, yet despite all the wonders of nature and art, all the magnificence of color and the beauty of the creations of man, nothing stirred them to passion. They seemed further off from love than ever. At times they even felt guilty because the southern skies gave forth such a sensuous call to happiness and joy. They were out of harmony with the "land of the laurel and the citron," and therefore felt still more sharply their physical and spiritual unrest. Apollinaria was secretly dreaming that Salvador would come back to her and imagining how she would punish him. Dostoevsky, after every moment of transitory intimacy and ease, could not help remembering Maria. "About the details of my trip I will tell you by word of mouth," he wrote Michael. "Plenty of various adventures, but the ennui is awful, despite A. P.! Here the reaction even to happiness is painful, since one has drawn apart from all those whom one has up to this point loved, and on whose account one has suffered many times." However, he would have thought less often of his wife if happiness had really been close at hand. But during his moments of lucidity he realized that his wanderings with Apollinaria resembled a Via Crucis rather than a lovers' journey. At such times all that had happened seemed like a retribution for having broken the laws of Christian compassion and justice. "To seek happiness, having abandoned everything, even that which one might have served usefully, is egoism, and this thought now poisons my happiness (provided there really is such a thing)." With this melancholy doubt he ends his letter from Turin, dated the twentieth of September: his life with Apollinaria had been particularly hard to bear in that city.

At the end of September, 1863, they found themselves in Rome, and from there Dostoevsky wrote to Strakhov, asking him to remit some money: "There are other circumstances as well; that is, there are other expenditures here, which I find it entirely impossible to do without." This muted reference to Apollinaria is the only one in his letter to a stranger. It also contains intimations of the first plan of *The Gambler:* the character of the hero is far more complex than the eventual one, and nothing is said of his relations with Polina. During these same weeks, toward the end of his tour, Dostoevsky was beginning to work out *Notes from the Underground.*

From Naples they came back to Genoa on the sixth of October, and while on the steamer they met Herzen, the famous Russian writer, and his family. Dostoevsky presented Apollinaria to them as a kinswoman. "He behaved toward me like a brother—even closer than a brother—which must have puzzled Herzen somewhat," she wrote. To judge by a letter of Herzen's, dated June 17, 1865, he found Apollinaria "very clever." "On the day we left Naples," she tells us in her diary, "Fyodor Mikhailovich and I had a quarrel; but on shipboard, under the influence of the meeting with Herzen, which inspired us, we had an explanation and made up (the argument had been over the emancipation of women). From that day on we no longer quarrelled; I treated him almost the same as before, and felt sorry about parting with him."

What is the meaning of these lines, in the last entry Apollinaria wrote concerning the trip to Italy? Her further remarks about her friend may lead us to suppose that that physical intimacy for which Dostoevsky strove so hard had finally become a reality, and that this was what she could never forgive him. However, there was something else she could not forgive. After more than twenty years, in answer to Rosanov's question as to why, after all was said and done, she had parted with Dostoevsky, she had replied: "Because he didn't want to divorce his consumptive wife, since she was dying."

"But then, she *was* dying."

"Yes. She was. She died half a year later. But I had already ceased to love him."

"Why did you?"

"Because he didn't want to get a divorce. . . . For I had

given myself to him, loving him, without asking questions, without calculations, and he should have acted the same way. He didn't, and I left him."

They parted at the end of October, when it was imperative for Dostoevsky to return to Russia. From Turin they went to Berlin, from there Apollinaria set out for Paris, where she arrived on the twenty-second of October. Dostoevsky went on to Hamburg, where he again plunged into gambling and lost the last of his money. On the twenty-sixth of October Apollinaria received a letter from him imploring her for help. At this juncture she herself was rather low in funds and had to pawn her watch and chain in order to set the hapless gambler on his way. Without her prompt co-operation he would not have succeeded in arriving on time at Vladimir, where Maria, by now looking like a ghost, was expecting him.

IN TELLING ANSTEY, THE ENGLISHMAN, AROUT HIS RELA-
tions with Polina, the hero of *The Gambler* remarks: "Everything was fantastic, unsubstantial, and like nothing on earth."
These words sum up perfectly Dostoevsky's tour through Europe. Nevertheless, and perhaps precisely because of this, he
came home more engrossed with Apollinaria than ever. According to an almost mathematical law, the attraction of love
is in direct proportion to the experiences which the "object of
love" provides us with, no matter whether they are joyous or
sad. The value of a woman we love increases in keeping with
the dream and intensity of the emotions and thoughts we have
expended upon her. Coarse natures tot up, while they are at it,
the money they have spent, while economists compare love
with an investment of capital, in proportion to which, naturally,
the value of the enterprise goes up. And, of course, Apollinaria
had become even dearer to Dostoevsky since she symbolized
all the bodily and spiritual strain and unhappiness of the last
few months.

But most important of all was that fusion of imagination
and physical desire without which it was impossible for him
to experience genuine passion. Apollinaria intrigued his intellect and emotions just as strongly as she aroused his flesh.
Gumilev has written of the woman "whom we are fated first
to be tortured by, then to have our fill of delight from." In the
case of Apollinaria the delight had come first, but hardly had

Dostoevsky taken his fill of it than his martyrdom began. The irritation of constant nearness, the remembrance of recent physical intimacy, jealousy of the man to whom she had just given herself, offended masculine pride, the promise of joy with each glimmer of tenderness on her part, followed by despair because of her frigidity and indifference—he had gone through this whole drama of helpless love and unfulfilled desire. At times, in an access of resignation and self-abasement, he was ready to accept everything, to bear everything, if she would permit him merely to kiss her feet or the hem of her dress. But after this excruciating and dear humiliation would come the rebellion of pride, and indignation at his own weakness. Reason and experience warned him that it was out of the question to resurrect the past, that Apollinaria was about to leave him, if indeed she had not already left him. But he could not bring himself to accept his dismissal; he wanted to believe in her despite everything. Recalling her infidelity and her conduct in Italy, he would clench his fists in resentment and impotence; he found this love a crushing obsession, he implored God to give him the strength to free himself from Apollinaria. Yet an hour later the thought that he would lose her for good, that he might never see her again, made him ill for the whole day. He writhed between dreaming of her and struggling against her, and could find no peace in anything.

He was especially drawn by her self-assertiveness; it was both more complex and more significant than simple egoism —she considered herself entitled to commit any action she found reasonable, since she rejected all moral conventions and taboos. Nor was her theoretical rejection as complete and shocking as her actual one. But the crux of the matter lay not so much in her nihilism, her face-value acceptance of the slogans of her age, as in her nature. She was a rebel through her inner make-up and her authentic Russianism. She was constantly seeking freedom, but understood it after a fashion of

her own, renouncing obligations to others and not considering
herself bound to anyone. During the very height of the drama
with Salvador, she had written in her diary (and then, most
probably, read the entry to Dostoevsky): "Today I did a great
deal of thinking and was almost pleased because Salvador does
not love me much: I have more freedom. . . . The life I had
in mind will not quite suit me. One must live with more fullness
and breadth." These words are not the usual vaporings of a
romantic young girl; all her actions prove that she could overcome obstacles and take barriers by storm.

To a certain extent her resoluteness and autocracy had
detonated something in Dostoevsky's inner self. After his collision with her, there emerged all those deviations of his thought
and emotion which until then had existed only in the background; in the foreground had been pity, a sentimental hu-
maneness, the religion of the suffering individual—the last is
evident not only from his first works but from the entire history
of his first love and marriage. But now he was swept up by the
religion of the daring individual. In his works belonging to
this period, the idea of revolt ranges from a theoretical negation
(*Notes from the Underground*) and a challenge to fate (*The
Gambler*) to overt action (*Crime and Punishment*)—and all
these works are bound up with Apollinaria. The problem of
free will and the insurgence of man—insurgence metaphysical,
moral, social—was becoming his basic theme; in Apollinaria
the revolt was embodied in her emotions and her sex.

Of course, the whole question depends on the extent of
Apollinaria's influence upon him in the 'sixties, when he was
writing his novels, the extent to which she colored the beginning of his second period of creativity. Did his affair with her
crystallize his ideas concerning the personality that rejects the
norm? Or did she cast a spell over him precisely because all his
interest as writer and thinker was directed toward the problem of self-assertion and self-will, of moral anarchism and law-

less action? Apollinaria is amazingly like a heroine from a Dostoevsky novel, and her traits are scattered throughout a succession of Dostoevsky's women: a few in Dunia, Raskolnikov's sister (in *Crime and Punishment*); a few in Nastasia, that blend of Apollinaria and Maria, and Aglaia (both in *The Idiot*); beyond a doubt in Akhmakova (in *The Raw Youth*); in Nathalia, the heroine of *The Eternal Husband*; in Lisa (*The Possessed*) and—again partially—in Katherine (*The Brothers Karamazov*); to say nothing, of course, of Polina in *The Gambler*. This merely sketchy list shows how truly Apollinaria had "transfixed" Dostoevsky.

But it also should be asked: Do the women in his novels resemble Apollinaria because his heart was full of her, because he could not help remembering her, or had he fallen in love with her, was he tormented by her, because she resembled the images born of his imagination and desire—since she corresponded to that vision of woman which owed its being not to life but to creative fantasy? Certainly it was not a case of his works copying his biography and nothing more; rather, he chose from life women who could have been the heroines of his novels, revealing his dreams and secret aspirations. But to answer these questions fully would mean solving one of the most complex and contradictory problems in the psychology of artistic creativity.

What is perfectly clear is that Apollinaria revealed just those aspects of her character which Dostoevsky generally considered the crucial ones in any study of human complexity; she was capable of revolt and audacity and she accepted and combined in herself the most contradictory tendencies. Her temperament showed itself alike in love and hatred. She became quickly infatuated, formed ideal images—and was quickly disillusioned. And since she was incapable of forgiveness and did not know the meaning of tolerance, this disillusionment was immediately transformed into irony and implacability, into rage and cruelty. At times she herself suffered because of this; her demands upon life and people inevitably doomed her to defeats and shocks, and this cast a tragic shadow over her whole existence. Dostoevsky had found this out in Paris, and it made him love her more than ever. The aura of trouble (almost of catastrophe) which enveloped her, this natural inclination of hers toward the absolute, the inordinate, and her inability to accept limitations—all these were flesh of his flesh and blood of his blood. At times, when he contemplated this young girl, he seemed to be peering into a mirror: the things he was trying to put into his novels were seething within her, and there was about her more of the Dostoevsky touch than in a whole string of his heroes and heroines. But she knew nothing of this, did not give it a thought and, after all, she no longer loved him.

However, he did not feel assured even of that. He was constantly uncertain as to her feelings and moods and simply could not read clearly the heart of his mistress. Was she really about to forsake him? Was this the end, or was it a temporary interruption, after which she would be entirely his? And Dostoevsky, the psychologist and seer, who understood all the mysteries of mind and soul, stood in despair and impotence before the enigma of this self-willed girl of twenty-three. When it came to dealing with Apollinaria everything was quaggy and incomprehensible, just as though he had lost his way and at every moment risked falling headlong into a fatal quicksand. But perhaps Maria also had never loved him, and it was true that, during a quarrel in Tver, she had reproached him: "There isn't a woman living who can love an ex-convict!"

Dostoevsky was bringing his wife from Vladimir to Moscow, settling her in a new place, talking things over with doctors, corresponding with Michael about *The Epoch*, which had begun to come out in place of the suppressed *Time*, writing articles, working on *Notes from the Underground*, but he was beset by the same persistent questions: How could he explain the conduct of Apollinaria, how much did she still feel of her former love; and what would be the end of his affair with this woman who was dearer to him than anyone else, whom he was now ready to call, as he never called anyone before or afterward, his Eternal Mate?

DOSTOEVSKY CAME TO VLADIMIR AT THE END OF OCTOBER, 1863, and immediately decided to bring Maria to Moscow: to settle with her in St. Petersburg was impossible, while to leave her in Vladimir was obviously out of the question. Maria was so worn out by fever and, in general, was in so critical a condition that even the removal from Vladimir to nearby Moscow appeared difficult, probably dangerous. "However," Dostoevsky wrote Michael, "owing to certain extreme circumstances, there are other reasons so pressing that it is utterly impossible to remain in Vladimir."

What was the nature of these reasons? Was it some question of work or business or, as was often the case with Dostoevsky, did the terse phrases screen certain complications in his life, certain secret moves in his personal relations and psychological complexes, which will always remain among the riddles of his biography? Could it be possible, as Dostoevsky's daughter hints, that Vergunov was located in Vladimir? But perhaps Maria suspected her husband of infidelity and did not want to be separated from him, while he had to choose between Moscow or St. Petersburg, and under no circumstances could bury himself in provincial Vladimir. It is possible that Maria had quarreled with the relatives or friends who had been taking care of her all this time. In any event, Fyodor considered it his duty to make the last months of Maria's life easier for her and to create the best possible external conditions for her, and this was far easier to accomplish in Moscow.

At the beginning of November, 1863, the Dostoevskys settled in Moscow. Fyodor had come into a small inheritance and was under less of a strain financially than he had ever been. He passed days and nights at his desk, but his writing was going poorly. Two seizures interrupted his activity for several days, but the greatest obstacle to his work was the necessity of looking after his wife. Her disease had made her so irritable that she could not endure anybody, not even her son, who had come from St. Petersburg to see her. However, Pasha was so frivolous, studied so badly and committed such follies that by now (he was in his teens) he was altogether unbearable.

Dostoevsky was quite aware that Maria's end was near. "I feel dreadfully sorry for her," he wrote Michael in January, 1864. "There is not a moment when Maria hasn't her death in mind; she grieves and falls into despair. Such moments are very hard for her to bear. Her nerves are all on edge. Her chest is bad and she has wasted away to a matchstick. It is horrible! It is painful and hard to look at her." Maria was dying agonizingly; the novelist's thoughts were evidently haunted by her sufferings and moods when he described Hippolyte's agony in *The Idiot*. And all the ailing characters (for the most part consumptive women) in his works bear some of the features of Maria.

How strange and difficult his life was in the winter of 1863, by the side of his dying wife whom he tended, making her last days easier, taking care of her (and perhaps, even dreaming of her death as a deliverance), yet all the time with Apollinaria in his heart and in the very depths of his flesh. Maria was coughing blood in the bedroom, and he was expecting a letter with a French stamp, Apollinaria's letter, from Paris. She sent him a new story of hers, and he immediately dispatched it to St. Petersburg: *One's Own Path* appeared, under the usual initials of A. S-va, in the sixth issue of *The Epoch*.

Meanwhile he had begun to write *The Gambler,* in which he exposed his passion for gambling and for a crackbrained young girl, and did not even change her name; his heroine is Polina—and he had always called Apollinaria that.

The novel was making very slow progress, however. This is quite understandable; it was torture for him to write about Polina and relive the weeks he had spent with her abroad and at the same time watch his wife die day by day. He was forced to deceive and pretend all the time; not once could he take off his mask. Nobody—not even his brother Michael, the confidant of his romance with Apollinaria—knew what was going on inside him during these frightful months. Clenching his teeth, subjecting himself to a firmly established regimen of work and domestic duties, he allowed nothing to betray the scorching whirlwind of passion and doubts, of repentance and regrets, that was raging in his soul. With every day his mood became darker; he was lonely and unhappy, witnessing the agony of a woman he had once loved; death and madness were in the air he breathed. Maria would sit for hours in her easy chair, without moving, plunged in her thoughts, then suddenly spring up, rush into the parlor, come to a stop before a portrait of her husband and, threatening it with her fist, would shout, "Convict! Vile convict!" There were days when her hatred turned into frenzy, only to disappear without a trace. She was often tortured by hallucinations and nightmares; during the last few weeks before her death she became semi-insane, with occasional moments of lucidity.

As early as February, 1864, it became clear that Maria would not live through the spring: she was literally melting away. Dostoevsky wrote on the twenty-sixth of March, 1864: "Maria is so weak that A. P. [her physician] by now does not feel certain of even one day. She will *under no circumstances* live through more than two weeks. I will try to finish my short novel as quickly as possible, but judge for yourself: is this a propitious time for writing?" Maria, however, as is often the case with someone on the deathbed, had by now ceased to understand that her condition was hopeless, and was dreaming of going to her father in Astrakhan, or to Taganrog, where the Constants had a house. She dreaded any mention of Pasha, since she had stated that she wanted to see him only to bless him before her death. Yet during the very days when she was giving herself up to all these dreams of going away and re-covering, Fyodor asked Michael to see about getting some black garments for her son and wrote: "I will send you a telegram as soon as Maria dies." This acceptance of coming events and calm, almost businesslike discussion of the inevitable did not continue long, however. In April, Maria's prolonged and fright-ful death agony began. "All my different torments are now so hard to bear," Dostoevsky wrote on the second of April, "that I don't want even to mention them. . . . My wife is dying, *literally*. Every day a moment comes when we expect her death. Her sufferings are horrible and affect me, because. . . . As for writing, it is mechanical labor, and yet I write and write, in the mornings."

On the fourteenth of April, Maria had a hemorrhage; blood spurted from her throat and flooded her chest. The next day, toward evening, she died—died quietly in her full senses, and gave her blessings to everybody. "She had gone through so much suffering that I do not know who could have refused to become reconciled with her." These words (in a letter notifying him of Maria's end) were addressed to Michael, whom Maria had always considered her "secret enemy." He, in his turn, had disliked her very much and felt positive that she had ruined Fyodor's life.

A year after the death of his wife, Dostoevsky wrote of her in the following terms to Wrangel, the man who not only had known her but had witnessed the first period of their love: "My wife, a being who loved me and whom I loved immeasurably, died in Moscow, where she had moved a year before her death from consumption. I followed her to Moscow, did not leave her bedside all through the winter of '64, and on the 16th of April, last year,* she died in her full senses . . . and, as she was saying her farewells, she remembered you. Let your memories of her be good, kind. . . . This was the most honest, the most noble and magnanimous woman of all those whom I have known in all my life. When she died—even though I had been tortured for a whole year watching her die, even though I appreciated and felt excruciatingly what I was burying with her—I simply could not imagine the extent of the pain and emptiness that came into my life as they were strewing the earth over her. And now a year has gone by, yet the feeling is still the same; it does not decrease."

Dostoevsky loved her for all those emotions which she had awakened in him, for all that he had given her, for all that was bound up with her—and for whatever sufferings she had caused him. Yet he loved her for her own sufferings also, with that complex interweaving of human pity, tenderness, carnal passion, and an intimacy, at the same time filial and paternal, which bound him to the ailing and hysterical Maria more strongly than the joys of a successful marriage could have done. In certain respects they resembled each other: in both there easily flared up a certain fire of frenzy, too great for the usual frameworks of serenity and habit, with both everything brimmed over, knew no measure. But what raged as the fire of genius in Dostoevsky merely flickered in irritating little flames as a deadly malady in the case of Maria.

The mark left by Maria can be found in many of Dostoevsky's works. Natasha in *The Humiliated and Wronged*, Marmeladov's wife in *Crime and Punishment*, Nastasia

* Dostoevsky's data are not quite correct here: Maria moved to Moscow in November, 1863, and died on April 15, 1864.

(partly) in *The Idiot*, and Katherine in *The Brothers Karama-zov*: all these images of women with pale cheeks, feverish gaze and impulsive movements were created under the influence of the woman who was his first, his great love.

What Dostoevsky wrote his old Semipalatinsk friend, Wrangel, concerning Maria and his feelings toward her was, of course, the strictest truth. But he did not mention that while he was tending his dying wife, the torture of compassion and attachment was not the only emotion experienced. He was suffering also from a sense of guilt, perhaps of shame, because his heart and his mind were divided, and because he was dreaming, at the head of Maria's deathbed, of another woman, and yearning to see her with all the force of passion, jealousy and desire within him.

DURING MARIA'S AGONY THE NEWS FROM PARIS COULD bring no consolation to Dostoevsky's tormented spirit. His grief was only intensified by what Apollinaria herself wrote him and what he could guess by reading between the lines or from the slips she made. He loved her more and more, but she was receding further and further from him; their destinies were taking different paths. At times they quarreled in their letters, with almost the same heat as in Italy not so long before. Their correspondence was exceedingly lively. Only an insignificant part of it, however, has come down to us; most of the letters have disappeared or are buried in unknown archives. Dostoevsky perceived that Apollinaria was approaching some sort of inner crisis, yet he could not help her; they were separated by thousands of miles and there was no possibility of his escaping abroad before summer, while she did not want to return to Russia.

After their parting in Berlin in October, 1863, Apollinaria had come back to Paris. At first she was still taken up with Salvador: she was pondering how to "avenge" herself or bring him back to her, but nothing came of all her attempts, and she was devoured by depression and boredom. She had no love for the West, and her negative attitude toward European life reflected some of Dostoevsky's diatribes against the vanity and hollowness of the French and the smug sanity of the Germans. "Everything in Paris is so meretricious," she wrote, "everything is so contrary to nature and common sense, that I, as a barbarian, will say what a famous barbarian once said of Rome: 'This people will perish!' " French ideals of financial comfort and security aroused her indignation: "I would tear all of them apart!" At times, when she became fed up with the French, she dreamt of a trip to America, to a new land. Two Americans came to live at the *pension* where she was staying: "I like them; one in particular—his face is so energetic and serious. He was looking at me closely and seriously; at the same time I myself kept looking at him. These must be real people, glory be to God! But perhaps I won't become friendly with them." This was no idle doubt: she really found it difficult to become friendly with people and did not know what to do with herself. Her heart was bitter, she had no definite place in life, and she longed for new faces and impressions.

For the sake of diversion she cold-bloodedly used the men who crossed her path. "After lengthy reflections I have worked out a conviction that one must do everything one considers desirable." She flirted with an elderly Englishman, with a Dutch medico who spoke Russian (evidently a brother of that same revolutionist Benni about whom Leskov writes so touchingly and racily), with a Georgian by the name of Nikoladze, with Robescour, a Frenchman (before the eyes of his wife)—and all this international collection afforded her just one pleasure; the consciousness of her power over the man she infatuated. It seemed as if she were the prisoner of her own force, for which there was no outlet, of her own needless conquests. She made the acquaintance of two Russian women writers living in Paris: Countess Salias de Tournemir (Eugenie Tour) and Maria Markovich (Marco Vovchok). She was on friendly terms with the first and showed her some of her own attempts at writing fiction. But she had no talent: her stories were dry, colorless, poorly worded. She

was utterly devoid of any feeling for form and style—like so
many other authors and critics of that epoch, which is rather
noted for aesthetic poverty.

It was probably during these months that she wrote the
novelette, *A Strange Woman and a Man of Our Own*. Losnitski, her hero, comes to see Anna, his beloved of twenty-two,
and they repeat in detail the Paris meetings of Apollinaria and
Dostoevsky. In her story, Apollinaria utilized the expressions
she has recorded in her diary and letters: "Why have you
come?" asks Anna. "You have been a trifle late in coming,"
and so on. The episode of Dostoevsky wanting to kiss her foot
is also given exactly. Losnitski marries, but later goes to the
south of France, where the ailing Anna is living, and pursues
her passionately. When he happens to be in a gay mood he
tells her of his love adventures and remarks that "such relations of a man toward a woman are very natural and ex-
cusable, and are even necessary, and not only do not interfere
with higher love but actually both augment and sustain it.
Unfortunately, there's not a woman who can grasp this."
Undoubtedly, the author had heard similar speeches from the
lips of Dostoevsky.

At the end of the novelette Anna throws herself in a river.
This suicide was a reflection of Apollinaria's somber mood
at the beginning of 1864. Every new encounter intensified
her dissatisfaction; she was wasting herself in a barren game
with a dozen men, and could not become completely engrossed either in the radical ideas current in Countess Salias'
circle or the cerebral nihilism and utilitarianism flaunted
by the young people arriving from Russia. She met revolutionaries but could not join them, and remained lonely in
a dismal and confined world of her own.

DOSTOEVSKY HAD HOPES THAT 1864 WOULD BRING HIM luck, but in reality it proved one of his most difficult and unfortunate years. Maria died in April and, in July, came the death of Michael, his favorite brother and his partner in literary enterprises. September was marked by the death of Apollon Grigoriev, poet, critic, a prominent contributor to *The Epoch* and a close friend of Dostoevsky, who subsequently wrote to Wrangel: "After her [Maria's] funeral I hurried to St. Petersburg, to my brother—he was the only one left to me—but three months later, he, too, died. And so I was suddenly left alone, and I became simply frightened. My whole life has snapped in two. One half, that which I have traversed, held everything I had lived for, while in the other half, still unknown to me, everything was alien, everything was new, and had not one heart that could replace for me the other two. Everything has become cold and desert-like around me." Apollinaria might have become that heart, and spanned the two halves of his life for him, but Dostoevsky does not mention her. Evidently even in her letters she had very little kindness for him. Besides, she neither could nor would be consoling; she could hardly regret the death of Maria and, finding weakness and sentimentality unbearable, understood Dostoevsky's grief only poorly. She had summoned him to Paris and was very angry because he had not come. He gave his circumstances as an excuse, but such arguments did not move her; she believed that strong people know how to overcome obstacles.

In St. Petersburg, Dostoevsky was running around in circles. He had to take care of his stepson, Pasha, an impudent and annoying youth with black pomaded hair and yellow skin; he had settled in the same quarters with Pasha, and the latter ran the household in such a way that there was never any money. Dostoevsky was saddled with the family of his brother as well: Emilia, Michael's widow, with her numerous adolescent children, believed that Fyodor ought to take care of all of them. His other brother, Nicholas, who was an acute alcoholic, was constantly turning to him for help. In addition, he had taken upon himself all of his dead brother's debts, both in the periodical and the cigarette factory, and in the process was giving promissory notes right and left without going into the merits of the claims; among the creditors there proved to be not a few whom Michael had already paid in full. He was faced with having to pay these debts for the next thirteen years, almost up to the day of his death. He could not manage the periodical by himself. His affairs were going badly; he was ailing and in a most depressed state. He wrote to Apollinaria, hoping to persuade her to return to Russia, but she showed no inclination at all to come back and nurse him. On the contrary, her feeling of vexation—even of hatred —toward Dostoevsky was growing. She denied his right to be her mentor or give her lectures on the Christian virtues. She had ceased to believe in his "nobility." Knowing his temperament and inflammability, she could not bring herself to believe that he was not sleeping with other women, especially after the death of his wife, and there was something about this thought that was unpleasant and unclean. She suddenly disliked those very traits of tolerance and gentleness which she had valued so much when she needed his help in her affair with Salvador. Now she wrote: "What is it I want from Sal-

vador? That he should confess, repent—*i.e.*, that he should
be a Fyodor Mikhailovich? What would happen then—yet
now I have moments of such triumph, of such consciousness
of power."

Dostoevsky's weakness and the fact that he repented of
his actions during a certain onset of sexual passion evidently
provoked Apollinaria's contempt. She grew indignant at his
inability to be resolute and to renounce moral and other
prejudices. At the same time she accused him of having infected her with his scrupulousness, of having instilled doubts
into her, of having sapped her strength. Like Hamlet, she
was ready to say: "For there is nothing either good or bad, but
thinking makes it so." "They speak to me of Fyodor Mikhailovich," she writes in September, 1864. "I simply hate
him. He has made me suffer so much, when it was possible
to do without suffering."

She had in mind not only their trip through Italy, but
also the beginning of their affair in St. Petersburg and, perhaps,
their entire correspondence, which filled her with irritation
and an obscure consciousness of being in the wrong. "Now
I feel and see clearly that I cannot love," she adds, "that I
cannot find happiness and delight in love, because the caresses
of men will remind me of affronts and sufferings." However,
on this point she should also have accused both Salvador and
herself. The search for thrills, for sensual amusement, for new
men, absorbs her for a very short time—only to be followed
by revulsion and indignation over her own empty life. She
goes the limit with one of her admirers, Dr. Benni, and cries
out: "Where has my audacity gone to? When I recall what I
was two years ago, I begin to hate Dostoevsky; he was the first
to kill this confidence within me. But I want to shake off
this melancholy." Dostoevsky had made her doubt that she
could attain a full and happy life by following those paths
of merciless egoism down which her instincts for domination

led her. But she was no longer able to renounce her experiments, she could not be regenerated, and she traveled through France, Switzerland and Germany, changed cities and lovers, and did not find anybody, anywhere, who could give her that uncompromising, indivisible happiness of which she had always dreamt. "Will pride ever forsake me? No, that cannot be; it is better to die."

While she was turning her back on everyday well-being and vainly trying to lose her depression at Versailles, Paris, the Spa and Zurich, Dostoevsky was ready to collapse from weariness under a double burden of care and loneliness, and was seeking the most fantastic ways out of his situation. In the winter of 1864 and the beginning of 1865 came the crisis in his relations with Apollinaria. She was as dear to him as one of his own flesh and blood, but she was far away and she no longer loved him. One could not count upon her. At first he tried to divert himself by taking whatever came to hand. A series of chance women again found a place in his life, a few of whom, like Martha Braun, were adventuresses, while others were still worse. Next he decided that his salvation lay in marrying a good, pure young girl. Just about this time he became acquainted with a pretty twenty-year-old from an excellent family, Anna Korvin-Krukovskaya, who was most suitable for the role of a savior, and it seemed to Dostoevsky that he was in love with her. He met her in March, 1865 and, by April, was ready to ask for her hand. But nothing came of this and, during those very moments when he was enjoying his idyll with Korvin-Krukovskaya, he was an especially frequent visitor at the home of Nadezhda Suslova, Apollinaria's sister, and was confiding all his troubles to her.

Nadezhda had just been expelled from the Academy of Military Surgery for her radical leanings and was getting ready to go abroad. She left in 1865 for Zurich and in two years finished at the university there, brilliantly defending a dissertation on the physiology of the heart. Subsequently she became the first woman doctor in Russia and played an important part in the history of higher education for women. In the 'seventies she married Theodore Erisman, a professor of zoology, and had a medical practice in Moscow. Dostoevsky had always been enraptured with the high moral and intellectual qualities of this young student (in 1865 she was twenty-two). "Here is a rare personality," he wrote about her, "noble, honest, lofty." Her mind and energy astonished Herzen as well when he made her acquaintance in Europe. And it was with her that Dostoevsky discussed her sister in the spring of 1865. At this time Apollinaria had left Paris and was undergoing medical treatment at Montpellier (was it for some feminine ailment, perhaps?) where she became quite friendly with Nathalie Ogareva-Tuchkova, the common-law wife of Herzen. She was sending caustic and supercilious letters to Dostoevsky, applying in correspondence the method she had found so effective when face to face with him. "She found pleasure," remarks the hero of *The Gambler*, "after having heard me out and irritated me until it hurt, in dumbfounding me by some sudden trick of the utmost contempt and disregard." When he asked how things were with her, or attempted to analyze her state, she retorted that he had always adored the tears and sufferings of others. After one of these sorties he could not restrain himself and uttered a few bitter truths about her "individualism"—more correctly, her heartlessness.

When Nadezhda arrived in Zurich in the spring of 1865, Apollinaria complained to her about Dostoevsky. Nadezhda immediately wrote him, repeating her sister's accusations. Dostoevsky's letter to Nadezhda in answer to these reproaches is a document of prime importance. Asking her to read a copy of what he had written to Apollinaria (it has not been preserved) he adds: "It will clarify all the questions you put to me in your letter—that is, whether I 'love to feed daintily upon the sufferings and tears of others,' and so on. And it will also clear up the points about my cynicism and filth. . . . Whenever things became too hard, I came to you to ease my soul, and of late I had been coming only to you, whenever my heart ached too much. . . . Apollinaria is a great egoist. Her egoism and conceit are colossal. She demands *all* from people, all perfections, she does not forgive a single imperfection when set against other traits which are good, while she absolves her own self of the least obligations toward others. She chides me to this day with my having been unworthy of her love; she complains and reproaches me incessantly, yet she herself meets me in Paris in 1863 with the phrase: 'You have been a trifle late in coming,' *i.e.*, that she had fallen in love with another, yet only two weeks before she was still writing that she loved me ardently. It isn't with love for another that I am reproaching her, but with these four lines which she sent to my hotel, with these rude words: 'You have been a trifle late in coming.' I could write a great deal about Rome, about our life together in Turin, in Naples, but what's the use? I love her to this very day—I love her very much— but by now I wish I didn't. She is not *worthy* of such love. I feel sorry for her, because I foresee that she will always be unhappy. She will never find a friend and happiness for herself anywhere. One who demands everything from another, yet absolves himself from obligations, will never find happiness.

"Perhaps my letter to her, against which she complains, shows my irritation. But it is not coarse. She considers as rudeness my daring to contradict her, my daring to mention how hurt I feel. She has always treated me condescendingly. She has taken offense because I at last wanted to speak up, to complain, to contradict her. She does not admit equality in our relations. About her relations with me there is no humanity at all. Come, she knows I love her to this very day.

Why does she torture me, then? She does not have to love me, but she need not torture me either."

This outcry did not remain unanswered. Nadezhda's intervention evidently had some effect on her sister, and a reconciliation of sorts took place between Apollinaria and Dostoevsky. At any rate, he renounced rather easily the idea of marrying Korvin-Krukovskaya and once more longed to go abroad. However, everything stood in his way. It was necessary to liquidate *The Epoch*. Creditors were besieging him on all sides, threatening him with lawsuits and imprisonment. There were so many worries and unpleasantnesses that he could not hold his pen. The epileptic seizures were of frequent occurrence; after each one he was unwell for several days and again could not write, and yet outside of writing he had no other means of livelihood.

The trip abroad assumed in his imagination the fabulous proportions of deliverance from all his troubles. He dreamt of roulette and of Apollinaria. Gambling was bound to bring him money, just as Apollinaria would bring him tenderness and love. His two passions were blending into a single complex and unwholesome longing.

In the late summer of 1865, after borrowing a small sum which could not possibly last the trip, he again set out for Europe in an unusually feverish state.

10

DOSTOEVSKY HAD NOT SEEN APOLLINARIA FOR TWO YEARS.
And what years they had been! It seemed to him as if ages
had passed since that day, in the fall of 1863, when for the
last time he had held her close to him on the smoky platform
of the railway depot in Berlin. Since then his love had fed
upon recollections, played on by his imagination: in these
his beloved seemed more beautiful and better than she was in
reality, but spectral, elusive, like a dream. He tried to picture
Apollinaria as she was now bound to appear, and could not.
He almost dreaded their long awaited meeting, which had
been put off so many times, and this fear, blending with a
tentative joy, brought him to the verge of a nervous break-
down.

By the middle of August, 1865, Dostoevsky was already
in Wiesbaden, where Apollinaria was due to arrive on her way
from Zurich to Paris.

When they met at last, he instantly perceived how she
had changed. Yes, this was the Apollinaria whom he knew and
loved, his darling, his mate. His whole body began to tremble
on hearing her throaty voice, on feeling her soft shoulders
under his avid fingers—but that voice sounded dry, haughty.
Her body, which had become still more beautiful and had burst
into full bloom, remained unyielding and unresponsive. She
had grown more frigid and more estranged. She remarked that
his lofty impulses were nothing but common sensuality, she

responded with disdain to his passionate kisses. Even when there were moments of physical intimacy, she bestowed them upon him like alms—and she always behaved as if this sort of thing were unnecessary and burdensome to her. At times he imagined that his embraces soiled and degraded her. And, in general, she was present and not present: she absented herself emotionally and erotically. There were two years of free life behind her in which he had no place; there was that world of hers, a world of yearnings and caprices which he rather guessed at than knew anything about. He understood very well from her letters and words that she had not passed these two years alone, yet could not even put the superfluous question to her as to whether she had been true to him all this while. She refused to acknowledge that he had any rights, even the right to be jealous. For her part she seemed to be indifferent to what he had been doing in St. Petersburg. In talking about their relations, she was apathetic about his emotions and sensations and hers—just as if the conversation had to do not with the two of them but with two utter strangers. It was obvious that she had already made her diagnosis: their love was dying, and there were no medicines to revive it. Nothing but the past drew her to him now.

He attempted to fight for this love which was crumbling into dust, for his vision of her—and announced to Apollinaria that she must marry him, since that was the only way out; no one could give her as much tenderness and understanding as he could. Particularly now, when everything was slipping away, he had to prove both to himself and her that it could be saved. He demanded the utmost: that they become one for all time. She answered harshly, almost rudely, as was her way. After the first days of comparative tranquillity they began to quarrel again. When she had seen her sister in Switzerland, they had talked endlessly about Dostoevsky, and she had promised to be indulgent and gentle with him. But hardly had she felt her power over him and sensed his agreement and slavish rapture under the lash, hardly had she unleashed his physical passion, than she experienced an unrestrainable desire to trample on him, to cause him pain, to take vengeance on him for all the humiliations and failures of her muddled existence. She thwarted him, made sport of him, or else treated him as a casual and uninteresting acquaintance. And at such times Dostoevsky would plunge into roulette in some sort of ecstasy —and this again insulted her: after assurances of eternal love and embraces (indifferent or actually disagreeable), he would suddenly forget her and dash off like one possessed for the gaming rooms. Roulette had become his mechanism for forgetfulness and consolation.

He lost all he had at gaming, and all she had, and when she decided to leave without knowing if there would be money enough to get her to Paris, Dostoevsky did not hold her back —just as though the possibility of her digging up in Paris the money he needed to recoup his losses, or perhaps even to win, was of greater importance than her physical presence. What called forth this strange behavior of his? The acknowledgement of a final defeat in love? Or unconscious self-defence? This meeting after two years of separation had taken an unexpected turn: it seemed as if the passion for gambling had crowded out and replaced the other passion. But the substitution proved to be only a temporary one. Hardly had Apollinaria left when, as though he had been set free from an evil spell, he came to his senses and began writing tender letters to her: "Dear Polia—in the first place, I don't understand how you ever managed to get to your destination. To my most abominable worrying concerning myself has been added worry about you. . . . I can't believe that I won't see you before you leave (she was preparing to go to Montpellier). A hard hug." Two days later he reverts to the same theme: "However, I don't want to believe that I won't be in Paris and that I won't see you before you leave. It just can't be. . . . I am all yours: A hug once more, ever so hard."

After her departure, he found himself in desperate straits. The hotel refused to give him dinners on credit; he subsisted on tea and bread and sat in the dark: he had no candle, since he had nothing with which to pay for one. He passed his evenings in bed, humiliated by shame and hunger, but was afraid to leave his room because of the contemptuous and mocking looks of the hotel employees. During the day he feverishly penned letters calling for aid: he wrote to Herzen, Turgenev, Miliukov, Wrangel, and magazine publishers in St. Petersburg to whom he offered an expansive plan of a future novel—eventually, *Crime and Punishment*. All his things were in pawn; the money sent him from Paris by Apollinaria he immediately lost at play. Finally he received fifty thalers (a German thaler was worth about seventy cents) from Turgenev, instead of the hundred he had asked for. This loan merely intensified the old enmity between the two writers. Turgenev never let slip a chance of reminding all and sundry how he had saved Dostoevsky and how the other had never made good. Actually, Dostoevsky did not repay his debt until 1876, ten years later, and this led to another dispute: Turgenev maintained that he had sent one hundred thalers to Wiesbaden at the time and not fifty, while Dostoevsky denied it, producing documentary evidence to prove his point, becoming indignant, losing his temper and saying uncomplimentary things about Turgenev.

The advance from his publisher Katkov for the first version of the novel, at that time still entitled *Raskolnikov*, did not arrive in Wiesbaden owing to a misunderstanding (Dostoevsky received it when he was already back in St. Petersburg); Herzen did not respond; Wrangel, that old faithful friend, came to his aid, but only when it was too late; and it was Ioann Yanushev, a priest of the Orthodox church in Wiesbaden, who saved Dostoevsky. He went surety at the hotel for the writer, whom he held in high esteem, and furnished him with seventy thalers. With such a sum it was out of the question even to think of a trip to Paris—it was barely enough to take him home. From Apollinaria, however, came a letter promising that she would soon be in Russia. With this hope, which consoled him to some extent after all the fiascos—in love, at the tables, his utter financial collapse—Dostoevsky set out on his return voyage.

Apollinaria had gone back to Paris dissatisfied both with Dostoevsky and herself. Her affair with him now struck her as a drag on her freedom, a disgusting ball and chain, insulting to her self-respect and her dignity as a woman. Without losing any time she renewed her flirtation with the medico, as if the meeting with Dostoevsky had aroused her sensuality and she had to direct it toward someone else. In this case, as usual, she alternated between frigidity and passion: "He wanted a great deal," she wrote, "but I would not let him." Dostoevsky's gambling fever had exasperated her no less than his lust; it seemed a weakness totally unworthy of him, even a vice, and with her usual impatience she condemned him. And, in general, everything he did and desired from her called forth her protest and indignation. She considered most of the people she knew her enemies, and she was ready to include Dostoevsky among them. About the middle of September she made an entry in her diary: "It is better to die from melancholy, yet die free, independent of external things, faithful to one's convictions, and to return one's soul to God just as pure as it was, rather than to make a concession, to allow oneself even for a moment to mingle with base and unworthy things; but I find life so coarse and sad that I endure it with difficulty. My God, is it possible it will always be thus? And was it worth while to be born?"

While Apollinaria was putting these questions to herself,

Dostoevsky was working at high pressure in St. Petersburg on *Crime and Punishment*. He had dropped *The Gambler*, since he found it painful to write about Apollinaria, and was combining in the new novel the various themes that had attracted him during the last few months. He was at a high tide of creative energy, and at times asked himself whether the death of his wife had loosed these extraordinary forces within him. But he was compelled to do his writing between serious attacks of epilepsy. After his return from abroad they were recurring almost every five days—probably both because of Apollinaria and the intense work on his novel. Before a seizure his melancholy and irritation would increase; he became morose and quarrelsome—at times he simply threw himself at people and yelled at them. He frequently heard voices, visions swept past him as if in a dream or delirium, or else he experienced a poignant, unbearable blissfulness, very much like a sexual orgasm although the act of love did not afford him such a piercing delight as this moment of rapture, this *aura*, as the physicians called it, which invariably ended in convulsions and loss of consciousness. After a seizure the symptoms of nervous shock passed very slowly; his head ached, melancholy and weakness took possession of him for several days. Almost always, in connection with his attacks, he was overcome by depression and anguish. According to the testimony of his friends, who quoted him, the nature of his depression "consisted of his feeling himself like some sort of criminal; it seemed to him that some unknown guilt, some great misdeed, hung heavy over him." During such moments he was ready to acknowledge his frightful sin against Maria—he had deceived her with Apollinaria; and against Apollinaria—he had robbed her of her innocence and driven her through the flames of passion.

The doctors were of the opinion that a cure was out of the question for him, but they said that it would be possible

to alleviate his general condition if he would give up writing
and all strong excitement. Dostoevsky's usual answer to this
advice was to shrug: they were offering him suicide as a
medicine. At that very moment he was being consumed by two
fires: he was trying to describe Raskolnikov, the murder of
the old pawnbroker and her sister, the death of Marmeladov,
the sickness and madness and self-justification of a criminal
—and he was waiting for Apollinaria. The whole tense atmosphere of *Crime and Punishment*, that novel of bold action,
bloodshed, physical corruption and spiritual cleansing, corresponded to his own inner state and the atmosphere in which
he had to work.

Apollinaria arrived in St. Petersburg at the end of October,
1865, and immediately the inevitable occurred. Dostoevsky
proposed marriage to her with still greater determination
than at Wiesbaden. He wanted to come to a definite understanding. "Halfway reconciliation with her was out of the
question," he wrote in *The Eternal Husband* of Nathalia,
who is so reminiscent of the Apollinaria of this period. His
proposal of marriage was nothing new, and he made no secret
of it with his friends. Apollinaria has an entry in her diary
that November: "He has long been offering me his hand and
heart, and he merely angers me by doing so." Still earlier,
in February, the young nihilist, Peter Ussov, a friend of Salias',
had asked Apollinaria why she should not marry Dostoevsky
and get hold of *The Epoch;* he thought she should turn the
conservative periodical into a radical one (such, evidently,
was his confidence in her sway over Dostoevsky). "Because I
don't want to," she had answered him. "Had I wanted to, I
would have been in St. Petersburg and not gone off to Montpellier."

But even when she found herself in Russia, she did not
change her mind; she not only had no intention of spending
the rest of her life with Dostoevsky but, during the four

months of her stay in St. Petersburg, brought their relations
to a point of irrevocable rupture. Even Dostoevsky was working for a crisis and a definite clarification—their meetings were
becoming far too depressing, they were being transformed
into an endless duel. "Today Fyodor Mikhailovich was here,"
Apollinaria recorded, "and we were bickering and contradicting
each other all the time." Everything about him displeased her
now: his religiosity and his excessively pomaded short hair,
his speeches on what was permissible in morals and his fondness for sweets. She made fun of his useless dandyism; he
ordered his suits from expensive tailors, yet everything hung
on him like a sack. Whenever he broached the matter of
marriage, she would laughingly remind him about his raptures
over Englishwomen—really, he ought to take a trip to London
and find himself a wife there, since he seemed to think that
Englishwomen were the most perfect type of feminine beauty.
And when, to use her expression, he began *to importune* her,
she caustically faced him with his encounters with loose women
or with his prospective brides—she had found out everything
about him from the St. Petersburg gossips.

And he, for his part, saw her in the merciless light of
truth. She appeared to him frigid and dissolute, like the
princess in *The Humiliated and Wronged*. He now had a
superb understanding of all the infernality of her nature. Later
on he was to describe Nathalia in *The Eternal Husband*: "She
was like one of those women whom the Flagellant sectarians
choose and adore as the Divine Mother, who herself believes
to the utmost that she really is the Divine Mother . . . a
passionate, cruel, sensual type. She detested licentiousness,
condemned it with frenzied wrath, and was herself licentious,
yet no facts could ever bring her to a consciousness of her own
licentiousness."

There was no use in hoping for anything; their love had
come to an end. But he was enduring the end painfully,

almost tragically, like a heavy blow. In his correspondence the break with Apollinaria is reflected only obliquely; he never mentions it directly. In December, 1865, he wrote his brother Nicholas: "All my seizures are of the severest kind, and they come more frequently than ever. The work is hard going, and on top of that I catch colds, and the house is all upset." And in the beginning of 1866, when the rupture had become a fact, he described his life to Wrangel in the following terms: "A novel is a poetic business; it demands serenity of spirit and of imagination for its fulfillment. But I am being tortured by creditors—that is, they threaten to put me in prison . . . illnesses torture me also—epilepsy and hemorrhoids; because of the latter I had to spend fifteen days in bed, without doing any work. . . . Dear friend, you at least are happy in your family [Wrangel had married about this time], but fate has denied me this great and unique human happiness."

In mid-April, 1866, when he wrote this, Apollinaria was about to leave St. Petersburg. She had not only rejected all his proposals of marriage but, after three years of love, infidelities, quarrels and reconciliations, had announced that it was time for them to separate entirely since there was no future for them together.

These words, of course, came as no surprise to Dostoevsky: everything was rolling downhill, and this was merely a confirmation of something he had seen and sensed beforehand. He was experiencing pain, shame and—despite everything— actual relief. He had become so weary because of Apollinaria, she had mangled him so badly, the hopelessness of their future friendship had become so evident, that amputation seemed better than a protracted illness. He preferred at that moment the bitter reality of her departure to false hopes; loneliness promised him less suffering than dreams that never materialized.

In the spring of 1866, Apollinaria went to her brother's place in the country. She and Dostoevsky made their farewells, knowing only too well that their paths would never cross again. If we are to believe Dostoevsky's daughter, they did in fact meet once more, toward the end of the 'seventies, when *The Diary of a Writer* had greatly increased his popularity. One day he was informed that an unknown visitor wanted to see him. A lady wearing a veil entered his study and took her seat before the master of the house, near his desk.

"Whom have I the honor of receiving?" he asked.

With an abrupt gesture she lifted her veil, revealing her face.

"Please be kind enough to tell me your name," he continued in a dry voice.

"You do not recognize who I am?"

"No; tell me your name."

For answer the visitor dropped her veil without a word, arose and went out of the room. And only when the house door had slammed to behind her did it dawn on Dostoevsky that this was Apollinaria.

In telling his wife about this occurrence, he is supposed to have added, "She hasn't changed, but she has disappeared from my life and memory so completely that I failed to recognize her."

And the daughter goes on to explain: epileptics are queer folk, and their memory is likewise queer. But even considering his disease, this melodramatic story is not very credible and differs very little from other similar cock-and-bull stories transmitted by this same Liubov Dostoevskaya. It is possible that her father, having come across Apollinaria somewhere, did fail to recognize her at once, and this would certainly have been sufficient to offend Apollinaria mortally. But if the incident ever did take place, it was undoubtedly not in the manner reported. For after all, how could Dostoevsky forget or fail to recognize someone whom he had loved with a serious, rapturous and anguished love, for three years, someone who had left a mark as searing as a wound upon his soul and flesh? And is it possible that ten years of separation could erase her image from his memory? He used to start whenever her name was uttered in his presence, he kept up a correspondence with her, concealing it from his new wife, he invariably reverted to describing her in his works, he bore to his very death the scars of her caresses and rebuffs, he remained for all time—in the innermost recesses of his heart and flesh—faithful to his seductive, his cruel, unfaithful and tragic mate.

APOLLINARIA HAD COME BACK TO RUSSIA TO EXTRICATE
herself from the slough of vulgarity which, it seemed to her,
was sucking her down in Europe. In St. Petersburg she broke
finally with the past when she broke with Dostoevsky whom
she imagined to be the cause of all her sufferings. Now she
was free and could begin a new life. However, what we know
of her later on indicates that this freedom brought her very
little joy.

At first she busied herself with social welfare and realized
her long-cherished intention of working for the people. After
passing an examination as a teacher in 1868, she organized
a school for peasant children in the hamlet of Ivanovo, in
the Vladimir province. Local authorities lost no time in re-
porting this to St. Petersburg: Apollinaria Suslova was under
police surveillance and her home was repeatedly raided in
search of subversive material; her brother was afterward arrested. The school was closed down two months later, on
orders from the capital. In the Secret Police report it is mentioned that she wore blue spectacles and bobbed her hair;
there are other accusations as well: "She is too free in her
opinions and does not go to church."

In the archives of Section III, Case No. 260 for 1868, it
is noted by one of the agents that the said Apollinaria Suslova
"is one of the foremost she-nihilists, openly proclaiming her
teachings, and while abroad had close contacts with persons

inimical to the government." These persons were, evidently, Nathalia Ogareva-Tuchkova, the wife of the *emigré* Herzen, Peter Ussov, Countess Salias, and other representatives of the revolutionary and radical intelligentsia.

At one time Apollinaria went in for literary work: in 1870 appeared her translation of M. Munier's life of Franklin— she remained true to her interest in America. About her personal life during this period nothing is known. She was an ardent champion of the emancipation of women, and in 1872 showed up at the open courses Vladimir Herrier was giving in St. Petersburg—the first Russian institution of higher learning for women. She was thirty-two at the time. Dressed in dark silk, grave and absorbed, she aroused interest by her air of mystery. She did not finish the courses, however; learning evidently bored her just as quickly as everything else did.

For some time she lived at her brother's place in Tambov province and visited Moscow and St. Petersburg frequently, but there is no record of what she did or how she occupied her days during the next seven or eight years. At the end of the 'seventies, she was again in St. Petersburg, where she made the acquaintance of a provincial teacher, Vassily Rosanov, the future journalist, writer and philosopher. She married him in 1880, still during the lifetime of Dostoevsky, whom her husband deified. Subsequently in his works, which constitute a most peculiar chapter in Russian literature, he proclaimed himself Dostoevsky's disciple. He, too, was tormented by ideas of God, by questions of good and evil and, in particular, by the problem of sex. There was always the stifling odor of the flesh hanging heavy over him, and with an insistence that bordered on obsession he reduced religion, as well as politics and philosophy, to the symbols of male and female genitalia and the ritual of copulation. His marriage with Apollinaria took on for him the character of a physical sacrament. The mere thought that he was going to sleep with the very same woman whom Dostoevsky had slept with in the past threw him into a mystical-sensuous ecstasy. He declared himself "smitten" by Apollinaria's appearance. She was his senior by sixteen years (he was twenty-four and she was forty or forty-one) but, according to him, she still preserved the traits of a once striking beauty. In a portrait of this period she is sitting very straight in an armchair, wearing a lace headdress; her hair is parted and frames a small, very handsome head; the regularly featured face, looking as if it were carved, is somewhat stern; the gaze of the large eyes, just a trifle sad, is frank and proud; the imperious mouth, just a trifle too wide, is sharply defined; she has splendidly beautiful hands, lowered in a languorous, just a trifle mannered gesture of fatigue.

Echoing Dostoevsky's *mot* about the heroine of *The Eternal Husband*, Rosanov writes that her character was that of "a Russian Katie de Medici" or a Divine Mother of the Flagellant sectarians belonging to the Pomorski Accord. On St. Bartholomew's Eve (to quote him) she would have stood by a window and aimed straight at the Huguenots, nor would her hand have trembled.

Her heart, too, trembled only rarely, and he soon experienced this himself.

She married him, in all probability, out of boredom and curiosity. And perhaps there was also an admixture of something hidden, secret—some physical desire, going back to the days of her intimacy with Dostoevsky. For Rosanov as well, physical love was transformed into a stifling captivity, into a delighted self-annihilation. There was in him some sort of sexual mania; he, too, was possessed, even as Dostoevsky had been, but in another fashion, unlike that of a genius. Yet in his speeches about the holiness of the embrace, about the mysteries of the marriage bed, there was to be felt such a persuasiveness, such a genuine worship before sexual fusion, that intimacy with him may have held forth for Apollinaria

the promise of some higher justification and sanctification of
her own sensuality—the transformation of sin into a pathway
to God.

These hopes, however, were not justified. Her marriage
with Rosanov proved unsuccessful and turned into an unbearable ordeal for both husband and wife. Even at the very
beginning Rosanov, to use a graphic expression of Zinaida
Hippius, the poetess, "bathed in water mingled with tears."
At first Apollinaria persecuted him with her monstrous jealousy
and staged savage scenes for his benefit. She used to waylay
him on the one street of the very small town (either Eletz
or Riazan) where they lived, and on one occasion when he
left his school in the company of a woman teacher she threw
herself on the innocent girl in a frenzy and cuffed her until
her ears rang. Apollinaria quickly became disillusioned by the
sexual mysticism of Rosanov: in her opinion he simply used
it as a screen for his slavering and sticky sensuality. But, with
age, her own desires increased, and she cast lingering glances
at young students. She took to making scarcely equivocal
advances to one of them, a friend of her husband's, and when
he did not respond, she sent a letter to the police informing
on him. The young man was arrested, and Apollinaria was
quite calm in telling about her revenge.

Rosanov affirms that she fell in love with his friend
Goldovski, a young Jew, and when she failed *to get somewhere*
with him, forbade her husband to be on friendly terms with
the man who had insulted her. According to another version
of this story she left Rosanov for Goldovski. It is difficult to
tell whether this is still the same person who figured in the
affair of the police exposé. At any rate, in 1886, after six
years of marriage, she cast off Rosanov, declaring that she
was tired of his lies and unfaithfulness, and settled in Nishni
Novgorod. As far as Rosanov was concerned, the truth was
probably on her side; she had such power over him, however,

that he tearfully began to implore her to come back to him. She replied to his letters and demands with that cruelty, even coarseness, so natural to her; she wrote that he was no dog, and hence there was no use in his "yowling." But when Rosanov took up with another woman and had some children by her, she categorically refused to give him a divorce, and for fifteen years contrived all sorts of unpleasant things for him: this new union of Rosanov's, brought about by her own fault, was considered "unlawful cohabitation," and his children were deprived of civil rights.

The struggle between Apollinaria and her former husband continued with suspensions, military ruses, stratagems and intrigues, right up to 1897, when Rosanov at last agreed to let her have a separation: he had not done so up to then, hoping in this way to compel her to consent to a divorce. But five more years passed before Apollinaria made the concession: she was intractable and obstinate with the friends whom her hubsand sent for parleys; she spoke to them bitterly, almost with hatred, and called him a prostitute and a liar. However, Rosanov's duplicity and moral filth were so repulsive that she had full grounds for her comments.

Everyone who had to do with her suffered in the extreme from her imperious, unbearable character. We are told that, after leaving Rosanov, she adopted a child to bring up, but that the young girl apparently found her life too hard to bear and drowned herself. Apollinaria's father, an old man when she came back to his home in Nishni Novgorod, wrote concerning her: "The Enemy of Mankind has now come to dwell in my house, and there's no living in it myself." In a short while, however, she moved to the Crimea and settled down in Sebastopol, in a house of her own, which she kept exceptionally clean and in apple-pie order. Zinaida Hippius for some reason calls her an "evil-tempered, white and stout old woman," sly and depraved. Stout she never was; in her old age she was remarkable for her leanness, her straight and proud bearing, and her exceptional appearance created an unforgettable impression. As far as her slyness, craftiness and licentiousness are concerned, it is possible that all these vices increased toward the end of her life.

Passion probably did not cease to stir her even in her declining years. In 1914, during World War I, she unexpectedly proclaimed herself an ardent patriot and joined reactionary organizations—or, at any rate, supported them. Life with Rosanov, a collaberator on *The New Time* sheet, an anti-Semite and a monarchist, had evidently not left her unscathed; she had adopted certain views of his.

She died in 1918, at seventy-eight, hardly suspecting that she had for a neighbor one who, fifty years before, had taken her place in the heart of her first lover, had become his wife, and who was now finishing her days on the same Crimean littoral, in the very same year: Anna Grigorievna Dostoevskaya.

PART THREE
ANNA:

▲

The Happy Marriage

BESIDES THE POWERFUL INSTINCTS AND DESIRES THAT HE kept secret (some of which found release in life while others expressed themselves in creativity, in the catharsis of writing) Dostoevsky had an open curiosity concerning all the refinements of vice, the variations and combinations of the passions, and the abnormalities of human nature which showed its origins in evil. This curiosity lent a certain oddity to his behavior, which his friends were quite familiar with, and supplied an explanation for his great interest in "fallen creatures." He knelt in adoration before the "purest beauty" of innocence, he adored the Sistine Madonna as a symbol of immaculate womanhood and idealized "young ladies in muslin," yet at the same time got along quite cosily with streetwalkers—and not only with the victims of poverty and slum life, but with cynical professional women who had chosen their trade and quite frankly offered themselves for what they could get. Their erotic gestures held an irresistible fascination for him.

His interest in the professional woman, from the tart to the courtesan, in no way reminiscent of that sainted prostitute Sonia Marmeladova in *Crime and Punishment,* determined the nature of his affair with Martha Brown. He made her acquaintance toward the end of 1864, at a time when he was still brooding over the loss of his wife and saw it as a misfortune and a punishment of God, and when the everlasting separation from Apollinaria condemned him to loneliness. During those depressing autumn and winter months, he willingly took whatever offered itself in the way of distraction and entertainment, and may well have turned to loose women as a kind of drug.

Martha Brown, nee Panina, from a family of gentlefolk, had received quite a good education but had left home in her early years and "taken the wrong path." A born adventuress, she had crisscrossed all Europe, had stayed in Paris, Marseilles and Gibraltar, had lived in Austria, Spain and many other countries, trafficking in her youth, changing her lovers with extraordinary rapidity and getting involved in the most fantastic scrapes. She numbered among her friends cardsharps, counterfeiters, international *chevaliers d'industrie* and even professional holdup men who did not shrink from using steel or firearms. Her ties with the criminal world were so flagrant that the police expelled her from Belgium and Holland. Most of the time she managed to live fairly well, but her luck ran out in London; she lost both her money and her protector, walked about in rags, and had to spend her nights under bridges in the company of other prostitutes and thieves.

At last she was arrested and clapped into prison. Eventually she was released, after considerable difficulty, by some Methodist missionaries who had taken an interest in her. They fed, clothed and shod the stray lamb, supplied her with soul-saving tracts which she read with a zeal that enraptured them, and sent her to the Isle of Guernsey. There they persuaded her to marry an American sailor from Baltimore by the name of Brown. When her husband signed on for a long voyage, however, Martha fled from the Isle of Guernsey to the continent and set out on her travels again, determined to make her way home to Russia by hook or crook.

She made her appearance in St. Petersburg in the 'sixties. She had just passed thirty, was still interesting and attractive to look at, had seen and gone through a great deal, had read much, and wrote not at all badly. But her affairs were not prospering, somehow. At first she became the mistress of one Fleming, a gambler and a typical representative of the capital's underworld. From him she passed on to Peter Gorsky, a minor contributor to Dostoevsky's *Epoch*. Her new friend, a dipsomaniac and bohemian without a copper to his name, became strongly attached to her, was exceedingly jealous, and at one time even attempted to lead her back to the path of righteousness, *i.e.*, the circles where she belonged by birth. He brought Martha to the editorial rooms of *The Epoch*, obtained some work for her as a translator—she knew English well—and kept persuading her to write up her "travels," something she stubbornly refused to do, on the by no means groundless theory that the more colorful of her adventures were hardly meant for print.

Through Gorsky she gained access to Dostoevsky, who immediately became interested in this extraordinary woman. He found her somewhat shopworn, but not the least embarrassed either by her own professional airs or by her tempestuous past. Her extremely frank accounts of her London adventures reminded him vividly of pages from his beloved Dickens—in particular, of *Oliver Twist*—and in a short while they became very close friends.

Toward the end of 1864, Martha found herself in the hospital of Sts. Peter and Paul; there was, however, nothing seriously wrong with her. But Gorsky did his utmost to keep her there. Just then he was going through particularly lean times and was afraid that if Martha discovered this on coming out of the hospital, she would drop him for good and all. And so he pleaded with the doctors and thought up all sorts of maneuvers to postpone her release. However, she herself was in no great a hurry to come out: after all, it was peaceful in the ward and they fed her well, whereas her release meant returning to Gorsky's filthy hole-in-the-wall or taking to the streets.

She mentioned all these things in her letters to Dostoevsky, confiding to him the particulars of her quarrels with
Gorsky and her complicated relations with him. In one of his
answers Dostoevsky proposed that she move to his rooms and
live there temporarily. He was not, apparently, prompted solely
by pity and the desire to shelter the homeless. It was not so
much a matter of living at his place as of living with him—and
he must either have told her so without beating about the bush
or let her understand it quite clearly. At any rate, Martha's
last letter from the hospital contains this significant passage:
"Whether or not I succeed in satisfying you in a physical
way, and whether or not that spiritual harmony upon which
the continuation of our acquaintanceship depends material-
izes, I still ask you to believe that I shall always remain grateful
because you found me—if for a moment, or for any time at all
—worthy of your friendship and your good will."

How far the good will went, and whether or not Martha
Brown succeeded in satisfying Dostoevsky physically, we do not
know. Even if the arrangement was carried out, it did not last
long, since two months later he became infatuated with a
young girl who was the complete antithesis of the runaway
wife of a Baltimore sailor. It is possible that here again the
law of contrast and polarity which always played such a role
in the life and thoughts of Dostoevsky was at work.

The episode with Martha Brown put an end to his tavern
friendships. The intense interest he had cherished since youth
in the "lost personalities" of the St. Petersburg underworld
apparently petered out about the mid-'sixties, and he gradually
gave up frequenting dens and bawdy houses in the rougher
districts. On the whole, his passions quieted down, and much
of the fire within him burned out about 1865, after his parting
with Apollinaria. In individuals such as Dostoevsky erotic
desires and even perversions do not become habits. There
comes a moment when they attain the limit of their intensity,

flare up into a conflagration, and then burn out or become transmuted. They lose their acuteness and pathological force, their virulence weakens, the high temperature of the blood falls, they undergo a change into something new or remain as a heavy cargo of recollections whose only power is to create sexual phantasms.

Beginning with 1865, Dostoevsky's masochism and sadism, his complexes about minor girls, his sexual curiosity—in short, all the pathological aspects of his erotic life—lost their obsessive and maniacal nature; they became blunted, and he consciously strove for what may be called the "normalization" of his sexual activity. In connection with this his dreams of marrying were intensified and he began to gravitate once more toward marriageable young girls.

IN THE SUMMER OF 1865, DOSTOEVSKY RECEIVED A STORY,
The Dream, with an introductory letter from its author, Anna
Korvin-Krukovskaya, who resided in Palibino, a large estate in
the province of Vitebsk. Her father, Vassily, the leader of the
gentry in that province and a retired lieutenant general, traced
his lineage back to Matthew Korvin, King of Hungary, whose
descendants had migrated to Lithuania, and were related to
the Czars of Russia through the Glinsky nobles. A gentleman
of the old school, he had given a worldly education to his
two daughters, with foreign *bonnes* and governesses, and had
tried to instill into them his own ideas of family pride. However, he had not succeeded in shielding them from the liberal
tendencies of the 1860's. His elder daughter, the dreamy and
romantic Anna, had decided to become a writer and, keeping
her aspirations a secret from her immediate family, had sent
her first attempt to the editor of *The Epoch*, whose novels
she ardently admired.

Her story dealt with a young girl who, because of social
considerations, does not dare to give her heart to a poor
student. A prophetic dream reveals to her her true feelings;
she decides at last to scorn conventions and prejudices, but
learns that the man she has loved is dead. In a short while
she herself dies, regretting her wasted and loveless youth. The
story, very typical of the period, was weak artistically, but
its sincerity and freshness were ingratiating, while the young

author's letter made such an impression on Dostoevsky with its enthusiasm and faith in life that he decided to publish *The Dream* in the next issue of his periodical and immediately wrote her, asking her age and "circumstances."

Evidently he had a poor memory and had forgotten his earlier experience with another literary debutante and how dearly it had cost him.

The correspondence which sprang up between the twenty-year-old girl and the forty-three-year-old editor was carried on either through the housekeeper at Palibino or through a friend of Anna's, the daughter of Evreinov, Commandant of Peterhof, in the utmost secrecy, so as not to arouse the wrath of Anna's father. According to his younger daughter, the lieutenant general believed women writers were the root of all evil; he regarded them with a naïve horror and indignation, considered every one of them capable of the worst depravity and used to point to George Sand, in breeches, with sputterings of fury. One can imagine what things were like when he learned that his favorite Anna wanted nothing better than to be a writer.

He made the grievous discovery under the most discouraging circumstances, during a grand ball arranged to mark his wife's birthday: he came upon a registered letter from Dostoevsky, enclosing the honorarium for *The Dream*. The very thought that his daughter was capable of corresponding with a stranger, an ex-convict, and of receiving money from him besides, seemed so monstrous and disgraceful to Korvin-Krukovsky that he felt faint. A terrible row broke out. The father refused to forgive Anna until she promised him not to carry on with such an indecent business as contributing to periodicals. She refused to do so and remained stubborn; the mother kept running between father and daughter, bullying and coaxing. At that time such disagreements were common in families of the gentry; there was an unprecedented discord between parents and children, and the struggle of the younger generation (especially the daughters) for their independence took on the character of open warfare against parental authority and the old traditions of obedience and silent submissiveness.

The lieutenant general at last consented to hear his daughter read her story, found nothing scandalous in it but, on the contrary, was greatly touched. His wrath turned to forgiveness. Anna succeeded in convincing him that times had changed and that traditions might be changed too. Under the pressure brought to bear upon him by his wife and daughters, he had to retreat on all fronts: Anna's second story, dealing with a novice by the name of Michael who had been reared in a monastery by his uncle, a monk, was brought out in the September, 1864, issue of The Epoch, and payment for it was made in December. The correspondence with Dostoevsky went on, although the young author had to submit all her letters to the father. She was even granted permission to see the ogre on her next visit to St. Petersburg. But, while he consented to this, Korvin-Krukovsky warned his wife: "Remember, Dostoevsky doesn't belong to our social circle—what do we know of him? Only that he's a journalist and an exconvict. A fine recommendation, I must say! We have to be very careful about him."

Early in 1865 the mother, with the twenty-year-old Anna and the fourteen-year-old Sofia set out for St. Petersburg. They had 110 miles to cover before they would reach the railway station. A troika with jingle-bells went in front, carrying the maids and the baggage; the squire's wife and the squire's two daughters rode in a roomy sleigh-coach drawn by six horses.

Toward the end of February the Korvin-Krukovskys settled in the house of some elderly aunts on Vassilievsky Island and Anna at once invited Dostoevsky to call. The first meeting was not much of a success. The mother, bearing her husband's warnings in mind, did not leave her daughters unchaperoned for even a moment. The septuagenarian aunts and even Anna and Sofia eyed the writer as if he were some rare and curious animal. He was embarrassed and felt resentful in this atmosphere of grandes dames and little maidens. On that particular day he looked old and ailing—as he generally did whenever he was out of sorts. He kept plucking nervously at his scanty blondish beard and biting his mustache, while his whole face was twitching. Nothing came of their attempts at salon conversation; he answered in monosyllables with premeditated rudeness.

Five days later, however, he put in an unexpected appearance. There was no one in the house but the two sisters. He took Anna by the hand, made her sit down next to him on a divan, and the ice was broken. They immediately became friends, while the dark-eyed Sofia, who was gaping from the wings, fell head over heels in love with him.

Anna Korvin-Krukovskaya was going on twenty-one at the time, was good-looking, lithe and graceful, had a splendid complexion, sea-green eyes and a mass of silky flaxen hair in two braids that reached below her waist. She was considered a beauty in the family and nicknamed Russalka (Lorelei). She was a far from foolish, excellently educated young woman of the world, witty and vivacious, somewhat naïve and impractical, yet open-hearted and resolute. She was taken up with the new ideas of freedom, equal rights for women and social progress and deeply devoted to them, enthusiastically sharing the views of Russian radicals and French socialistic thinkers. The materialism of Buchner and Moleschott—the two most popular philosophers of the 'sixties—was mingled in her mind with the collectivistic teachings of Fourier, Saint-Simon, Proudhon and Cabet, the author of the communistic utopia, *Voyage en Icarie.*

Dostoevsky had read their works in his youth, when he was a member of the Petrashevsky circle, but by now he had left them far behind. Besides that, he disliked very much their current followers, the she-nihilists with bobbed hair and tartan plaids thrown over their shoulders, who spoke roughly and inhaled cigarettes deeply to show the independence of their ways. But in this instance the she-nihilist turned out to be an exquisitely dressed young woman with magnificent braids, who instead of tobacco smoke gave off the scent of fine French perfume.

Fyodor was bewitched. He liked to call on her, to talk with her. He used to visit her three times a week, and they became very close friends. Her mother and the aunts were often out paying calls or attending some theatre, and he would find himself alone with both sisters. When he enjoyed the company and close attention was paid to what he was saying (Anna and Sofia lived up to both requirements) he became animated, delivered lengthy monologues, outlined his ideas for novels or, occasionally, related scenes from his own life. He was probably more confiding with these two young girls than with his old friends. He described to them how, from the spot where he stood on Semenovsky Square awaiting his execution, he had seen the sun come out from behind the clouds, strike brilliantly on the cupola of a church, and how he had stubbornly watched that glow, watched the bright sunbeams, thinking that within five minutes he would blend with them and feeling a physical revulsion against death.

To the astonishment of his hearers he also spoke—with perfect frankness—of his epilepsy. According to him it had begun at Semipalatinsk. One Easter Eve an atheistic friend had called on him; they had spent all night in conversation and argued warmly about religion. "There is a God—there is!" Dostoevsky had shouted, beside himself with excitement. Just then a church bell rang for early Easter mass, and it seemed to him that heaven had descended upon earth and engulfed him. "Yes, there is a God!" he cried out and, falling into convulsions, had lost consciousness.

While telling all this he addressed himself to Anna, without noticing that the black-haired Sofia was hanging on his every word. She did not take her piercing eyes off him for even a moment: he used to describe them as "gypsy eyes." She had fallen in love with him with the ecstatic love of an adolescent, in which childish adoration is mixed with a premonition of feminine passion. She was in torment, she wept, she dreamt of him, and in her reveries went through a stormy romance with the utterly unsuspecting writer who was three and a half times her age. This very young girl who was so enamored with Dostoevsky later became one of the most famous Russian women, a scholar and a professor of mathematics at Stockholm and, as Sofia Kovalevskaya, was celebrated not only in her native land but throughout Europe. Her life was short yet very full, brilliant and even romantic, and she remained true to her early attachment to Dostoevsky: she kept up her friendship with him, saw him frequently and was an ardent admirer of his to the day of her death in 1891.

But during March and April, 1865, her rival—and a fortunate rival, at that—was her own sister. Dostoevsky devoted himself entirely to Anna. During those two spring months he was so captivated by her that he thought no one else could be the chosen one of his heart and the architect of his happiness, as the sentimental novels of the period used to phrase it. As soon as this thought occurred to him, however, his whole attitude toward her changed. He became captious and nervous, reproaching her if she happened to attend a ball or did not fully appreciate Pushkin, grew angry over what he called her frivolity and scolded her for being trivial. In short, a bystander might have imagined that he was ready to quarrel and break off with her. All this was camouflage so typical of him; he treated her especially atrociously on those days when he was trying to get up enough courage to confess his love and to ask for her hand. At the same time it was hardly love at first sight: he was simply reacting to the enchantment of youth and the availability of an endearing and beautiful young woman.

After all he had gone through with Apollinaria, his friendship with Anna Korvin-Krukovskaya offered such hours of simple and quiet delight that he came to believe he had found his salvation, his deliverance. Anna was far from being weak —she decidedly did have character—but there were no hints of those violent and vengeful traits he had found in Apollinaria. On the contrary, Anna was self-sacrificing and all her energies were directed toward serving others. She always spoke of service to "work and ideals," but he felt her idealism could be channelled into domesticity as well. And since marriage was a necessity to Dostoevsky and he was dreaming of it, and since Apollinaria was away and he believed he no longer loved her, he transferred all his hopes to this girl he had so recently met, and soon convinced both her and himself that he was in love with her.

One evening when they were alone he told her how he felt and asked if she would consent to be his wife. It is possible that she answered evasively, or at any rate not definitely, and that Dostoevsky took for consent what was no more than a vague promise. But at any rate he considered himself engaged, and she must have felt momentarily both exhilarated and troubled because such a man as Dostoevsky was offering her his heart and hand. She had dreams of becoming a writer, and marriage to the famous author of Poor Folk and The Humiliated and Wronged suddenly seemed to be the real fulfillment of her dreams. She did not think of his age or appearance, while his poverty and ill health were mere vexatious details not worthy of any serious attention. With his usual soaring fantasy Dostoevsky tried to persuade her that he had loved her from the first moment he saw her—and even before that: her letters had already made him feel that this was to be no ordinary friendship, but that he would love her with all his being.

In reality, however, their relations did not go beyond mutual sympathy. He had a most typical predilection, half paternal and half erotic, for friendship with young girls, while her regard was a mixture of womanly pity for the sufferings he had endured and awareness of his overpowering excellence as a writer. What they called love was a half-cerebral, half-literary friendship, and because of this it suffered a great deal both from disputes on abstract themes and from Dostoevsky's attempts to approach Anna with certain emotional demands.

A definite understanding with Anna should, one would think, have given Dostoevsky wings and made him happy. But instead his suspiciousness increased; he began demanding an account of her every move and did not conceal his dislike of everybody she enjoyed. He was invited to a gala evening arranged by Anna's mother and aunts and appeared in formal dress, but his coat hung atrociously and made him rage inwardly. "He began working himself up into a temper from the very moment he crossed the threshold of the reception room," Sofia tells us. "Like all nervous people he felt an annoying embarrassment whenever he found himself in the society of strangers . . . he evidently wanted to vent the annoyance aroused by this feeling on someone." Hence he was quarrelsome with the guests, carried a chip on his shoulder and behaved maliciously, impertinently and ridiculously. This conduct did not improve his position in Anna's eyes, and soon there were more serious disagreements.

No matter how much Anna may have admired Dostoevsky's genius, she could not accept all his views blindly. They were forever quarreling over his negative attitude toward new trends. Anna defended her faith in progress, science and socialism, while Dostoevsky ridiculed these "ideals of the age." Besides that she had begun to suspect that her love for him was not at all the sort marriage calls for. From doubts concerning her own feelings, she passed on to the question of whether their characters were really compatible. "What he needs is a wife altogether different from me," she told her younger sister, who felt a mad joy at this confidence. "His wife will have to dedicate herself wholly—wholly!—to him, to give up her entire life to him, to think only of him. But I can't do that—I want to live myself. Then, too, he is so nervous, so demanding. He seems to be enveloping me all the time, to be absorbing me into himself: in his presence I am never my own self."

A showdown between the engaged couple finally took place before Anna's departure from St. Petersburg and, as he put it, he released her from her word. Here is how he told the incident later on: "Anna Vassilievna is one of the finest women I have met in all my life. She is exceptionally intelligent, very cultured, well versed in literature; she has a splendid and kind heart. She is a young woman of high moral qualities —but her convictions are diametrically opposed to mine, and she cannot yield where they are concerned; she is much too straightforward for that; because of all this it is hardly likely that our marriage would have been a happy one. I have released her from the word she gave me and wish with all my soul that she may meet a man who holds to the same ideas as hers and that she may be happy with him."

His good wishes came true: four years later, in Paris, Anna married Victor Jaclar, a French revolutionary, took part in the Commune of 1871 and then, after many hardships and adventures, returned to Russia with her husband. To the day of her death in 1887, she kept her leftist convictions, but they did not stand in the way of her continuing friendship with Dostoevsky. In the mid-'seventies, when Anna was living in

St. Petersburg, she saw the Dostoevskys quite frequently. He liked to talk with her and was an eager caller. One summer, a year before his death, she and Fyodor passed a summer in the small town of Staraya Russa as next-door neighbors, and at that time he used to drop in on her almost daily. Evidently their brief romance had left neither resentment nor bitter recollections but, on the contrary, had laid the foundations of a firm friendship. This is simply one more proof that the affair was not marked by either passion or any particular depth.

ALTHOUGH HIS SUIT FOR ANNA KORVIN-KRUKOVSKAYA'S hand had ended in a fiasco, the idea of marrying did not leave him. Marriage became an *idée fixe* with him not only because of his loneliness and his need for someone near to him, but because of the very conditions under which he was living. Disorder (something he always detested) reigned in his home; the house was run in a haphazard fashion; he could not contrive a comfortable setting for his work and there was nobody to look after Pasha. Dostoevsky knew all the shortcomings of this insufferable, annoying young man, but treated him as a son and felt keenly responsible for his future. During the first half of 1866, he devoted himself wholly to the writing of *Crime and Punishment*, and passed the summer in the Liublianas with the family of his sister, Vera Ivanova. She, too, was urging him to marry and had even proposed a bride for him—Elena Ivanova, a sister-in-law of hers. Elena was married, but her husband was so gravely ill that he was expected to die at any moment—this, however, did not stop him from lingering on for three years more. On his sister's advice Dostoevsky asked Elena—a charming and simple woman but in no way remarkable—whether she would marry him if she were free. Elena put him off with a vague answer—one that could be interpreted favorably if need be—and this very haziness caused Fyodor some unpleasant moments later on. She understood very well that love was out of the question here and that this was a business proposition, a marriage of convenience.

That summer, in a letter to Anna Korvin-Krukovskaya (dated June 17, 1866) he described to his ex-fiancée the circumstances that were particularly depressing him and even interfering with his work just then. Just a year before, when he had been exceedingly hard pressed (his creditors were besieging him and he needed money to go abroad to see Apollinaria) he had signed an extortionate contract with the unscrupulous publisher F. Stellovsky, letting him have for three thousand rubles the right to publish a three-volume collection of his works and obligating himself to submit a new novel of sixty thousand words by the first of November, 1866. In the event of his failure to fulfill the second clause, Dostoevsky was to pay a cash forfeit in addition to foregoing his royalties on the three volumes for a period of nine years.

It was perfectly clear that this provision was precisely what Stellovsky was banking on. He knew very well that Dostoevsky would be taken up with a serial novel for a periodical and that he would never manage to write a new work at the same time. The advance from Stellovsky had been immediately spent—it had gone in part to pay off promissory notes which Stellovsky himself had bought up from Dostoevsky's creditors for the proverbial song. And only when the last ruble of the advance had vanished did Dostoevsky realize what a noose he had put about his neck. In order to find some escape from the trap he decided on an extreme measure.

"I want to do an extraordinary and eccentric thing," he informed Anna, "to write 150,000 words in four months, working on two novels, one of which I will work on in the morning and the other in the evening, and thus finish them on time. Do you know . . . such eccentric and extraordinary things actually appeal to me to this very day? I don't fit in the category of people who lead regular lives and. . . . Forgive me: that was bragging! . . . I am convinced that not a one of our litterateurs, past or present, has written under such conditions as those under which I am *constantly* writing —Turgenev would die from the very idea."

One of these novels was *Crime and Punishment,* which he had to finish by a certain deadline for *The Russian Messenger;* the proposed second work was *The Gambler,* for which he had only notes, outlines, and several chapters in rough shape.

After his summer in the Liubianas, where he had worked long and well, Dostoevsky moved to St. Petersburg and, following the advice of a good friend of his, Alexander Miliukov, the teacher and writer, decided to engage a stenographer to help him carry out his "eccentric" plan. Stenography was a novelty at the time, comparatively few had mastered it, and Dostoevsky appealed to Peter Olkhin, a stenographic instructor. Olkhin offered the commission to his star pupil, Anna Grigorievna Snitkina, but cautioned her that the writer had a "strange and gloomy character," and that he could pay only fifty rubles for all the work on his long novel.

Anna Snitkina was quick to accept, not only because earning money through her own efforts was a dream of hers —as it was to most young women of the upper classes in Russia during this period—but also because she was familiar with Dostoevsky's name, had read his works, wept over his *Notes from the House of the Dead,* was in love with Ivan, the modest and noble hero of *The Humiliated and Wronged,* and instinctively identified him with the author. The opportunity of meeting the celebrated writer and even helping him in his literary work made her happy and excited. She considered her assignment an unusual stroke of luck.

Anna's father, a government clerk neither too high nor too low in the service, had died the previous year and she was still in mourning for him. He had left to his wife and children (two daughters and a son) two small wooden-frame houses out on the Peski ("The Sands") near Smolny Mon-astery—at that time in the extreme outskirts of St. Petersburg. The Snitkin family lived in one house; the other they rented out. Anna's mother, a Finn of German extraction, had been very pretty in her youth but too choosy; she married Gregory Snitkin when she was twenty-seven, without any particular rejoicing, since he was over forty. Although there had been no extraordinary passion on either side, the marriage had been a successful one: both were simple folk, unpretentious, decent and kind. She had the business ability and energy of a native of the north, while he was dreamy and easy-going, like his Ukrainian forebears.

The chief event of his youth, placid and in no way re-markable, had been his falling in love with the great tra-gedienne Barbara Asenkova, who died at an early age. This had led to his lifelong interest in literature and the theatre. He had been a great and avid reader, and it was from him that Anna had first heard Dostoevsky's name. She and her father had been great friends, she had shared his tastes and dreams, she was even religious as he was, observing all the holidays and rites and praying zealously in church.

She had finished the *gymnasia* with a silver medal, some-thing she was always proud of, and had attended teacher-training courses, but had dropped out in favor of some more practical profession which would be sure to earn her a living. Stenography was just coming into fashion then, and Anna had taken it up. She had no liking for she-nihilists and was conservative in her political views, but just the same she con-sidered herself one of the progressive women of the 'sixties, and was an ardent supporter of the radical youth in their movement for equal rights for women, education and financial independence. She also sympathized with the general protest of her generation against conventions, social prejudices and the soulful poses of the aristocrats, which usually went hand in hand with laziness, plus the Hamletism of the superfluous men.

Anna Snitkina was twenty, tall and rather thin, with an oval face and very fine gray eyes, penetrating and deep. People who liked her praised her open forehead, her slightly prominent chin and her nose with an exquisite little hump at the bridge, her beautiful teeth and ash-blonde hair. Her detractors drew attention to her hands, coarsened and calloused by constant work, and the poor color of her face, somewhere between grayish and sallow; she was frequently pale with the pallor one finds in persons living under great stress. Stoyunina, one of her woman teachers, maintained that Anna had been noted from her girlhood for a lively, ardent temperament: "Hers was one of those fiery natures with a quivering heart that knows not a single calm beat." Other contemporaries of Anna's emphasized her sense of humor and her self-possession, despite an outward impulsiveness.

After getting the assignment from Olkhin she slept poorly all night, trembling in anticipation of tomorrow's interview with so learned and clever a man as Dostoevsky. Writers in general appeared to her as superior beings; furthermore, she imagined him to be extremely old. Her idealized image of him, the crystallization of her admiration (and even love) for him, was thus formed before their actual meeting.

The next day, October 4, 1866, she came to the house in Stolovaya Lane, at the corner of Little Burgher Street. This was a large building of many apartments, occupied by persons of middling means—tradespeople and artisans, for the most part. Alonkin, the owner of the building, himself a merchant and an earnest and deliberate old man, held his writer tenant in very great respect. He always saw the light in his windows late at night and used to comment: "A great lover of work, that!" It is possible that Alonkin served as the prototype of the old merchant who was Grushenka's patron in *The Brothers Karamazov*.

Dostoevsky at this time was living with Pasha and their servant, Theodosia, a not too intelligent woman but a devoted one. The furnishings of the apartment were modest, even poor. The barren study had only few ornaments, among them the portrait of a lady in black, Maria.

When Dostoevsky came into the room where Anna was waiting, the young woman's attention was drawn to his odd eyes. He held himself straight; his light chestnut (or even somewhat reddish) hair was slicked down with pomatum; he had on a well-made but rather worn suit, and his linen was snowy. Although he looked considerably younger than she expected, she found him a little disappointing. He was nervous, impatient, absent-minded, kept forgetting her name all the time, repeated his questions only to forget the answers the next moment, and simply could not get down to business. In the end he suggested that she come in the evening. And, as he was saying goodbye, he astonished her by remarking unexpectedly, "I was glad when Olkhin suggested sending me a girl and not a man—and do you know why?"

"Why?"

"Because a man would surely take to drink but you, I hope, won't do any such thing."

She could barely restrain her laughter, and, on the whole, the impression he left was unfavorable. However, it changed again when she came again that evening. Tea was served; he told her that he had liked the way she had behaved in the morning—seriously, almost sternly, refraining from smoking and, in general, without looking like the free-and-easy and self-reliant girls of the new generation. Then he got into a talkative vein, recalled his sensations while awaiting his execution before the firing squad and how, after his reprieve, he had paced his cell and kept singing—singing ever so loudly —as he rejoiced over the gift of his restored life.

She wondered how such an apparently reticent and morose man could speak so frankly to a young woman, almost a girl, whom he had met that day for the first time in his life. Only later on did she comprehend how very lonely he must have been at this time, how great his need for human warmth and sympathy was. He must have immediately sensed the current of interest and friendship in her, and this had made him unusually responsive. His simplicity and frankness proved very much to her liking, and her heart was touched by the words of this intelligent, strange being, obviously made unhappy by general neglect. Later on she told her mother of the complex feelings Dostoevsky had aroused in her: compassion, amazement, fascination. He was an individual who had been wronged by life, remarkable, kind and unusual. She held her breath as he spoke; everything within her was changed because of this meeting.

For this nervous, somewhat high-strung girl the acquaintance with Dostoevsky was an event of the first magnitude: she had fallen in love with him at first sight without even realizing the fact.

Next day when she arrived she found him extremely agitated; he had not made a note of her name and address, and since she was late he imagined that she had lost the stenographic notes she had taken home for transcription and that she would not come any more.

From then on they worked several hours each day. He was jotting down *The Gambler* at night, while in the daytime, from noon until four in the afternoon, he rearranged what he had written and dictated it to her. At home she transcribed her notes in longhand, and the next day Dostoevsky would correct the manuscript she brought him. His original embarrassment soon vanished; he was eager to talk in the breaks between the periods of dictation and told her of the hardships of his youth and of the last few years. He became more used to her with every day, called her *my dear* and *darling,* and she rather liked these terms. It soon became obvious that the work was going well. There was a possibility that *The Gambler* might by ready by the deadline. Fyodor found this very encouraging and was grateful to his collaborator, who spared neither time nor energy in helping him.

By now she no longer feared him, asked him about his marriage with Maria and about Pasha, and advised him on domestic matters. She used to mourn over the disorderliness and poverty of his life. One day she noticed that a pair of Chinese vases he had brought from Semipalatinsk was missing from the dining room; another time, one evening, she saw Dostoevsky eating his soup with a wooden spoon. The silver ones were in pawn, as were the Chinese vases. Quite often there was literally not a kopeck in the house, but he regarded troubles of this sort good-naturedly, apparently attaching little importance to them, and, when she could not help scolding him, he would tell her that such trifles meant nothing to him after the hardships he had known in the past.

"Why do you recall only the misfortunes?" she happened to ask him. "It would be better to speak of the times when you were happy."

"When I was happy? Why, happiness has not come my way as yet—at least not such happiness as I have always dreamt of. I am still waiting for it. Just the other day I wrote my friend Baron Wrangel that, despite all the woes I've gone through, I'm still dreaming of beginning a new and happy life."

He himself said he was capable of as many new lives as a cat, and was astonished by his ability for making plans and starting a new chapter of his biography at the age of forty-five.

One day Anna found him in a particularly disturbed state. He told her that he had reached the crossing of three roads: he would either travel to the Orient, going through Constantinople to Jerusalem (he had even procured letters of introduction to the Russian consul in Turkey) and, perhaps, remain there for good; or he would go abroad to play roulette and plunge with all his soul into the game which he had always found so engrossing; or finally, he might marry a second time and seek happiness in family life. She did not stop to reflect why he had put on an equal footing three such unique things as a withdrawal into sanctity, a leap into gambling and the founding of a family, and advised him to marry a second time.

"So you think I can still marry?" he asked. "That someone would consent to marry me? What sort of a wife should I choose, then—a clever or a kind one?"

"A clever one, of course."

"Well, no. If it comes to a choice I'll take a kind one, so that I may have her sympathy and love."

Then he asked her why she did not marry. She answered that there were two suitors for her hand, both of them fine men—but, while she respected them very much, she did not love either one. And she did want to marry for love.

"Marry for love, without fail," he concurred warmly. "Respect alone is not enough for a happy marriage."

They had become so fond of these heartfelt talks, had grown so used to each other during the four weeks of their work together, that Dostoevsky felt panicky as *The Gambler* neared completion. He simply could not reconcile himself to bringing his friendship with Anna to a close. He had been perfectly sincere when he said he would prefer a kind wife to a clever one: womanly kindness was the one thing lacking in his life, and what he had sensed about Anna first of all was her tender heart. After Apollinaria (and even Korvin-Krukovskaya) he wanted to love a woman who was, above all else, of a kindly nature. Maria, of course, had taken pity on him during the first months of their acquaintanceship, but her kindliness had been short lived. Then their roles had changed, and he had had to take pity upon her. Besides, more than a decade had passed since then. And for the first time in that decade he had met someone who showed him genuine sympathy, who was always thinking of his comfort, worrying about his eating and sleeping habits, and concerning herself with his health and his writing. In short, she took a constant interest in his material well-being and his peace of mind.

He was an absolute stranger to such solicitude. Her concern for him both touched and embarrassed him, but it was a pleasant, gladdening sort of embarrassment. And besides, he perceived how much he needed her—and this, too, was a novelty. They had found a common meeting ground in literary collaboration. She had actually helped him as no one had before, and this was another first experience for him. A young woman had proved herself friendly and helpful in what was his primary concern: his creative work. Other women had generally hindered it; this one actually participated in it. Could he find a better helpmeet? Nevertheless he still hesitated: could he dream of anything more than friendship? He understood very well how exceedingly pitiful and comical an elderly, homely man can be when he is trying to win the love of a young girl. Yet he could not bear to be comical; his self-pride was like a raw wound and he had no wish to add a new rejection to the wrongs done him in the past.

On the twenty-ninth of October, Dostoevsky dictated to Anna the last lines of *The Gambler*. In twenty-six days he had dictated something like fifty thousand words; his plan had worked. On the thirty-first of the month the manuscript was sent to Stellovsky through the police. The dishonest publisher had purposely left town to trick Dostoevsky, and his clerks had refused to accept the novel when the author brought it in his own hands to the office.

A few days later, on the eighth of November, Anna came to see Dostoevsky to talk over finishing *Crime and Punishment*. He was plainly overjoyed at her coming, yet he was, by turns, sad or strangely excited. Instead of talking business he became confidential about his literary projects or burst into improvisations: he wanted to write a novel about an elderly and ailing artist and his meeting with a young girl by the name of Ania. He described in detail not only the artist but his life and his creative quests. When he mentioned the name of Ania, Anna immediately thought of Korvin-Krukovskaya: he had already told her about this affair and had just received a letter from abroad. The stenographer had for the moment completely forgotten that her own name was also Anna. Having confided the plan of this novel to her, Dostoevsky asked her whether she considered it psychologically feasible for a young girl to feel any love for such a man, old, unattractive and sickly. Anna, quite taken up with the projected work, set about proving that it was altogether possible if the heroine had a kind heart. In that case there would be no sacrifice whatsoever on her part, and as for illness and poverty—they were not so frightening; after all there was such a thing as loving somebody for reasons other than physical appearance and wealth.

He kept silent for a while, as though hesitating, and then said, "Put yourself in her place; imagine that I am that artist, that I have confessed my love to you and have asked you to be my wife. What answer would you give me in that case?"

His face as he said this wore an expression of frightful confusion and most heartfelt torment. Anna, on recovering from her astonishment and surprise, grasped that they were no longer talking about a new literary project.

"My answer would be that I love you—and will love you all my life," said she, looking up at him.

Exactly a year before, Apollinaria's answer to a similar proposal had been a mocking rejection.

DOSTOEVSKY HAD BEGUN WRITING THE GAMBLER BESIDE
Maria's deathbed; the novel dealt with Apollinaria, and he
had finished it with the help of Anna. Thus this work bound
together with strange and invisible threads the three great
loves of his life.

However, at the time when he was proposing to his
stenographer, he did not yet suspect that she would take a
place in his life greater than any other woman he had known.
He was obeying his instinct, that stifled inward voice which
always guided him during grave moments. Yet he was also
following practical considerations. He trusted Anna; he felt
that she was near to him and kind, but he was not in love
with her—he merely believed in a promise of love. His hopes
fortified the rational arguments which had impelled him to
take such a decisive step. She was kindhearted, he needed
her, he was languishing in his loneliness and was seeking
spiritual strength in marriage, for only married life could
liberate him from the impermanence of sensuality, from the
seesaw of sex with its ups and downs.

He respected marriage as a cohabitation sanctified by
church and God, furnishing a religious basis and justification
for passion and also marriage appeared to be the best guarantee
against betrayal and unfaithfulness. He saw marriage as a
definite strengthening and formulation of his existence. He
longed to attach himself to something, to have something

constant at last, something he could rely on when he was
torn by the contradictions of his impulses and theories. In
his youth he had been on the verge of psychic disorder; the
shock of his arrest and transportation had probably kept him
from going over the edge. He now needed a remedy of a different sort—emotionally, physically, sexually, he had to have a
wife and a family in order to escape from his fantastic world
of visions and ideas, from his ineradicable desires and masochistic sufferings. Besides, he had always had a secret yearning to renounce his own oddity, to cease being a genius, an
epileptic, a seeker after God, a convict, a voluptuary, an
idealist—and to become like everybody else. And, especially,
to become like his parents, to live according to the way they
had established, to repeat their experience and thereby to
resurrect the peaceful feeling of childhood.

Marriage was a necessity to him and he realized this and
was ready to marry Anna "out of practical considerations"—
as he described the whole web of his conscious arguments and
instinctual drives. It would hardly do to say that love had
struck him down like lightning—it had taken him long
enough to perceive that Anna was a woman as well as a businesslike and accurate secretary. He had made this momentous
discovery only after the completion of *The Gambler*, when
she came to congratulate him on his birthday and happened
to be wearing a new dress—lilac, instead of her customary
black. It made her look taller and more graceful and for the
first time he became aware of her feminine attractiveness. He
had not had the slightest inkling before that she could awaken
any desire in him. Up to then he had been intrigued far
more by her mixture of gravity and joyousness; she worked
like a much older person and yet, when he began calling at
her home, could be as playful as a child. However, in a short
while it was precisely in this combination of the childlike
and the staid that he found a source of erotic attraction. He

was, as always, drawn by youth—for, after all, Anna was only twenty. This aroused him and held a promise of future physical pleasure.

Yet the very difference in their ages implied danger and called forth his doubts, while his relatives tried to use it as an argument as soon as they heard about the engagement. Dostoevsky was the chief provider for two households. Pasha, as well as Emily Dostoevskaya (the widow of Michael) and her children, considered this proposed marriage a serious threat to their own well-being and did not conceal their dissatisfaction. They all began working on Dostoevsky's apprehensions: Could he possibly, at his age, fail to understand that it was too late to start a new family? That a twenty-year-old girl was hardly likely to remain true to an ailing husband of forty-five?

Anna's mother, on learning of the engagement, did not stand in her daughter's way, yet at the same time she did not show any special pleasure; while her kindred and friends began trying to persuade Anna not to marry a poor man and an epileptic "burdened with debts and family obligations" and, on top of that, according to rumors, ill-natured and hot-tempered. Their main argument was likewise the difference in age. The best answer to this was made by Anna herself— twenty years later. When her own daughter asked her how she could possibly have fallen in love with a man old enough to be her father, the mother had replied with a smile: "But he *was* young; he was more interesting and lively than the young people of my time. They were all wearing spectacles and looked like old and boring professors of zoology." So greatly was she enchanted by him that she simply did not notice his wrinkles, or his tic, or the tired expression of his eyes, or his graying temples. And he, despite all the warnings of his relatives, knew very well that he could derive joy and a hope for happiness only from the society of a very young woman.

During his brief courtship they were very pleased with each other. Dostoevsky called on his fiancée every evening, brought her candy and told her about his work. In November, he had finished the third part of *Crime and Punishment* and he ascribed this to her happy influence. He confided to her certain secrets of his past, yet remained reticent about a good many things: he made practically no mention of Apollinaria, for instance. He did, however, tell her about Korvin-Krukovskaya and Elena Ivanova; he was constantly apprehensive that his sister's family might feel he was committed to the proposal he had made her. His epileptic attacks became rare, and his nervousness as well seemed to be decreasing. Anna found him cheerful and good-natured and was in her turn lively and laughed a great deal; he seemed to have shed his years and was hardly ever too grave. Sometimes he assumed the role of the Prince, "the little ancient who would be young," from his own *Uncle's Dream,* and assured her that he had given his own traits to this literary creation, which statement Anna found somewhat nettling.

November and December, 1866, were idyllic, with only one thing worrying Anna: no sooner did Dostoevsky come into any money than all his relatives developed the most pressing needs, and whatever payments and advances he received would evaporate within a few hours. He had, for instance, received four hundred rubles from *The Russian Messenger*—next day there were only thirty rubles left to meet all his expenses. He did not know how to refuse anybody and was utterly incapable of keeping track of his money. One December evening he arrived frozen and shivering, in a light topcoat: he had pawned his fur-lined coat on the advice of Pasha, Emily and his brother Nicholas, all of whom needed money. Anna protested vehemently that he would catch cold and began to cry from vexation. Her tears overwhelmed him. "Now I am convinced how ardently you love me," he told her.

However, he was receiving other proofs of the strength and sincerity of her feelings every day.

Both wanted to marry as soon as possible, but the chief obstacle lay in Fyodor's lack of money. Anna had a couple of thousand rubles of her own bequeathed to her by her father, but Dostoevsky refused to spend them on the wedding, insisting that they should be used exclusively to buy things for the bride. He was very fond of choosing her dresses, making her try them on, and she asked his advice in everything and felt certain that he had excellent imagination and taste in women's clothes, although she knew very well that he distinguished colors poorly. Anna's mother bought fur coats, furniture and silver for her.

Dostoevsky set out for Moscow to negotiate an advance from Katkov, Editor of *The Russian Messenger*, as a stake for their new life. *Crime and Punishment*, serialized in Katkov's monthly, was quite a success with the readers and the critics—even though it was not a hit—and Dostoevsky had good hopes for obtaining money from the publisher.

His letters to his bride at the end of December, 1866, and the beginning of January, 1867, are very tender, and certain expressions in them are quite characteristic: "Yours, infinitely loving and with infinite faith in you. . . . All yours. . . . You are all my future—and my hope, and faith, and happiness, and bliss—my all. . . . I kiss your little hand a thousand times, and your tiny lips (which I remember so well). . . . Soon I shall be clasping and kissing you, your little hands and feet (which you do not permit me to kiss). And then the *third* period of our life will begin. . . . Love me, Ania; I will love you without end."

At last everything was in readiness: the apartment rented, the furniture moved, the dresses fitted, and on February 15, 1867, at eight in the evening, in the presence of their friends and kindred, the two were married in the Troitsko-Ismailovski

Cathedral. According to the Russian belief, whoever is the first to step on the rug laid before the priest will rule the family. Anna deliberately let Fyodor be the first to step on the rug: "I always submitted to him in everything," she wrote later on.

The first few days after the wedding passed in gay turmoil. The relatives and friends invited the newly married couple to evening parties and dinners, and they had never drunk as much champagne in all their lives as they did during that fortnight. But they had no real honeymoon. Pasha, Emily, Fyodor's brother Nicholas and all of Fyodor's nephews did not leave them alone for a moment; the house was thronged with visitors until late at night—when Dostoevsky would sit down to his writing. There were days when they did not have a chance to be by themselves for even half an hour. Instead of intimacy and heart-to-heart talk, mutual serenity and adjustment, they found themselves in an absurd and humiliating situation. Anna was surrounded by intrigues and plots; the in-laws criticized the way she was running the house, did their utmost to trip her up in practical matters and, having found out that she was extremely self-centered and likely to take offence over trifles, baited her unmercifully with sneers and painful innuendoes.

She easily succumbed to flattery and because of this committed not a few blunders. Pasha and Emily intrigued to set Fyodor against his young wife, and she saw with horror how naïve and blind he was, hardly defending her. His relatives convinced him that Anna felt far more lighthearted with his young nephews than she did with him, and he locked himself up in his study so as not to interfere with her, at the very moment when she was crying her eyes out in their bedroom from humiliation and helplessness. She could not issue any orders in her own home, Pasha always stood between her and the servant; the nephews, the brother's widow, the guests, the intimates, always intervened between her husband and herself.

She was especially humiliated because the marriage had not brought about any real intimacy between her and Fyodor, because their physical relations were not leading to any happiness. Owing to the general bustle and continual company, their embraces were somehow casual and sketchy; everything stood in the way of the realization of that sexual freedom without which a genuine union is so difficult to attain.

Some sort of block seemed to prevent the very development of their emotions; they could not get used to each other physically, while certain prosaic details proved altogether discouraging. Fyodor frequently worked late at night in his study and, when he became tired, would lie down on a divan and fall asleep, while she slept alone in a bed which she was coming to regard as a vestal's. Despite the flare-ups of his physical passion, there was no rapturous love in their marriage, and for that reason it might have taken any direction, depending on circumstances. But its beginning was certainly inauspicious. They understood each other poorly: he thought she was bored with him, while she became offended because he was apparently avoiding her. She had no feeling that the fusion of their bodies was a continuation of any spiritual fusion as she had dreamt—and at the same time, owing to her inexperience, she was not quite certain whether everything was as it should be, or whether she was right in feeling that something was amiss. She loved him, and this formula is no worse than others to ensure a happy marriage. It did not take her long to discover how constrained their love-making was. Love, it seemed, was a lot more difficult than she had supposed, and at the same time it required favorable conditions and a peaceful setting.

A month after her marriage Anna was in a semi-hysterical state. It was early spring, and just about this time the usual talk began about taking a villa for the summer and living there with all Fyodor's relatives. Faced with such a prospect,

Anna burst into tears and made her husband understand that she was miserable and that they would have to go abroad if their love was to be saved.

Dostoevsky was genuinely shocked. He himself was aware that domestic happiness, as he had imagined it during the idyllic weeks following their engagement, was simply not materializing, that everything in the house was topsy-turvy and that the atmosphere was strained. He hardly ever saw his wife alone, and realized that for some reason they had lost the spiritual closeness which had come into being during his dictation of *The Gambler*. But he simply had not taken into account how very critical such a situation could become: this seer and connoisseur of the human soul often showed himself amazingly blind and deaf in his personal life. Neither of them had been able to organize their life together; he, owing to his lack of talent for that sort of thing and his habits of an absent-minded and lonely man, so absorbed in his work and thoughts that he did not notice his surroundings; she, because of her inexperience, timidity, youth and infantile vanity.

The idea of going abroad appealed to Dostoevsky very much: it would give him an opportunity to stave off for a few months the creditors who were breathing down his neck; besides that, he hoped that his work would be better there, and living expenses cheaper. But in order to travel it was necessary to get a new advance from *The Russian Messenger*, and with this end in view he set out for Moscow and took his wife along. Pasha, brother Nicholas and Emily and her children, realizing that he was taking this trip to raise money, offered no objections; they knew nothing, however, of his plans for going abroad.

New trials awaited Anna in Moscow: she met with anything but a friendly reception from the family of Vera Ivanova, Fyodor's sister. After all, Vera had wanted him to marry

Elena, her sister-in-law. However, had not Elena herself told him, when she had last seen him in December: "There, you see how good it was that I hadn't given you any definite answer?" This had made Dostoevsky very happy and relieved him from a feeling of guilt, since it had seemed to him all the time that perhaps she was counting on his proposal.

Fortunately, the opposition of the Ivanovs disappeared quickly. They had thought of Fyodor's wife as a short-haired and be-spectacled nihilist; but their new kinswoman proved to be a modest young thing, almost a girl, who, far from being aggressive, was rather shy with everybody and obviously deified her husband. The clan softened and took her to its bosom.

Dostoevsky's jealousy proved to be another thorn: he made scenes over the merest trifles. When they returned one night from a visit to the Ivanovs, he lost no time in accusing Anna of being a heartless flirt: she had been far too amiable all evening to the man sitting next to her, thereby torturing her husband. She attempted to justify herself, but he, forgetting that they were staying at a hotel, shouted at the top of his voice; his whole face became distorted, he was terrifying to look at and, frightened in case he was going to beat or kill her, she burst into torrential tears. Only then did he come to his senses, began kissing her hands and confessed that he was monstrously jealous. After this night's scene she gave him her word that she would be "on guard against subjecting him to such painful impressions." This is very characteristic of her; there was no indignation against his unjust and fantastic accusations, she did not argue with him and, before all else, thought not of herself but of him and his peace of mind.

His jealousy is very revealing. He had made no scenes for Maria's benefit or Apollinaria's, although there was immeasurably more cause in either case. Of course, he had been tortured by jealousy and had suffered in both instances, yet he had not shown his jealousy—either because he had not dared to do so, or because he knew that his accusations would do him no good. At any rate, he had restrained himself. With Anna he was already himself, without concealment or restraint, without any curbs whatsoever—and in fact, he always had an alleviating feeling of freedom and naturalness when he was with her. He could permit himself to act as he felt— for instance, to show he was jealous with all the frenzy which invariably marked all his emotional outbursts. But it is also possible that his experiences in the past had intensified his suspiciousness. His inferiority complex and his feeling of injured self-esteem were a source of perpetual irritation in sexual matters, and compelled him to doubt the love of the women in his life. This lack of confidence turned into jealousy and erupted in savage flare-ups; for deep within them was a real fear of infidelity and sufferings, a fear which had tormented him after his experiences in Kuznetsk, Tver and Paris. He was forever questioning if he was loved, and forever striving for and demanding proofs of love. Even in regard to Anna, who was wholly devoted to him, he experienced the same emotions; he was afraid of losing her and convulsively clung to her, eternally apprehensive of being deprived of his nearest and most necessary possession.

All these complex emotions were interwoven in Dostoevsky with a keen sense of ownership which was strongly developed in him in sexual matters as well as in many of his everyday concerns. Anna had to belong to him indivisibly, body and soul, like the things on his desk which no one dared to move about or even touch. And, finally, his jealousy had grown with age: the thought of the twenty-five years' difference between him and Anna always aroused his apprehensiveness. Despite all her assurances, he remained to the very end subject to raging, utterly unjustified fits of jealousy.

Scenes and difficult situations did not, however, conceal one fact from the married couple: in Moscow their relations improved markedly, since they were left alone together much more than they had been in St. Petersburg. This realization confirmed Anna in her desire to go abroad and to spend at least two or three months alone with Fyodor; it was the only certain means of their calming down, of resting after the excitement they had gone through, and of Anna's getting used to her husband both physically and morally.

When they came back to St. Petersburg, however, and announced their intentions, there was great and noisy indignation among the Dostoevskys. Within two days it became clear that Fyodor would have to leave eleven hundred rubles to placate his relatives and the more clamorous creditors, and yet his whole advance from *The Russian Messenger* amounted to no more than a thousand. Pasha and Emily began dissuading him from his "insane" plan and tried to convince him that he had no right to spend the last of his money on his young wife's whim. And when the talk veered to the moral debt Fyodor owed to the family of his late brother Michael, his spirits sank, he wavered and was about to give up his trip abroad. The project of all renting a house together for the summer was restored to the agenda of family councils.

This was the point at which Anna showed the hidden strength of her character and decided upon an extreme measure. She instinctively knew that her life with Fyodor hung in the balance, and she was ready to sacrifice everything to save it. Her mother understood and supported her, and Anna did something for which her friends never forgave her; she pawned everything she had spent her dowry on—furniture, silver, clothes—everything she had chosen and bought with such pleasure and hope. This business was transacted in two

days and on the fourteenth of April, 1867, to the amazement
and indignation of all Fyodor's relatives, the Dostoevskys left
for abroad.

They were planning to spend three months on the continent, but actually they did not return until more than four
years later. During these four years, they had succeeded in
forgetting the inauspicious beginnings of their life together,
and had established a close, happy and firm friendship.

AT THE TIME OF THEIR DEPARTURE IN THE SPRING OF 1867, the nerves of both were very much on edge. Dostoevsky had little money left; his hopes for future earnings were dim; everything before him was vaguely wavering, as if in a fog. His health was exceedingly precarious. The events of the last two years had exhausted him physically, while the efforts expended upon *Crime and Punishment* and *The Gambler* had drained his creativity. Like many artists he felt empty and depressed after the completion of a long work. He did not know what to do with himself, what to write about, how to arrange his life, how to clamber out of his debts. He was now traveling through Germany, yet still mulling over the recent interests of his life in St. Petersburg, telling his wife about his creditors, the arrangements made for his nephews, about his various periodicals and publishers.

"I went abroad with death in my soul," he confessed in a letter to Maikov four months later, "alone, without material means, with a youthful being who with a naïve joy was striving to share my nomadic life; of course I perceived a great deal of inexperience and a fresh fervor in this naïve joy, and this confused and tormented me very much. I was afraid that Anna would become bored in my company. And, really, up to the present we are all by ourselves. And I had no great reliance on my own self: I am of an ailing nature, and I supposed that she would get tired of having to bother with me. *Nota bene:* It is true that Anna proved both stronger and of greater depth than I had known or considered her to be, and on many occasions was simply my guardian angel, yet at the same time there is about her much of the child-like and that which pertains to the age of twenty, both of which are splendidly and naturally *unavoidable*, yet to which I hardly have the strength and ability to respond. All these haunted me at departure and although (I repeat) Anna proved both stronger and better than I thought, I am nevertheless uneasy right up to the present. Finally, our modest means embarrassed me."

They spent some time in Berlin; then, traveling across Germany, settled in Dresden. It was here that their intimacy really began and shortly dispelled all his apprehensions and doubts. They were two utterly different individuals; in age, temperament, interests, intellect—but they also had a great deal in common, and the happy combination of similarities and differences assured the success of their married life.

It was Anna's first trip abroad and she found everything of interest. Travel delighted her; she was enraptured with new lands. In this respect she differed somewhat from her husband. During their four years in Europe they visited Switzerland, Austria and Italy in addition to Germany, and Anna found all these countries enchanting, whereas Fyodor never ceased to revile everybody and everything, and also brought up all sorts of disagreeable facts about France and England, which he had visited before. All his wife had to do was to remark that she liked things abroad and he would burst into insults, heaping one grievance on top of the last. The Germans were stolid, rude and self-righteous; they had no genuine culture, but to make up for it they had an inex-haustible mother-lode of fools and dolts. Frenchmen were clever, yet they were nothing but a pack of knaves and huck-sters: all they set their minds on was form and dissipation.

The Swiss had no baths, they were filthy, and swindlers, the whole pack of them, and coarse and uncouth, besides. Their landscapes were remarkable, true enough, but Vevey on Lake Geneva was even worse than Zaraisk on Osetr River back home—there was no such thing as double window-frames in winter and consequently everybody had to freeze, all their fireplaces gave were smoke and colds. In short, everything about this famous West was worse than in Russia and boring as boring could be—and that went too for Paris the renowned, which was enough to turn one's stomach.

He had a kind word for Italy only, practically admitting that it had a smiling landscape and a few works of art—but even there, according to him, a stifling tedium prevailed. He acknowledged the splendor of the Swiss Alps (even though they depressed him and spoiled his spirits); he approved of the sky over Rome and the clear air of Florence; he valued highly the picture gallery in Dresden and the paintings of the Renaissance (he was indifferent to architecture), but still his praise was casual and grudging. He warmed up only when the chance arose to reel off the things he disliked. From the day he arrived in Europe he crusaded against it and counted each and every grudge: an incorrect bill at a hotel and the aridity of Protestantism, a draft in a railway car and the degeneration of Catholicism into Papal Imperialism. He admitted intellectually that Europe was a second fatherland to Russians, but emotionally he struggled against the West, even while acknowledging that it was "a land of sacred tombs." He had no desire whatever to penetrate into the heart of European life; during his four years on the Continent he did not form a single friendship with a non-Russian, nor did he express any wish to meet Western writers and thinkers. His sharply negative attitude toward all things European was one of the causes of his final break with Turgenev, a convinced Westernizer who lost all patience with Dostoevsky's wholesale condemnation of bourgeois culture in particular and of Western culture as a whole.

This hatred of all things foreign was a blend of various motives. On the one hand his Slavophilic views were continually growing stronger: "We have a far more direct and noble faith in good, as well as in Christianity, and by no means in a bourgeois solution of the problem of comfort," he wrote from Geneva in 1868. "There is a great renewal being prepared for the whole world through Russian thought, which is firmly welded with Orthodoxy . . . and all this will be consummated in a mere century or so: there you have my fervid belief."

On the other hand, Europe repelled him because of his own "plebeianism" and his disdain of material values. He had no love for wealth or luxury and disliked any leanings toward the external forms of life and conduct; he shrank inwardly from the eloquence, aestheticism, grand gestures and patent attainments of the West. And he felt an animosity toward the social movements and the art of Europe because they were founded far too much upon logic and reason; he mistrusted these fragile vessels of human knowledge. There was about his anti-Europeanism a considerable measure of provincialism; he often found himself in the position of a poor relation, and the pangs of his own self-esteem became mixed with a feeling of injured national pride.

Anna did not go into all these fine points; everything about the West held a lively interest for her, she behaved like an eager tourist and kept a notebook, and this schoolgirlish industriousness amused and delighted Fyodor. She found everything worth looking at, therefore she would not feel bored while he worked or wrote extremely long letters to his friends in Russia concerning his latest literary plans. And so he merely concealed an adult smile when she became absorbed in guidebooks and catalogues: What's the odds how a child amuses itself so long as it keeps from crying! "Anna has revealed an absolutely antiquarian streak in her character," he wrote Maikov, "and I find this endearing and amusing. It really occupies her, for instance, to go and take in some silly Rathhaus or other, to make notes on it and describe it."

In general he was touched because she was so simple and unpretentious. Anna's habits derived from a petty bourgeois, almost a burgher, environment, even though according to her passport she belonged to the gentry—and this created a common feeling of social equality between them. She was a modest and quiet young woman, and neither in childhood nor youth had she known any noisy diversions. There had been almost no important events in her family, and she was not demanding, had seen little and visited few places. When, on completing *The Gambler,* Dostoevsky had wanted to celebrate at a gala dinner in a restaurant in the company of Maikov, Miliukov and Strakhov, and had invited his stenographer, she could not find the resolution to come; never in her life had she been in a restaurant and she felt embarrassed about being seen in such a place—and in the company of strangers, at that.

Her ways of life and thought, her manners and habits, her dress and tastes all betrayed the daughter of a none-too-prosperous petty official living on the outskirts of St. Petersburg. There was not a little provincialism about her, and this was very much to Dostoevsky's liking. That he himself had a streak of the burgher in him was very well known to his intimates—although this peculiarity also struck those who met him for the first time and had pictured him as some sort of superman. The clever and observant Ellen Stakhenschneider, a fervent admirer of his (he was a frequent caller at her home toward the end of his life) has written: "Many who approach him in awe do not perceive how much of the burgher there is about him. Not anything vulgar—no, he is never vulgar—but he is *a burgher*. Yes, a burgher! Not an aristocrat, not a seminarist, not a merchant, not a happy-go-lucky fellow such as an artist ´or a scholar, but a burgher, precisely. And lo, this burgher is the profoundest of thinkers and a writer of genius."

He was a burgher in all the inclinations and habits of life, in his love of a certain order in his daily existence, in his very shortcomings against which he himself complained: "I lack gesture and form." The reasons for this could, of course, be found in his education, in the background of his childhood and the circumstances of his later life, as well as in his constant financial dependence upon others. About the manners and speech of persons accustomed from their earliest years to have money at their disposal and to spend it easily, one invariably senses an unconscious self-assurance. Even though they may not be imperious and aggressive, they do tread the earth with a trim step, and it is upon this moneyed self-assurance that their good manners and their gracious ways are based. Dostoevsky, that hired hand in the literary field, perpetually burdened with debts, borrowing fifty rubles here and fifty rubles there, not knowing what the morrow would bring and doomed beforehand to pleas and humiliations, had neither gracious ways, nor ease, nor any self-assurance, while his ideal of the "good" and "full" life went no further than the burgher's ideal of security: a four-room flat (at that time very modest housing for intellectuals), rather hideous furniture, bought on the installment plan: an overstuffed divan with a rug thrown over it in the study and, in the parlor, small vases and an oil chromo or two.

Dostoevsky was tormented by his own poor taste, his awkwardness in society, his susceptibility to insults and his petty self-pride. He envied the "lords of life," such as Turgenev and Grigorovich, and disliked them precisely for their confidence, their worldliness, their well-tied cravats, their well-polished speech, the freedom with which they could spend thousands and write whatever they had a mind to write and however they wanted to write it. His numerous quarrels with his contemporaries were often the result of his plebeianism; he was always getting his feelings hurt because he was poor and had to ask for favors. He attained everything the hard way; in order to be paid by the various periodicals that owed him money, he had to beg and all but go down on his knees, and this he did in the tear-gulping, "loutish" manner of his Marmeladovs and Lebedevs: his letters of this sort are anything but pleasant reading today.

Toward the end of his life he was entertained by grand dukes and notables, but both at court and in the aristocratic salons he did not feel himself at ease and behaved like a bear. He heartily detested receptions, banquets, appearances in high society; he liked most of all to sit in an overheated room, drinking tea with jam and reading some historical novel to his wife.

Maria had dreamt of playing a role in society, of being hostess at gala dinners, and even with her Fyodor had not felt sure of himself and always remained the poor provider. Apollinaria, too, had wanted to shine and to be somebody. But with Anna it was different. She never desired a worldly life, she did not want anything to do with the social whirl— it would have made her head spin and she would have felt as queasy as her husband. On this point they were remarkably alike. There was no cause for him to feel uneasy with her; she too was seeking a burgher's happiness and accepted her husband's dressing-gown and house-slippers not as a lessening of his dignity but as something quite natural—anything else was out of the question. And she shared fully his modest pleasures —a Sunday stroll and a pasty for dinner; a samovar on the round table at evening, an ever-burning lamp before the icon in a corner of the bedroom, in the winter a coat lined with wolf-skins for him and, for her, a coat of fox fur.

Anna was shy and became lively only when she was alone with her husband and was not afraid to express what he called her "inflammability." This he understood and appreciated. He himself was timid and confused among strangers, and he, too, felt free from all constraint only when he was alone with his wife. It was all so different from his early experience with Panaeva, with Maria or Apollinaria. Anna's youth, her inexperience and burgher ideals had a soothing effect on him; they made him feel hopeful and his complexes of inferiority and guilt disappeared. He was subject to spells of real melancholy, and after his flare-ups of morbid pride, when he used to shout that only future generations would appreciate his novels, he would be overcome by excruciating periods of depression and discouragement.

At such times he literally hated himself. He contemplated his hands with their bulging veins and liver spots, his hairy chest—his body that tormented him with its aches, illnesses and lusts, with all the peculiar independent life that was such a hindrance to his intellect and spirituality. And it was doomed to decay in the darkness of the grave, to becoming food for worms, and he saw eternity as a stifling, cramped shack infested with spiders. He gasped with horror before the realization of his own nothingness and his fear of death.

Very few people were aware how great his need was at such moments for a kind word, for the warm pressure of a woman's hand. The presence of a young person who loved him dispelled all his nightmares, while praise or even a hint of approval made his spirits soar, despite his moroseness and pessimism. He had suffered too often and too sorely; he was always anticipating failures and disappointments. But Anna had a firm belief in him, and from the day of their first meeting he had seen this written on her face and she had expressed it in all her words and actions. She looked up to him and, even if she did not agree with all his ideas, was convinced of their importance and value. Any doubt of his excellence simply could not occur to her. She could disagree with him over some of his judgments: he accused women, for instance, of not being persistent enough—and Anna, to disprove it, began collecting stamps and kept up her hobby for a number of years. He scolded the younger generation for its slovenliness and apparent coarseness, but she considered herself a woman of the 'sixties and warmly defended her contemporaries.

They quarreled over trifles as well and, after recriminations, refused to talk to each other, but such spells did not last long before they would make up. He reached the boiling point very quickly but was just as quick to simmer down; his tempests usually blew over without leaving any trace and he soon forgot all about them. She, too, took offence easily—and found it just as easy to forgive. Upon their arrival in Berlin, he had criticized her dress unmercifully, telling her that she was not properly dressed for the season and that her gloves were atrocious. She became very much offended and left him in the street, yet was really afraid that she might never see him again. When she met him later on, however, she realized that he had forgotten all about their disagreement.

There were days when he was so irritable that he scolded her continually or, if he was really wrought up, shouted at her. Why had she looked that way at the young man passing by? How clumsy she was—she had just jostled that German in the restaurant with the handle of her umbrella! Or else: Why did she have to confide to the waiter that she had forgotten to buy butter and tea? She bore all this and, during their stay in Dresden, decided not to show how much it hurt her, even though she used to cry by herself. She began to accept these tempests as an unavoidable evil. In general, she accepted everything about him without murmuring, and this simple and somewhat naïve approach of hers disarmed and touched Fyodor; toward the end of their life abroad their quarrels became far less frequent as he felt fully at ease with Anna. She was "submitting" to him, acknowledging his authority in absolutely everything, including the choosing of her dresses and hats, an indulgence he particularly enjoyed. Yet hers was no blind subordination: she was neither spineless nor a nonentity. She had a quite definite individuality that developed with the years; her character was firm and self-reliant, despite her gentleness, compliance and a certain naïveté that never left her.

Many years after her husband's death, in explaining the secret of their successful married life, she justly remarked that friendship is often founded on differences and not on similarities, and gave herself as an example. She and Fyodor were entirely unlike in make-up and spiritual outlook. Yet she did not try to analyze him, did not intrude on his inner life; she had no desire to "influence and correct"—the mistake so many women make toward their husbands and lovers—and this nonintervention inspired him with respect for her and strengthened his feeling of freedom. And at the same time he knew that she was his friend, that he could rely on her in all things; she would not betray him, would not deceive, would not sell him out or laugh at him on the sly. It was on this double foundation of nonintervention and free trust that their domestic happiness became firmly established.

After the hysterics of Maria and the imperial posturings of Apollinaria, Fyodor welcomed Anna's neutrality with profound relief: she, at any rate, did not try to direct him, to take the reins, to play-act. At the time of their wedding she was a rather young, none-too-well-developed average girl, not remarkable in any way, yet possessed of a lively mind and an unerring intuition wherever Dostoevsky was concerned. During the fourteen years of their life together, her intelligence and culture, and her knowledge of her husband of course increased greatly. She had always worshiped Dostoevsky as a writer. However, during the first year of their marriage, she still did not know the riches of his genius and simply accepted what was generally known—here was a noted novelist, perhaps great, and ailing—and only later on did she correctly guess what he was, at a time when his contemporaries were still hesitant; for, after all, he gained full recognition, in Russia as well as in the West, only after his death.

This growth in her admiration and understanding delighted him; he was constantly gaining stature in her eyes. Usually, in marriage, the partners receive an intimate education in each other's shortcomings, and this easily produces disenchantment. With the Dostoevskys, on the contrary, intimacy revealed more and more reasons for love—and Anna, who had become acquainted with the author of *The Gambler* and had married him, perceived that he was an altogether extraordinary person, a genius, frightening and difficult; while he, who had married his little secretary, discovered that, if he was the "patron and protector of a young being," she in her turn was his "guardian angel," his friend and comforter.

Anna loved him ardently as a man and an individual; she loved him with the complex love of wife and mistress, of mother and daughter. And this fusion of the sensual with the filial and maternal was a strong factor in his love for her. She was just as fine and devoted a companion to him as his mother had been to Dr. Dostoevsky—the marriage of Anna and Fyodor was a repetition of his father's love—yet at the same time she was so young and inexperienced that he felt stable and fatherly. She was thus a mother to him and represented a return to his childhood, but he also loved her as if she were his own daughter, and also like a very young, very

innocent little girl—and the mixture of all these elements
added the pungency of sin to his embraces. Certain admissions
in Anna's *Diary*, pertaining to the Dresden period, are characteristic: "He was reading, while I lay behind him (my
favorite place now, just as it was in my childhood, behind
my father)." Her feelings for him were simultaneously those
of a daughter for her father, of a mother for her child and
of a beloved for her lover. This kind of feminine attachment
is the strongest of all. Later on came the additional consciousness that he was the father of her children.

IN APRIL, 1867, THE DOSTOEVSKYS SETTLED IN DRESDEN, and within a fortnight or so Anna began to forget the unpropitious start of their married life and feel happy. Fyodor told her that, although he had loved her when he married her, he had not known her at all well. "Now," she noted down in those shorthand symbols which he could not read, "he appreciates me four times as much, when he understands how simple I am. . . . He says I subdue him by being so kind and uncomplaining." She really did have a great deal of kindliness and resignation about her. Her moments of childishness also touched him. She happened to break three teeth in his comb and burst into tears because she had damaged a fine article he happened to value. She missed her mother; whenever she recalled St. Petersburg she had to brush away a tear. But he would sit down beside her, console her, put his arms around her and kiss her like a little child.

He was becoming more and more used to her, finding a charm in the unhurried, just a trifle monotonous rhythm of their life together. They got up late and, after breakfast, went for a stroll; he walked with a measured, slow step, a reminder of his days in the army. Then they listened to the band in the city park. Spring was approaching; everything was beginning to bloom, the birds were singing loudly; a glass of wine in the Italian Village where they usually dined was enough to make Anna practically tipsy and she laughed

infectiously, with Fyodor urging her on. Gravity restored, they
went to the shooting gallery: he was a good shot and was fond
of this diversion. In the evenings they read, she in her corner,
he in his; they had cake and pastry with their tea; some
evenings Dostoevsky would sit down to his writing. She went
to bed early, almost always alone; he would come and wake
her later, to give her a good-night kiss and to make the sign
of the cross over her and, instead of going to his own bed,
very often remained with her until morning.

When she married him, it is hardly likely that Anna
had taken into account what was awaiting her, and only after
marriage did she grasp the difficulty of the problems con-
fronting her. There were his jealousy and suspiciousness, and
his passion for gambling, and his ailments, and his peculiarities
and quirks. And, first and foremost, there was the matter of
their physical relations. As with everything else, physical
harmony did not come about at once but was the result of a
protracted, at times an excruciating process.

At first he had failed to experience any passionate desire
for her and treated her with a certain caution and restraint.
It was probably for this reason that he would not let her read
frivolous French novels, frowned on her telling funny stories
that were at all off-color and, when she was around, condemned
operettas as utterly useless trifles. Because of all this she considered him chaste. Physically she was inexperienced and
naïve and accepted his sexuality without question, wondering
at nothing and even unfrightened. She was ready to consider
what was pathological as normal; in her innocence she believed
that everything was proper and responded naturally and calmly
to what another woman, more experienced or instinctively
more understanding in sexual matters, would have considered
strange or offensive—and perhaps even monstrous.

Many years later, a year before his death, when he was
almost sixty and she was thirty-five, he wrote her from Ems:

"You write, 'Love me!' But then, don't I love you? The only thing is that it goes against my grain to put this into words for you, but you might have seen a great deal for yourself; it's a pity, though, that you don't know how to see. Why, my constant (no, it's more than constant—it grows with every year) marital delight in you might have indicated a great deal to you, but you either don't want to understand that or, through your inexperience, altogether fail to do so. Why, show me any other marriage you like where this phenomenon exists with such potency as in our marriage, which has lasted twelve years by now. As for my delight and admiration, they are inexhaustible. You will say this is but one aspect, and that the coarsest one. No, it is not coarse; in reality all the rest depends upon it. But that's the very thing you don't want to grasp. To end this tirade, I attest that I thirst to kiss over and over again every tiny toe on your little foot—and I'll attain this end, you'll see. You write: 'But what if someone reads our letters?' There's that, of course, but let them: let them feel envious."

Modesty, to the regret of biographers, compelled her to cross out the licentious words and phrases in his letters, which she preserved for posterity. But this was because she considered it indecent to let outsiders peer into the mysteries of the bedchamber: in the bedchamber itself everything was permitted. No wonder Dostoevsky spoke of his 'growing' connubial delight. He was wary of initiating her into the world of voluptuousness and of his own secret inclinations: if anybody did, he knew well both his sadistic and masochistic perversions and his frenzy whenever he was allowed to kiss little feet or to simulate corporal punishment during the sexual act. He was apprehensive of frightening her. Certain moments of sexual intercourse were for him just as blinding, just as full of unbearable strain as the moments preceding an epileptic seizure —and the strictly physical ecstasy of sexual climax gave him a sensation of breaking through into eternity. To join with a woman he loved in the consonant rhythm of intercourse drew him closer to God and left him with a mystic sense of self-affirmation and self-oblivion. All the tempests of his sensuality were resolved in an instantaneous contact with the ultimate truth: the universe poured in upon him, he became dissolved in the universe; the fusion of bodies led to a re-creation of a disrupted unity. Out of two, one—one flesh. In this lay the secret of peace, a premonition of universal harmony.

All this religio-mystical aspect of Fyodor's life was perfectly alien and incomprehensible to Anna; her feet were far too firmly planted on the ground. If she did have anything otherworldly about her, it was altogether unconscious and instinctive, as with all simple natures who preserve a kind of sixth sense, a prehistoric echo, a hearkening back to that first-created dawn when men still lived like animals. For instance, she had the power of second sight. She said that it came to her from her mother—a gift of the women-prophets of the North. But even in this matter she was far removed from Dostoevsky, with his premonitions, symbols and fateful dreams. He assured her that he always knew when a misfortune was impending; he would see his father in a dream—or, worse still, his late brother Michael.

She may have been unable to understand thoroughly the sexual rapture of Fyodor—and may even have been frightened a little by the prostration, so very like the immobility of death, which overcame him after the act of love—but she saw nothing horrifying in the tempestuous manifestations of his passion and responded to him naturally and ardently since she was after all a young and loving woman. And it was precisely this response of her body, her simplicity and desire to please him just as much at night as during the day, which proved so priceless to Dostoevsky. He could do with her what he willed, he could train her as a companion in his erotic fantasies, and hence felt no shame when he was with her, despite all her obvious signs of modesty.

He may have felt embarrassed with others but with her everything was permissible and he soon ceased to restrain himself—or to make any attempt at restraining himself. With her he could play the husband, the lover, the father, the child. This ever-expanding freedom was purely physical, not cerebral, and he had never had to fight for it as in the case of Apollinaria, who knew very well what licentiousness was. Besides, it was a freedom neither cynical nor bought as with Martha Brown, but voluntary—that is, the fullest and most genuine freedom. Anna offered him this freedom. According to her own expression, she "permitted" him a very great deal, and not only because she liked his "tricks," but because in her great love for him she was ready to endure everything, to bear anything submissively.

That this was far from always easy and pleasant was known only to their very close intimates. In 1879, in the thirteenth year of Dostoevsky's marriage, a close friend A. Maikov wrote to Mrs. Maikov: "Just what is it, then, that Anna told you, since you won't even write about it? That her husband is insufferable is beyond all doubt; there is nothing new about the impossibility of his character, with its coarse manifestations of love, jealousy, of all sorts of exactions in keeping with his momentary fantasy. What, then, could have overwhelmed you and shocked you so?" Evidently the matter concerned such unusual and odd forms of love-making, such exceptional habits or perversions, that Maikov's wife had not ventured to describe them in writing. Anna, in her naïveté, may well have spoken of them, or even complained about them, without realizing that there was anything pathological in their nature.

Dostoevsky was happy with her because she had given him a natural outlet for all his desires and those very fantasies

Maikov referred to. Her role was a liberating and cathartic one; therefore she released him of his burden of guilt, and he ceased to feel like a sinner or a voluptuary. Tolstoy maintained that there is no physical depravity where the woman is not made solely an object of pleasure. Dostoevsky loved Anna, and in his case sexual pleasure became all the keener if it was coupled with other emotions of an erotic or ideal nature. When his idealistic emotions came in conflict with his erotic ones and acted as a brake on them, however, he suffered from a terrible sense of dichotomy, and in his youth had distinguished sharply between the physical and the sentimental origins of love. Now both halves were blended into one whole, the union had been consummated; every increase in friendship, tenderness and attachment automatically heightened physical desire and sexual potency. In this respect his second marriage gave him for the first time a certain normalization of his sexual life.

It must not be forgotten that Anna can hardly be spoken of as the *type* of woman Dostoevsky specifically needed. The theory of "types" in sexual selectivity is on the whole inapplicable here; it is perfectly evident that he was not attracted by one invariable feminine type to the exclusion of all others, since he had been passionately drawn to such women as Maria and Apollinaria, neither of whom resembled Anna in either physical or spiritual make-up. The history of his major loves shows that there were three basic types of women in his life —and perhaps more. And Anna only "made a conquest" of him when she had become a habit and he grew convinced that he could trust her, that she was utterly his, and that everything he had been apprehensive about, or had been ashamed of, or had feared, was at last sanctioned and justified by their relationship.

This gradually came about as the result of their long cohabitation. Essentially, their travels abroad constituted their honeymoon trip, but a trip that lasted four years. By the end of that time Anna had begun bearing him children; the spiritual and sexual adaptation of husband and wife to each other was concluded, and they could safely assert that their marriage was a happy one.

However, during their stay in Dresden in 1867, Anna was still not quite certain of this. Rumblings of thunder continually threatened their idyll, and at times she grew actually frightened. She knew, for instance, that Dostoevsky had been intimate with Apollinaria, even though she does not have a word to say about that lady in her *Recollections*. But probably she was not aware that, even before they were really settled in Dresden, Fyodor had sat down to answer the letter from Apollinaria he had received just before he and Anna left for abroad.

He might have repeated the words of the Russian poet: "Oh, memory of the heart, thou art more powerful than the sad memory of the mind." He told her about his marriage, even though he knew that in all probability she had heard of it from other sources: "My stenographer, Anna Snitkina, was a young and rather comely girl of 20, of a good family, who had graduated with excellent marks from the *gymnasia*, and of a kind and serene character. Our work went along superbly. *The Gambler* was done in 24 days. When the work on the novel was finished, I perceived that my stenographer was sincerely in love with me, although she never said a word of it to me, while I was getting to like her more and more. Since, after the death of my brother, life had become dreadfully tedious for me and hard to bear, I proposed marriage to her and now we are wedded. The difference in [our] ages is dreadful [twenty and forty-four] but I am becoming ever more convinced that she will be happy. She has a heart and she knows how to love."

After this "muted" story, deliberately omitting his own romantic and emotional rôle and even containing factual errors (he was forty-six and not forty-four, and *The Gambler* was done in twenty-six days), he confided to her in full detail the state of his finances and his literary plans, and ended with the following declaration: "Your letter left a sad impression on me. You write that you feel very sad. I don't know what your life has been this last year and what has gone on in your heart but, judging by all I know about you, it is hard for you to be happy.

"Oh, my dear, it is no cheap, *indispensable* happiness I am suggesting to you. I respect you (and have always respected you) for your demanding nature, since I know that your heart cannot help but demand life, yet you yourself consider people as infinitely radiant or, just as precipitately, as coarse and dishonest. I judge in accordance with the facts. You can draw the conclusion yourself. Goodbye, eternal friend! Farewell, my friend; I clasp and kiss your hand."

He sent off this letter on the twenty-third of April, and four days later Anna confided in her diary: "I came home to read a letter I had found on Fedia's desk. Of course, it's a bad business to read a husband's letters, but what could I do— I could not have acted otherwise! This letter was from S[uslova]. After reading the letter I was so agitated that I simply did not know what to do. I had chills and fever, and even wept. I was afraid that the old fondness would be renewed and that his love for me would vanish."

Several days later a new letter from Apollinaria arrived, in answer to Dostoevsky's informing her of his marriage. He was gambling in Homburg at the time. Anna took a sharp knife and carefully unsealed the letter of her hated rival. It struck her as stupid and vulgar, but just the same her whole face grew hot with emotion. Apollinaria was, evidently, extremely irked by Fyodor's marriage and the tone of her reply was ironic; to show her contempt she purposely mangled Anna's maiden name. The young wife became so wrought up that she decided to answer the letter herself and asked her friends in St. Petersburg for Apollinaria's address.

However, she put this off until her husband should come home and she could see how he reacted to the wretched letter. On his return from Homburg she handed it to him, resealed, with an air of innocence: "For a long, long time he kept reading the first page over and over, then at last read the whole through and turned all red. It seemed to me that his hands were trembling. I pretended ignorance and asked him what Sonechka [a niece of his] had written. He answered that the letter was not from her and smiled a bitter sort of smile. I had never yet seen him smile that way. It was a smile of either contempt or pity—I don't know which, really, but some sort of a pitiful, distraught smile. Then he became simply horribly absent-minded, hardly understanding what I was talking about."

Apparently Apollinaria wrote no further letters to Dostoevsky and Anna's fears quieted down. She soon came to the conclusion that she had ousted the "eternal friend" from her husband's heart for good and all.

Her struggle against another passion of his proved far more difficult. She knew that he was a gambler, but had never imagined the insane power roulette had over him. She was inclined to regard it as a whim or a masculine diversion, just as incomprehensible to her as hunting or fencing (Dostoevsky had no patience with either sport). Therefore, when he began assuring her that to win at roulette was their only possible hope of escaping from their embarrassing financial situation, she consented to his going off by himself to the spa at Homburg, where there was a gambling casino.

At Homburg things took their inevitable course, but for Anna it was a baptism of fire. Dostoevsky at first won a little, then lost everything down to his last thaler and wrote his wife that he was coming back to Dresden, but that he did not have the money to settle his hotel bill and buy a return ticket. Anna submissively scraped together all the money in the house and sent it off to Homburg. On receiving the draft from her, he at

once dashed off to the casino and again gambled everything
away. Next day, instead of her husband, Anna was astonished
to receive a tearful letter: "Ania, my angel, my *only* happiness
and joy, will you forgive me for everything and for all the
sufferings and troubles I have made you go through? Oh, how
I need you! . . . Will you ever respect me now? Why, this
has rocked our marriage to its foundations. . . . I count the
hours. Forgive me, my angel, forgive me, my heart." And, several
hours later, on the heels of the first, a new letter arrived: "I
clasp you hard, my treasure; I kiss you countless times; love
me, be my wife; forgive me, don't remember the evil things—
why, we have to live together all life long." Anna pawned her
valuables and again sent him money, imploring him to return.
But he went on sending her letters that sounded like the ravings
of a man possessed: "I have stolen your money; I am worthless,
I dare not write you."

Anna had wept when he left; she broke into sobs again
when he returned, unshaven and haggard. She did not reproach him, however, nor make any scenes for his benefit—
and in this she showed her instinctive wisdom. He was not
only moved to tears by her kindness, which made him feel
his guilt all the more keenly but, as is so often the case with
erring husbands, strove to show his love in every way: by May,
Anna was pregnant.

As for their marriage, it not only remained unshaken but,
on the contrary, became stronger than ever. He no longer had
anything to conceal, she now knew his very last secret, his
dark passion, and through her kindness and understanding
had relieved him of still another burden of shame and freed
him from another complex.

For this, he was very grateful, no less than for her sexual
acquiescence. There were no longer any barriers between them.
He could trust her all the way, without concealing anything,
without being wary of anything. And he sighed with relief and

began convincing her that his losses in Homburg had been due to his loneliness and worry. He had been, in general, upset on her account; he had miscalculated at the tables because of the pressure of time and the responsibility he had taken upon himself. But, if they were to manage a trip together to some place where he could play roulette, if they could stay there a while, if he could play without having to hurry or plunge, following a system . . . Whether she believed him or merely pretended, she at last gave in to his arguments, and in June they set out for Baden-Baden, the place of his last meeting with Apollinaria. He was bound to recall a great many things as he strolled with Anna along the walks in the park and through the familiar streets.

They spent five weeks in Baden-Baden, which she later described as a nightmare. She was left alone all day long and suffered over everything: Fyodor's frenzy as he shuttled between hotel and casino in some sort of gambling fever; the uncertainty even of having dinner on the morrow; her poverty and her inability to dress well—she had to wear one poor black dress, while the ladies she saw on the promenade were dressed with great elegance. It seemed to her that a catastrophe was inevitable and impending, and this feeling of doom never forsook her until the day they left the spa.

Dostoevsky had an all-consuming belief in a system which would "turn the wheel of fortune." He might, perhaps, have scored some modest winnings had he applied this system coolly and calculatingly, but he was far too impatient to do so. He was instantly swept away, lost his head and, as always, went to extremes.

A week after their coming all their cash was gone and they took to pawning their things. Every day he had to scurry to the pawnbrokers with his watch, or a ruby-and-diamond brooch (his wedding gift to Anna), or his wife's earrings; their clothing went next—his overcoat, his suit, her shawl. On one

occasion he won four thousand thalers—almost a fortune—
and, deciding to be prudent, turned the whole sum over to
Anna. But every hour he kept coming home to replenish his
funds and hurrying back to the casino, and toward evening
nothing remained of his winnings. He and Anna had to move
from their hotel to a miserable cubbyhole over a smithy and
lived there to the accompaniment of the hammers and the
wheezing bellows.

In a short while they found themselves in a situation
similar to the one Dostoevsky had been in two years previously
when he had left Russia with Apollinaria. He again went
through the whole business: letters appealing for help, the
arrival of a long-awaited remittance, new losses, despair, attempts to clamber out of the pitfall. Anna at first wondered
how a man who had borne with such fortitude so many misfortunes and hardships in his life could have so little will
power. How could he fail to restrain himself? How could he
risk their last thaler? She saw something debasing and unworthy in it all. "But in a short while I understood," she wrote,
"that this was not simply a question of weak will but a passion
that absorbed a man wholly, something elemental against which
even the firmest character cannot struggle."

She could not, of course, put into words the fact that this
passion of her husband's was becoming almost mystical. Most
people who gamble consistently find in it an escape from worries and disturbances, sexual or otherwise; games of chance
offer an attractive substitute for release and liberation. A psychoanalyst would no doubt discover in Dostoevsky's gambling
mania a secret compensation for his sexual nervousness and
lack of satisfaction. But there was another element in his passion: it captivated him as an escape into the irrational, as a
contact with the world of chance. Winning and losing at the
roulette wheel were not subject to the laws of logic—they were
related to that inscrutable dark beginning of the universe where

neither morals nor the spatial limitations of Euclidean geometry existed. And gaming offered an unparalleled opportunity to right the wrongs of birth, poverty, status and circumstances through some magnificent stroke of luck, through a challenge to fate. For was not the whole process of gaming a challenge to the powers which oppress man, a break-through into the captivating anarchy of spontaneous action and hazard?

Anna sensed something of all this and, having called it a disease, accepted and bore as a cross all the complications and consequences of his gambling fever without even trying to cure him: "I never reproached my husband for a gambling loss, never quarreled with him on this account (my husband appreciated very much this trait of my character), and gave him our last money without a murmur." The only things she regretted enough to cry over were the earrings and brooches they did not manage to redeem from the pawnbroker, but she grieved over them in secret so that Fyodor might not notice. Not many women would have been capable of such self-control: in fact, she never attempted to put a stop to this passion through the arguments of reason and logic—which are every bit as effective as bailing water with a sieve.

He, of course, noticed her sufferings, punished himself in secret, and loved her still more for her meekness and did touching things to prove how tenderly he felt about her: he brought granulated sugar for the lemonade she was so fond of; if he won even two thalers he would buy flowers for her or surprise her with pastry for tea—and these things made her far happier than if he had prudently set the money aside for food and rent. This was one area where she forgot her burgher traits just as Fyodor did, even though she was a stranger to her husband's prodigality and knew how to count every copper. But in certain instances she neither scolded him nor even seemed aware of his extravagance: she remained convinced to the very last he was an endearing, simple and naïve man, and that one often had to treat him like a child. For his part he saw in her attitude on this matter only a manifestation of her love and, in all likelihood, he was right.

"Ania loves me," he wrote her mother from Baden-Baden, "and I have never been so happy in my life as I am with her. She is meek, kind, clever, she believes in me and her love has made me so attached to her that it now seems to me I would die without her." Even during the gloomiest spells of the Baden-Baden period she cheered him up with her little jokes and laughter. For, despite all their mishaps, she had just passed twenty and could hardly restrain her joyousness and the bubbling vitality of youth.

Yet with what relief did she leave sinister Baden-Baden behind her! They were going to Geneva by way of Basel—and there she received another proof of how expansive and contradictory Fyodor's nature was. Only yesterday he had taken no interest in anything save *rouge-et-noir* and the odd and even, but now, in the Basel Pinacotheca, he stood rooted before Hans Holbein's *Descent from the Cross*. The Christ it depicted had already undergone decomposition; the sight of his wounded, bloody body was horrible. Anna went away so as not to disturb her husband. When she came back twenty minutes later, she found him still standing there spellbound; his face was so agitated and distorted that she was afraid he would have an epileptic seizure at any moment. But, true to her policy of noninterference, she went off to one side without uttering a word or making her presence known in any way.

IN GENEVA SHE NOTICED THAT HIS IRASCIBILITY HAD LES-
sened even though he did not give up complaining it was a
dismal town, the climate was atrocious, the place was full of
Protestants, there were so many drunkards that there was
no counting them, and everything was boring as boring could
be! They were living on whatever Anna's mother could send
them and toward the end of each month invariably had to
pawn their belongings. Except for Nicholas Ogarev, the exiled
poet, not a soul came to see them: every so often they had to
borrow ten francs from him to tide them over until the next
remittance. Their isolation did not upset Anna, however; she
said she was "awfully happy." And Fyodor wrote Maikov: "I
was very, very glad because Anna was not at all bored, even
though I'm not a very jolly fellow to be living alone with for
all of six months, without any relatives and acquaintances."
His constant fear was that she might become bored on their
"uninhabited island" and regretted not having any money for
a trip to Paris. Certain biographers have advanced the notion
that he did not take her to Paris because he had been there
with Apollinaria. But then, he did take Anna with him not
only to Baden-Baden but to Berlin and Florence—the very
places he had visited with his eternal friend.

Toward the end of 1867 and the beginning of 1868 they
were leading a very modest and normal life in Geneva. Dostoevsky always believed strongly in a regularly scheduled day.

They got up about eleven, just as they had done in Dresden; after that Anna strolled or took in some sight or other while he wrote; about three they met in some restaurant for dinner, after which she took a siesta while he sat for hours in the Café du Monde reading Russian and foreign newspapers. At seven they usually took a stroll together along the quais and main streets, stopping at the shop windows lit by gas or small fire-pots to pick out the things he would have given her if he were rich—this window-shopping amused them very much. On coming home, he made the fire and they had tea; in the evenings, he either dictated to her what he had written the night before or read—he loved Dickens and used to read *Nicholas Nickleby* aloud. He also reread Hugo's *Les Misérables* with pleasure: it was a masterpiece he held very highly. And he made her read Balzac, his favorite author: he had purposely brought *Le Père Goriot* from St. Petersburg for her. Anna was expecting her child soon and was forever sewing or knitting in her free hours. He was at work on *The Idiot*.

Even at that time Anna had grasped that he was organically incapable of a long idyll, that he still had to interrupt the self-imposed regularity of his existence with bursts of strong sensations. He had to have orderliness for work and disorderliness for inspiration. He withdrew into a burgher's life to escape the overpowering throb of his imagination and thoughts. But without thunderstorms and tempests he suffocated, while roulette was one of his spiritual lightning rods. And Anna did what hardly any woman of greater experience and lesser sensitivity would have dared to do: when she saw that he was depressed and that his work was not making much headway, she herself proposed that her husband take a trip to Saxon les Bains where he could find roulette. At first he protested but eventually went—and everything took its due course: the winnings, the losses, the pawning of his wedding ring and winter overcoat, despair, hunger and cold, tearful letters to his long-suffering wife and the homecoming on a third-class ticket.

But the result was infallible: after this shake-up he wrote almost a hundred pages of *The Idiot* in November. He maintained that never had any idea of his been richer and more sound than the one that emerged with such clarity in this novel, but he was not satisfied with the way it was taking shape. "It is an enormous problem," said he of the moral and ideal basis of *The Idiot*, that tragedy of Christian compassion and love in conflict with the passions and abominations of the world. "But its execution is unsatisfactory." However, this was always the case with him: he went into ecstasies over the themes and ideas of the works he conceived but grew morose in the process of writing them and kept repeating that nothing was coming out right—nothing was well enough turned or vivid enough. Concerning *The Idiot* his doubts were quite serious and he wrote Maikov: "My only reader is Anna; it is very much to her liking, actually, but she is no judge of *my* trade."

She was disqualified as a judge not only because she approved of everything her husband did and seemed to lose even the most elementary critical perception when listening to or reading his works, but also because she was essentially limited in her artistic tastes. He avoided the discussion of theoretical themes with her and did not look for any philosophical or religious profundity on her part. During the first years of their marriage she simply could not rise to his level. She was, however, willing to learn; he found this touching, while her attentiveness and her attempts to improve his working conditions actually benefited him. "Anna is my true helper and consoler," he wrote. "Her love for me knows no limits although, naturally, there are many differences in our characters." But despite these differences (or, more probably, because of them), they were constantly drawing nearer to each other, in good times and bad.

In February, 1868, a daughter was born to the Dostoevskys and the father hugged the Geneva midwife so hard in
his excitement and joy that all she could do was to shrug resignedly and keep repeating: *"O, ces Russes, ces Russes!"* The
girl was named Sonia, after a daughter of Vera, Fyodor's sister.
He was most tenderly attached to this niece, who was the same
age as Anna. He pampered her and was jealous of her, and undoubtedly there was a subconscious erotic element in his
avuncular love.

Dostoevsky was proud and deeply moved at being a father
and became passionately fond of the child. This did not deter
him from taking another trip to Saxon les Bains, from which
he sent back soul-rending letters: "Forgive me, Ania—forgive
me, darling! For, no matter how vile, how low-down I am, I
still love both of you, you and Sonia (the second you) more
than all else in the world. I can't live without the two of you."

But the little Sonia, the "dear angel," did not survive,
and in May they lowered her tiny coffin into a grave in a
Geneva cemetery. This was a fearful blow not only for Anna
but for Fyodor as well. He despaired and sobbed like a woman,
was inconsolable for weeks, and simply could not reconcile
himself to what he called the "senselessness" of death. His
letters of this period mournfully question whether there is any
universal justice, any Divine wisdom, any justification for suffering: doubts subsequently formulated by Ivan Karamazov,
who cites the torments of children as evidence of the indifference of Providence and the high cost of universal harmony.

After the death of their little daughter, Geneva became
unbearable for them. They went to Vevey, also situated on
Lake Geneva, and on the steamer Dostoevsky astonished his
wife by his first complaints against fate, against all the afflic-
tions he had suffered and all the wrongs he had endured in the
past—in fact, against the injustice of heaven. At that moment

he had neither resignation nor Christian faith: there was only the agony of a man crushed by overwhelming forces.

They spent the summer in Vevey. Fyodor was at work on *The Idiot*, grieving over his dead daughter, ailing, complaining that it was impossible to create anything good among these lowering mountains. In the end they decided to move on to Italy. As at every move of theirs, it was necessary to twist and turn to find the money, and so the pleading letters and telegrams were again winging northward; only when this financial drama was resolved (not without the help of Anna's mother, who had come to Switzerland to see them) did the Dostoevskys manage to start out. They took a post chaise through the Simplon Pass. Where the road was too steep the passengers had to alight and walk. Anna, in a long black dress with a crinoline, leaned on her husband's arm; the postillion must have wondered who this bearded, bitter-looking man was who so solicitously led forward the young woman in mourning. The journey diverted them to some extent and restored Anna's health: she had been anemic, pale and, after the death of her child, had become altogether run down from her grief and upset nerves.

In Italy they rested. Dostoevsky admired the Cathedral at Milan and the paintings of the old masters, but they were driven out of Lombardy by the autumn weather and settled in Florence. They found a place across the Arno, near the Palazzo Pitti, where they lived for ten months. This was, in all probability, the happiest and most peaceful period of all their travels. Dostoevsky, as usual, complained that he was awakened in the morning by the braying of donkeys, that the streets were far too noisy, while in the summertime it was too hot. It turned out, though, that the noise did not interfere with his working, while the heat was beneficial to his health; his attacks of epilepsy became rarer in Florence, and his general physical condition improved considerably. They strolled through the Boboli Gardens with their fountains, grottoes and statues, and plucked roses in January before the Palazzo Pitti —something that made them almost rhapsodic. Crossing the Ponte Vecchio they came to the square before the Cathedral, and Dostoevsky broke into raptures over the scenes from the Old and New Testament carved on the bronze doors of the Baptistery by Ghiberti and Donatello. He dreamt of having a reproduction of them in his study in Russia.

He also loved the Pitti Gallery and made appointments with Anna to meet him before the Venus de' Medici or Raphael's Madonna of the Chair. Sometimes they would take excursions to Cascine, a park on the outskirts of the city, and went frequently to the Viesseux Lending Library. Dostoevsky took out Voltaire and Diderot to read at home (he had a rather good knowledge of French): he was studying the Encyclopedists in connection with one of the numerous literary plans he had matured during his isolated life in Florence. He had conceived a long novel, to be called *Atheism,* in which he intended to show the temper of the young people of that time, but abandoned it shortly afterward; he was too far removed from his native land to write it. Then he began working on *The Life of a Great Sinner:* he was prepared to devote two years to writing it and meant it to express all his most cherished views. In his outline the traits of Stavrogin, of Zossima the Elder, and individual autobiographical details were blended into a single general theme; parts of this novel later found a place in *The Possessed* and *The Brothers Karamazov.*

But although images and ideas were raging like the four winds through his head, he was nervous and vacillated among his various projects. Anna blamed this on their being all alone; they knew no one in Florence and met absolutely no one, and his ignorance of Italian merely intensified his feeling of utter isolation. Their life was as cloistered as if they were in a monastery, and Anna decided that her husband felt the lack of social contacts strongly. Besides that, she was pregnant again and did not want to bring a child into the world where her husband could not even make himself understood by the doctor or midwife. For that reason they resumed their wanderings in the summer of 1869, despite a most depressing lack of funds. Dostoevsky said they were very much like Mr. and Mrs. Micawber, *David Copperfield* being one of his great favorites.

At first they went to Prague by way of Venice and Trieste, in the hope of meeting the Czech leaders of the Slavic Renaissance. But in Prague they were unable to solve the housing problem and in the end came back to Dresden, since they knew that city well and were in love with it. Here their second daughter was born in September, 1869, and was christened Liubov. Her parents trembled over her, but she kept growing lustily; Anna, who had regained her strength in Italy, nursed the infant herself, while Dostoevsky felt again all the joys of fatherhood.

"Ah, why aren't you married," he wrote Strakhov, "and why haven't you got a baby? I swear to you that three fourths of life's happiness lie therein—and only one fourth, perhaps, in all the rest." But his material situation was very difficult: when Liubov was born the Dostoevskys had only ten thalers in the world; the rooms remained unheated; Fyodor had to pawn his jacket and sell his linen to keep his wife and baby going. "How can I write," he complained to Maïkov, "when I am hungry; when to get two thalers to send a telegram I had to pawn my trousers? However, to the devil with me and my hunger. But she is nursing the baby; what of her going *herself* to pawn her last warm woollen skirt. . . . And yet it's snowing here for the second day—she may catch a cold." His letters are one continuous cry of despair. "Send me two hundred rubles —save me. The word *save* is to be taken literally."

They really were starving; there was no money for the

baby's baptism; when the manuscript of the second part of
The Idiot was finished at last (he had worked on it without
a stop and had turned out almost fifty thousand words in two
months), he could not scrape together the five thalers to send
it by registered mail to *The Russian Messenger*. Only thanks to
the unflagging spirits of Anna, steeled in this school of poverty
and struggle, did they manage to arrange their desperate affairs
somehow or other. Their situation improved considerably
when Anna's mother came to Dresden. Shortly afterward her
brother arrived also—he had been attending the Petrovskaya
Academy in St. Petersburg, where a little while before the
student Ivanov had been killed by the followers of the revolutionary conspirator Nechaev.

His story of this notorious affair furnished Dostoevsky
with the central plot of *The Possessed*, in which he decided to
expose the revolutionaries and their destructive rôle. His political conservatism, as well as his acceptance of autocracy as the
foundation of Russian society and the stabilizing factor in
Russian government, had by then assumed a definite form.
In the concept of socialism and revolution he saw the greatest
danger to the religious and spiritual development not only of
Russia but of all the world, and he considered it his duty to
expose the fallacies of the young revolutionary movement at
home. He therefore deliberately constructed *The Possessed*
as a polemical novel, a novel of ideas. But, as always, in the
execution of his plan he broadened its scope, elevating the
meaning of the particular message to metaphysical and psychological heights. His Slavophilic views, and his hopes for the
mission of Russia, which he imagined to be the regeneration
of the perishing West, had become even stronger during his
years abroad.

The Dostoevskys passed all of 1870 in Dresden. By this
time their marriage had become stable, had taken on its final
shape both as the physical union of two people close to each

other and as a family organism. Convincing proof of this was the final trip which Dostoevsky took to Wiesbaden. Anna herself suggested that he "divert" himself; he had been working very hard all year, had finished *The Eternal Husband,* and was concentrating on the writing of *The Possessed.* This trip cost him dearly, but it put an end to his gambling passion. After a bout of the gambler fever and a losing streak, he wrote to his wife, begging her to mail him thirty thalers for his return fare —and, of course, sent that money down the drain after the rest. This was followed by a frightful vision and an access of repentance stronger than any he had ever felt before.

"I saw my father in a dream," he wrote his wife from Wiesbaden, "looking most horribly, the way he had appeared to me only twice in my life, warning me of some dreadful misfortune—and twice the dream came true. And now, when I also recall my dream of three days ago about your having turned gray, my heart stands still." In the same letter (dated April, 1871) he exclaims: "Ania, I am suffering so much now that, believe me, I have been punished too much already. I will remember it for a long time to come! If God would but preserve you now—ah, what is going to become of you? . . . I will recall this all my life and bless you, my guardian angel, every time. No; now I am surely yours, indivisibly all yours. But up to now I had *half* belonged to this accursed fantasy." The fact that in his frenzy he was actually confessing to her that the passion for gaming rivaled the passion of love indicates the extreme importance of the Wiesbaden episode. After that spring of 1871 he never again played roulette and was completely cured of his mania. The cure had come about with startling abruptness. Later on he made another trip abroad and was in Germany alone, without his wife, fully at liberty to set out for any town with a gambling casino; but he did not feel even the slightest urge to go back to the green-baize tables. Of particular interest to the psychoanalyst is the relation between his Oedipus complex and his sudden release from gambling, as well as the rôle played by the visions of his father before all the important crises (he speaks of *misfortunes*) of his life. Still more obvious is the erotic nature of the sudden "cure." Gambling, as a substitute for unsatisfied sexuality and a release from emotional instability and melancholy, was no longer necessary to him, since his sexual relations with his wife had become normalized and comparative tranquillity had been attained in his erotic life.

In the struggle to harness his instincts and subconscious drives, Anna had come off as victor, and he had an excellent understanding of this when he wrote that *now* he was indivisibly hers. *Now* signified the time following his revulsion against roulette. Henceforth he would devote himself to his family and wife, irretrievably and completely. It was this which constituted the symbolic meaning of Wiesbaden. It also signified the fall of the final curtain upon one of his rebellions; it meant that he had at last given up all attempts to "set nature right" by seizing luck on the wing, he would fling no more challenges at fate. The gesture had the metaphysical significance of a conversion. There was about it a ring of resignation—or, at least, of hope for it. From that day forward, Dostoevsky sought resignation, and if he wrote of rebellions, it was only to condemn them and to place in juxtaposition to them the ideals of religious submissiveness and Christian compassion.

It is also curious that, in the very letter in which he announced that he had sworn off gambling, he wrote: "If only one could get to Russia as soon as possible! Oh, with what hatred I shall recall this time!" Life outside Russia had given him all that it could, and he turned his back on it full of ingratitude, forgetting that it was precisely while he was abroad that his marriage had matured and come into full bloom. Also, since his life with Anna had already borne fruit, he was suddenly in a hurry to bring his isolation to a close.

They had many very basic reasons for returning to Russia. Although in 1870 and at the beginning of 1871 they were not as lonely in Dresden as they had once been and had made a few acquaintances among the Russians living there, Anna was nostalgic and worried about her house in St. Petersburg; it had fallen into the hands of such a bad manager that its loss seemed inevitable. As for Fyodor, he felt that he was drifting away from the actuality of Russian life; he found it difficult to finish *The Possessed* without plunging once more into the world of Russian discussions and reveries. "One suffers without one's native land, by God," he wrote Maikov. "Russia is necessary to me, it is necessary for my writing and work." He was even beginning to talk of the "ruin" of his talent away from his native soil, and Anna realized that they must leave Europe at once.

Even while they had been in Vevey, Dostoevsky had received an anonymous letter warning him that he was suspected of dealing with revolutionaries and that orders had been issued to open his letters and to submit him to the strictest search when he reached the Russian border. The public views of the author of *The Possessed* were such that any government endowed with common sense ought to have considered him its mainstay and to have been infinitely grateful for his defence of the Czarist regime and of Orthodoxy, not to mention all official policies. Nevertheless, he was still an ex-conspirator and an ex-convict as far as the dull bureaucrats of the dreaded Section III were concerned; and he remained under the most rigorous police surveillance almost up to the day of his death. In the year 1877–78 he became all stirred up and reproached his wife for not writing him regularly at a time when she was staying in the country and he was taking the waters at Ems, but the gaps in her letters were due simply to the time it took the local authorities to censor them. Only in 1880, after the celebrations in connection with the unveiling of the monument to

Pushkin, seven months or so before Dostoevsky's death, did he cease to be regarded as "suspicious"—and to bring this about had called for the intervention of grand dukes and of a grandee and arch-reactionary as imposing as Konstantin Pobedonostzev, head of the Holy Synod.

In June, 1871, before his departure from Dresden, Dostoevsky burned his manuscripts of the last four years, including the first drafts of *The Eternal Husband* and *The Idiot* and (according to his wife) "that part of *The Possessed* novel which represented an original variant." She succeeded in saving no more than the notebooks pertaining to these works— and that only by giving them to her mother to be smuggled into Russia.

The Dostoevskys actually did have to undergo a strict search at the Russian border. Anna was in the last days of her pregnancy and could hardly stand on her feet as she waited for the guards to look through all their books and papers and finish an endless interrogation of her husband. Yet this was taking place at the very time when all the leftist elements in Russia were attacking Dostoevsky for his harsh denunciation of radicals and revolutionaries in the serialized chapters of *The Possessed*.

They arrived in St. Petersburg on the eighth of July, 1871. A week later Anna gave birth to a son, who was christened Fyodor.

AS SOON AS HIS FAMILY WAS SETTLED IN ST. PETERSBURG, Dostoevsky resumed his work on *The Possessed*. By the end of 1871 he had completed a chapter of this long narrative which was destined to become the subject of a passionate controversy among his biographers.* In this chapter, written with terrifying intensity, the hero of the novel, the magnificent and enigmatic Stavrogin, nicknamed Prince Harry, tells how he raped a twelve-year-old girl and then impelled her to commit suicide. The editor of *The Russian Messenger*, the monthly in which *The Possessed* ran in 1872, refused to publish the chapter because of its "unbearable realism," and Dostoevsky read it to Strakhov, Maikov and many others to get their opinions. The story of the raped little girl had several versions. In the basic text Stavrogin accuses her of theft and she is birched while he witnesses her punishment.

In another variant the little girl is brought to Stavrogin by her governess while he is taking a bath. Certain friends of Dostoevsky were afraid that "such a dishonorable action on the part of the governess would cast aspersions on young women who earn their bread through honest toil, and will consequently be interpreted as an attack on the so-called feminine question"—*i.e.*, the emancipation of women. Perhaps be-

* This chapter was published for the first time after the 1917 revolution under the title "Stavrogin's Confession" and is usually reprinted in all the translations of *The Possessed*.

cause of these considerations, the author rejected the variant
with the governess. In the text of *Stavrogin's Confession* there
is no governess; the victim of the demoniacal Prince Harry is
a half-orphan from a poor family, and the rape takes place in
her home.

In a letter to Leo Tolstoy, Strakhov repeated the story
that Dostoevsky himself had supposedly boasted of having had
sexual relations with a little girl who was brought to him by
her governess while he was taking a bath. He cited as his source
Paul Viskovatov, a professor of literature, who had met Dostoevsky both in St. Petersburg and abroad. Dostoevsky's widow
wrote in her *Recollections:* "And so this variant of the novel,
this atrocious part played by Stavrogin, Strakhov in his malice
did not hesitate to ascribe to Fyodor Mikhailovich himself,
forgetting that . . . such refined depravity calls for considerable expenditures and is within the reach only of the very rich."
She is not content with this naïve argument alone, however,
and goes on to speak about the high morals of her husband
and the absence of depravity in his character and habits.

At any rate, not only the writer's widow but a succession
of biographers after her have believed that it was Dostoevsky's
own readings of *Stavrogin's Confession* in 1871, upon his return from Europe, which gave birth to the legend that he had
impaired the morals of a minor. As is so often the case, the
listeners had confused the author with his creation. It would
be a mistake, however, to suppose that the rumors of Dostoevsky's sexual excesses sprang up only in the 1870's, after
the publication of *The Possessed;* the "legend" (if it was no
more than that) was already making the rounds of St. Petersburg as far back as Dostoevsky's affair with Apollinaria. Yet
it is possible that even then it had literary origins.

In the winter of 1865, Dostoevsky had told the Korvin-
Krukovsky sisters of the idea for a novel which had come to him
when he was still a young man. Its hero, a splendidly educated

landowner, had sowed his wild oats in his youth, but in the course of time had acquired a wife and family and was now held in general esteem. On awakening one bright and sunny morning in a particularly serene and contented mood, he recalled a painting he had seen in Munich, with a wondrous beam of light falling on the bare shoulders of St. Cecilia; he was also pondering certain passages from a book of wisdom, *On Universal Beauty and Harmony*. And suddenly, at the very height of his pleasant reveries and thoughts, he was overcome by a disquieting, restless mood, like the nagging ache of an old wound. He was haunted by some urgent yet elusive recollection and strained his memory. And then, startlingly, the recollection did come to him, most vividly and realistically. He recalled a certain riotous night in his youth when, urged on by his companions, he had raped a ten-year-old girl.

Undoubtedly, Dostoevsky must have told this story to others besides the Korvin-Krukovsky sisters (it had horrified their mother, for one). The writer's widow, contradicting Strakhov and citing this variant of *Stavrogin's Confession*, adds that "the bath episode was an actual occurrence which someone had told to my husband." But he himself had been telling the story of a little girl's rape six years before writing *The Possessed* and *Stavrogin's Confession*, and at that time there was no word of a bath. And in the 1860's this rumor, in connection with his name, was already being whispered in the literary circles of St. Petersburg, generally with some comment on the "emancipation of the flesh" theories popular among his associates. Furthermore, the author of one circumstantial version was none other than Dmitri Grigorovich, the writer, who had been Dostoevsky's friend since his youth and had at one time shared quarters with him. According to Grigorovich, during a trial over the rape of a ten-year-old girl, Dostoevsky had become enflamed with passion for her and, even though he had never set eyes on the child before, had followed her out of court and *used* her. All this had supposedly taken place in the early 1860's.

Another person who did his share of the broadcasting was the littérateur, A. Faressov; he quoted K. Nazarieva, a contemporary of Dostoevsky's, who claimed she had heard the writer himself describe how he had seduced both the minor girl and her governess. And, finally, the present biographer heard in Petrograd, in 1916, when S. Vengerov and Dmitri Ovsyaniko-Kulikovsky, both well-known critics and historians of literature, that in the literary circles of the 1880's there were frequent rumors to the effect that Dostoevsky, before being sentenced to Siberia, had been involved with a minor girl; later he had repented but simply could not forget her—which would explain his unwholesome interest in this theme throughout his works.

This exhausts all the data concerning the "legend of corrupting a minor," before which all the investigators of Dostoevsky's life are brought up short in fear and perplexity. They are particularly confused by the fact that the writer did have an infantile complex. He was very fond of children, he drew them well and, according to the testimony of his friends, was always gentle and considerate with them. And children repaid him in the same coin and became quickly attached to him. A. E. Koni, a well-known attorney, has left an account of a trip Dostoevsky made to a colony of juvenile delinquents, where he immediately won the love and confidence of the inmates. The sufferings of children moved him very much, and he continually utilized this theme—in his early writings (*Netochka Nezvanova*), in his mature ones (*The Humiliated and Wronged, Crime and Punishment*), and even in his last works (*The Diary of a Writer* and *The Brothers Karamazov*).

But the extent to which his intense curiosity about the physical and moral hurt felt by children was of a pathological nature, and whether it was or was not coupled with erotic sensations, are very difficult points to clear up. One thing is indisputable: the theme of corrupting minor girls sounds so often in his works, and he reverted to it so frequently in his conversations, that it assumes a persistent, if not a truly manic character. Of course, there is no need to deduce from this that Dostoevsky had actually raped some little girl and that, tortured by his conscience, he was seeking release from his anguish through confession and creativity. It would be dangerous and even absurd to believe that an artist mirrors only what has actually taken place in his life, and to look only for living models and real occurrences in all his writings. Such an attitude is, unfortunately, far more prevalent than we are willing to admit, and it is precisely this which spawns a pseudo-literature founded on "facts." Dilettanti in their thousands feel certain that all a story or a novel demands is a "real" incident, a "life occurrence," while editors and publishers by the hundred and critics by the score accept all such anecdotes as *belles-lettres.* In fact, the delusion that all a writer does is show what "actually happens" denies the very grounds of artistic creativity and reduces to zero the part played by the imagination.

Leo Tolstoy once happened to remark concerning his novels, in which everybody was always finding portraits of his relatives and friends, that his work would be worthless if it amounted to no more than descriptions of people who actually existed. To copy things as they are is by no means a *sine qua non* for achieving artistic truth. It was not at all necessary for Dostoevsky to rape a little girl in order to make this a tremendous episode in the life of one of his characters—just as he did not have to become a murderer in order to describe how Raskolnikov did the old pawnbroker and his sister to death with an ax.

Yet what is the basis of creative imagination? To what extent is it determined (or limited) by personal experience, internal or external? Here, once more, it becomes necessary to distinguish between ideas and actions. Unrealized desires nourish artistic fantasy probably far more often than actual occurrences. And the way these desires appear in works of art explains, of course, what tendencies and impulses lurk in the depths of their creator's soul; they give us a key to his "secret abode." To a certain extent, for a certain fragment of time, every author identifies himself with the dramatis personae of his works, and his ability to reincarnate himself, just as in the case of a fine actor, grows out of his inner experience, independent of reality and fulfillment. In other words, it would have been enough for Dostoevsky to experience desire for a minor girl, without transforming it into an act, to be able in due time to describe Stavrogin's rape with staggering realism: he could have lived this scene through in all its details in his reveries or in the crepuscle of the subliminal.

We have the right, however, to consider the probable intensity and duration of such a desire. Apparently it not only stirred within him but must have appeared to him and tortured him again and again—otherwise he would hardly have reverted to it so persistently in his novels. Whether any ten- or twelve-year-old girl actually had come into his life, to the impairment of her morals, with or without the fancy trimmings of governess, Tiberian bath and so on, we do not know and probably never shall. But that a sexual fantasy of this sort dwelt within him and that he was hag-ridden by it appears undeniable to everyone who sets foot in the world of sensuality and perversion created by the imagination of this genius who was both torturer and tortured.

Dostoevsky repeatedly described the punishment and beating of children, and insisted that their complete helplessness—the opportunity it afforded to adults to do whatever they wanted with the small bodies, to pinch and flog them and tyrannize over them—engendered an evil delight and aroused the darkest instincts. Children cannot resist; apparently they are doomed to torture—and this, again, is a favorite theme of his. It is particularly upon children that adults vent their desire for absolute power, and such moral and intellectual sadism quickly turns into physical sadism.

World literature contains a good deal of data about the erotic nature of corporal punishment, about the connection between torture and sexual delight—from *Justine*, by the "divine Marquis" himself, and the *Confessions* of Rousseau, to Mirbeau's *Garden of Tortures* and Celine's *Journey to the End of the Night*—but in the case of Dostoevsky this theme (like almost every one he touched) becomes intensified and metaphysical. He laid the cause of flogging and other violence to the basic cruelty of man, the insuperable evil of man's corrupt nature, and traced the torturing of children almost as far back as the fall of Adam. And at the same time he stressed that evil inflicted upon children awakens evil in the children themselves. In the little girl he had raped, Stavrogin perceived through her innocence and purity an equivocal smile that horrified him—a premonition and foretaste of sin, a certain responsive fire; victim and tyrant were suddenly united by a common bond of sensuality, of bestiality; they shared the same impurity, the same awareness of the flesh, the same experience of transgression.

Interesting and significant is a certain dream of Dostoevsky's which up to now psychoanalysts have apparently overlooked: "Today," he wrote his wife in 1873, "I dreamed that Lilya (their daughter) had fallen into the hands of some woman who was torturing her; this woman had beaten her with birch-rods—huge ones, the kind used on soldiers—so hard that I found her breathing her last, and she kept saying all the time, 'Mamma dear, mamma dear!' This dream will drive me almost mad today!" To this it should be added that in his childhood, as has been mentioned already, he could have neither experienced nor witnessed any corporal punishment in his own family, since such things were unknown in the household of Dr. Dostoevsky—just as they were later on in his own. When Fyodor became a father he never laid a finger on his children.

This does not, of course, explain away his secret drives and impulses, nor certain aspects of his life he himself was very much aware of, and, perhaps even dreaded. Here again we come upon the duality of his nature and his inclinations. But it is best simply to allow for that duality without falling into the errors usual in the interpretation of his history, and without taking imaginary incidents for actual ones. In any case, whatever pathological drives he might have had earlier, they seem to have diminished after his marriage. By the time Dostoevsky returned home, in 1871, most of his violent desires had lost their fever, or at least were more consciously controlled.

A GREAT DEAL HAD CHANGED BETWEEN 1867 AND 1871, during the four years the Dostoevskys had spent outside of Russia. Physically, Fyodor had grown stronger and his attacks of epilepsy had become less frequent (they ceased altogether about 1877). True, he was by now beginning to have all sorts of trouble with his respiratory system; an infection which eventually led to his mortal illness. And he was overcome more and more often by the fear of death: he had unbearable moments of horror and revulsion at the thought that he would cease to be, that his body would decay, and his consciousness dissolve in an icy sleep. He wanted to believe in the immortality of the soul and could not, despite the fact that his religious tendencies had become stronger and he now styled himself a faithful son of the Orthodox Church. He had grown somewhat more gentle and tolerant of people and spoke of resignation and meekness as the highest Christian virtues. Anna thought that she had succeeded to some extent in blunting his irascibility and touchiness. At any rate, she did have a pacifying influence upon him. While abroad they had become closer friends than she had ever dreamt possible when the two of them, discontented and with their nerves on edge, had left St. Petersburg four years before.

Their union had matured and become firmly established during the hardships they had endured together. Poverty and humiliations, loneliness and hard work, the birth and death of their first daughter, Fyodor's mania for roulette and his complete recovery—all these had created an attachment which was exceptionally strong and profound. And Anna too had changed very much. She had left Russia a young and inexperienced girl and had come back as the "mother of a family," as her husband used to call her in his jokes, and her character had grown stronger and more rounded. In the presence of others, especially of men (she did not for a moment forget how jealous Fyodor was), she still tried to be aloof and reserved. But alone with him, *en famille*, and even among their close friends, she laughed willingly enough and was even playful—and he loved this liveliness of hers. He valued especially her down-to-earth quality and her optimism, since he himself was devoid of them, and felt that the contradictions of his consciousness and instincts, his preoccupation with the somber problems of evil, the vanity of all things under the sun, and the schism between God and man, sat on him like a malady and the mark of Cain. To live simply, unhesitatingly, treading the earth lightly, was beyond him, and the fact that the woman he loved was able to do so side by side with him seemed to him nothing short of a miracle.

To resume life in Russia was difficult: Anna's house had been auctioned off for next to nothing; the furniture and things they had pawned were lost because they had not paid the interest; Pasha had sold the library book by book on the flea market; creditors ringed them in like a pack of wolves. All they had to live on was the money for the last part of *The Possessed*, now running in *The Russian Messenger*. It was necessary to get an apartment and furnish it on the installment plan, and there were two children to take care of. It was at this point that Anna took over the negotiations with the creditors and assumed the responsibility not only of running the household but of managing all their money matters. At first she still confided her financial schemes and stratagems to Dostoevsky but later stopped doing so altogether. He reproached her for her secretiveness, but she was simply watching out for his peace of mind and trying to save him from trouble and worry. She made mistakes, of course, and was not without her shortcomings. For instance, either because of their life in furnished rooms while abroad, or because she was a "woman of the 'sixties" who paid no particular attention to surroundings and external comfort, she was not a very good housewife—and even a rather slipshod one: they changed apartments frequently and Dostoevsky accused her of being willing to sacrifice one essential comfort after another for the sake of saving a few rubles.

Yet the line she had taken was the right one: she was shielding him from everyday cares, knowing very well that if he were allowed to do so, he would get all stirred up over poorly washed linen or fall into despair over a grocery bill. Had it not been for her firmness and good management, he would often have worried himself sick: for instance, during their streak of ill luck in 1872, when their daughter broke an arm—it was poorly set and an operation became necessary—Anna's mother died, and Anna herself had abscesses of the throat and the doctors were afraid she might not live.

During the period from 1872 to his death in 1881, Anna put all her husband's affairs in order. By degrees she satisfied the claims of all his creditors, and although the liquidation of his debts went on right up to 1879, she relieved Dostoevsky of worrying about them. She became his agent and publisher. He had previously been offered pittances for his works (the publication of *The Eternal Husband* as a separate novelette brought him 150 rubles, while for *The Possessed*, in book form, he was offered 500 rubles, the payments to extend over two years), whereas she succeeded in turning them into a source of steady income. In 1874, Dostoevsky transferred to her all the rights to his works.* And it was Anna who advised Fyodor

---

* Leo Tolstoy followed a similar course, but for different and much-criticized reasons. He ceded his literary interests to his wife Sofia after he had, on moral grounds, renounced all property rights, including literary ones.

to take on the editorship of *The Citizen* in 1873, when he was tired out after finishing *The Possessed* and seeking a respite from strictly creative work.

She was also active as proofreader and administrator of Dostoevsky's *Diary of a Writer* in which, beginning with 1875, he published his comments on political, social and artistic events—and this journalistic venture proved particularly rewarding financially. When in 1877 he ceased publication of the *Diary,* which had enjoyed a great success, he found he had the means to devote himself to writing without any worry; beginning with 1878 he worked for two years on *The Brothers Karamazov* without having to interrupt his novel once for financial reasons, as he had always had to do during preceding works. For the first time in his life he had some security. Anna had also arranged through her brother the purchase of a small house in Staraya Russa, where they spent their summers, and where they lived during the winter of 1874, when he was writing *A Raw Youth.*

She had not been a practical person but had become one and had developed her business ability because circumstances had compelled her to. Her greatest difficulty lay, of course, in having to contend with Dostoevsky's inability to handle money and his extravagance. He was forever buying unwanted presents; the dining room could boast of an expensive Dresden vase— but the chairs were broken. Once he surprised Anna with a three-hundred-ruble bracelet when there was not enough money for household expenses; she had to tell him that it was magnificent but too small for her arm before he would consent to return it. There were times when, instead of bringing her an anticipated advance from *Notes of the Fatherland,* where *A Raw Youth* was running, he would arrive loaded down with toys for the children and expensive blouses for her, or binoculars, or a fan with ribs of ivory, and a bewildering variety of other articles for the family and himself. He was on such occasions very proud of his purchases and would ask his wife if she liked them. "I like them," Anna would say. "The only thing is, I haven't any money to buy dinner."

During the fourteen years of her life with Fyodor, Anna endured more than a few worries, griefs and misfortunes, including the death of their second son, Alexis, who died shortly after he was born in 1875, but she never murmured against her fate: the awareness that she was the life companion of a great writer, and that her love was making everyday burdens lighter for him, contented her. She tended him as if he were a child, sacrificed absolutely everything for him, including even the education of the children. She had brought a family into being for him, had taken upon herself the duties of his business manager and treasurer, transcribed his novels, was his first reader, critic and editor, stayed awake nights to listen to some literary project of the new chapters of a work in progress, consoled him during his spells of melancholy, of illness, of the fear of death. She had borne uncomplainingly the flare-ups of his gambling fever, his jealousy, irritation and persecution mania.

This was a genuinely heroic feat and she had dedicated herself to it, never quailing before taking on another burden and enduring sufferings as a nun might—to the very end, in the name of a duty which she regarded as the most precious in life. She and no other was a glowing example of the active love of which Dostoevsky spoke in his novels, and she deserved the tribute of *The Brothers Karamazov*, which was dedicated to her.

It is curious, however, that Anna's personality found no reflection in the world of Dostoevsky creations. In not a single novel written during their marriage is there any feminine type who is derived from her. Evidently she was such a stable and organic part of his existence that he felt no need of projecting her on the screen of fiction.

One may say with confidence that the years he spent with

Anna after their return from abroad were the most serene, tranquil and perhaps, the happiest in his life. He had attained the height of his creative activity between 1864 and 1871— the years when he wrote *Notes from the Underground, Crime and Punishment, The Gambler, The Idiot, The Eternal Husband* and *The Possessed*—the most significant and profound of his productions. Only the last four years of this period coincide with his second marriage—and even these he spent in the poverty and upset of his nomadic life abroad and not in the midst of domestic ease and comfort.

Between 1871 and 1878 he wrote only one novel, *A Raw Youth*, and that one is not among his best. Certain students of his life are therefore bothered by the questions: to what degree did domestic happiness help the creative work of the writer? And was he not one of those for whom serenity and security, a family and everyday stability, are by no means a fount of inspiration? But, in the first place, Dostoevsky was no longer young and therefore was in need of tranquillity. In the second, a family and a normal setting were absolutely necessary to him, since without descending from those metaphysical heights on which he had lived so long, his heart would surely have burst from the lack of oxygen. And, finally, it was under conditions created by the loving care of Anna that Dostoevsky wrote his most remarkable work—*The Brothers Karamazov*.

But there is also another, completely nonliterary consideration: did not Dostoevsky, who had endured so much in his life, have a right to any human happiness? Can it be that the trade of an artist excludes him from the ordinary, simple experiences and delights of life? The price the practitioner of any art pays for creativity is a high one, and it is hard to reconcile the illuminations of thought and art with the modest rewards of a burgher's happiness: yet it was precisely for these that Dostoevsky yearned—and attained, thanks to Anna.

The orderliness of his life and his sexual contentment,

both of which had by 1877 put an end to his epilepsy, hardly changed his character and habits. Anatoly Koni, in his reminiscences of Dostoevsky, gives a felicitous quotation from Heine to the effect that a great man is like the sun: he is best discerned not in the full blast of his activity but in his rise and his decline. Dostoevsky was well over fifty when he finally calmed down to some extent—if only outwardly—and became somewhat accustomed to domesticity. As before, he preferred to work in the quiet of the night, by the light of two candles. He was a late riser; when he appeared for breakfast he was fully dressed (he was constantly searching for any stains on his clothing—he disliked them very much). He drank tea, and wanted it prepared with such fastidiousness that even Anna gave up and he had to fuss with teapot and boiling water himself. He usually had two glasses of strong and much-sweetened tea and carried a third one with him into the study, where he sipped it while working.

Everything in his room had to be kept in an unalterable order and in the same position, and each morning Anna made sure that each piece of furniture was in its proper place and that his papers, the daily newspapers, magazines and books were on the desk—especially if they had had visitors the evening before and, God forbid, something had been shifted or disturbed. She alone had the right to dust his desk and books, and if anything was not just right Dostoevsky literally raised hell. Alongside his desk was a small one of her own with pencils and notebooks at which she took dictation and corrected proofs. Dostoevsky made hundreds of corrections in his manuscripts. He also had a habit of drawing profiles, little houses, designs and so forth on their margins; for the most part these casual drawings are neater and more precise and finished than the spirited and rather crude work of another great manuscript doodler—Pushkin. Dostoevsky had a drawer filled with raisins, nuts, Turkish delight and other sweets for the children whenever they managed to break through their mother's cordon and run into the study.

About four he went out for a walk and, on his way home, bought chocolates at Ballé's, or caviar and other delicacies at Elisseiev's. At six they dined; at nine the whole family drank tea, after which he either worked or went out. Occasionally he received guests—almost always his close friends. He liked having his intimates in, but Anna had by degrees discouraged Pasha and his other relatives from visiting; she had no sympathy for them whatsoever and in this regard was able to influence her husband. She was not fond of going out and willingly let him go alone.

By the end of the 'seventies, he had entrée into various salons, especially that of Countess Sofia Tolstoy, and had acquired not a few feminine admirers in the highest society. According to Anna he had many sincere friends among women, and they willingly made him the confidant of their secrets and asked his friendly advice, something which he never refused them. He could understand the things that interested women: "Rarely did anybody understand the feminine soul and its sufferings as profoundly as Fyodor understood and sensed them." Yet Anna was not in the least jealous. When he returned from his visits at two in the morning, he found her up waiting for him and ready to give him tea; after he had changed into a roomy spring coat that served him as a bathrobe, he would come into her bedroom (they usually slept apart) and would tell her in full detail how he had passed the evening, and at times their talks lasted until daybreak.

His quick temper and suspiciousness had not abated with the years. He frequently astonished friends and the society he was in by his bitter remarks; he became rancorous at the slightest pretext, was very sensitive to irony and was the first to launch an attack, as though afraid of somehow being wronged. Strangers often found his conversation insulting. Strakhov maintained that Dostoevsky could be called neither a good nor a happy man, since he was "envious, depraved, and had passed all his life among such excitements as had made him pitiful, and would have made him ridiculous if he were not at the same time so malevolent and so intelligent. But, like Rousseau, he considered himself the best of men and the happiest. . . . In Switzerland, in my presence, he harried a servant so much that the latter took offence and remonstrated: 'I, too, am a man.' Such scenes were a constant occurrence with him, because he was unable to restrain his rancor."

Other contemporaries denied these accusations and blamed whatever outbursts there were on the fact that he was shy and prone to take offence easily. Here is how Opochinin described him in 1879: "A trifle stooped, hair and beard reddish, the face gaunt with the cheekbones prominent, a wart on the right cheek. The eyes brooding; at times they show a gleam of suspiciousness and mistrust, but for the most part one sees some sort of deep thought and, apparently, sadness."

This face, which astonished many by its stamp of rebelliousness and suffering, became utterly transformed whenever he appeared at public gatherings. During the years 1879–80 he was often invited to read something of his own or others— and his readings always concluded with ovations. Despite his asthma and hoarseness, he read amazingly; his hearers lost all sense of actuality, forgot where they were and fell under the "hypnotizing sway of this emaciated, unprepossessing little ancient with a penetrating gaze that receded somewhere into the distance within his eyes." He became transformed; his inspired face seemed the face of a prophet. He used to come to these benefit performances accompanied by his "faithful squire," as he called Anna, who followed him with books, mufflers and cough lozenges. From the platform he observed

closely where she was seated and next to whom and at whom
she was looking; on one occasion he created an intolerable
scene because she had failed to wave a white handkerchief to
him from the auditorium. At sixty he was just as jealous as he
had been in his youth. But he was just as passionate in the
manifestations of his love.

THERE WAS ABOUT DOSTOEVSKY, AS ABOUT ALL MEN, A certain rhythm all his own in his love for his wife, his own high tides and low tides, and he understood very well that emotion and sensuality describe curves, and that things sexual and sentimental are alike subject to a regular rise and decline. But it was eroticism, precisely, that was the constant factor in their relations. He knew that love and infatuation are not one and the same, that it is possible to love deeply and faithfully without any longer experiencing the intoxication and sweep of infatuation, and was therefore astonished at his becoming infatuated with Anna over and over again. In fact, the physical vigor he showed during the many years of their life together was amazing—and this despite the approach of old age.

His sexual desire not only did not become blunted with the years but even acquired new force. In 1874, the seventh year of his marriage to Anna, after a separation of a fortnight (she was staying in the country and he was in St. Petersburg) he wrote her: "I must see you—dreadfully, dreadfully so, even despite the fever, although in one respect it relieves me, putting off . . ." Later on he went to Ems for the cure and confessed: "I think of you every minute, Anka; I am longing for you excruciatingly! . . . In the evening and on lying down to sleep (this is between us) when I think of you it is with agony; I embrace you in imagination and kiss *all* of you in imagination (do you understand?). In my dreams you come to me enticingly. You said that, in all likelihood, I would go after other women here abroad. My friend, I have found out through experience that I can't even imagine any other woman but you. I have no need whatsoever of others; it's you I need—that's what I say to myself every day. I've gotten too used to you and have become too much the family man. The things of old are all in the past. And besides, there's nothing better *in this respect* than my Annechka. Don't behave like a holy innocent when you read this—you ought to know me. I hope you won't show this letter to anybody."

The *things of old* evidently included not only adventures of the heart but far coarser experiments of the flesh. In describing the cure at Ems he begins by complaining that he had turned into a "mummy, there are no *desires* in me. For the first time in my life—is it possible this is also due to the cure? In that case . . . Nevertheless I kiss you, my angel, 1,000 times." But the absence of desire soon passes; he has "unseemly dreams" and they are accompanied by "consequences at night, which is very bad, since all things of that sort affect the chest."

Of course, his sexual tension can be explained by the fact that he was now used to the regular habits of marriage and also by the intensity of his eroticism and imagination, as well as his awareness that a thirty-year-old woman who had lived with him for all of a decade not only loved him but also found physical satisfaction in him. Anna wrote him in 1878: "I consider our family (despite certain spats) a model one, and you will hardly find in a thousand families one where the husband and wife have become so firmly united and understand each other so deeply; and, most important of all, the longer things go on the more we love and respect each other. I consider myself the happiest of women."

She knew what would make him rejoice and, a year later,

again from Ems, he sent her a new testimonial and declaration of his love: "You know that each time after a long parting I become infatuated with you and arrive infatuated. But, my angel, this time things are somewhat different. You probably noticed that I was infatuated even when I left St. Petersburg. After our serious quarrel I may have groused and, as I was packing for the trip, was impatient (after all, that's my nature), yet at the same time I was becoming infatuated with you and considered the matter right then, actually wondering at it. During all the years of our married life I was infatuated with you on four or five occasions, for some length of time on each occasion. Even right now I recall with enjoyment how, four years ago, I became infatuated with you at the time we had a serious quarrel and would not speak to each other for several days; we went visiting somewhere and I sat in a corner and watched you from there, and with a swooning heart admired how gaily you were talking with others. Just imagine, it occurred to me here that my infatuation with you in St. Petersburg during my last days there was also due in part to our sleeping together. It is a long time since we slept together, many years—beginning with the coming of the children—and this could have had a sudden effect on me. Don't say, Ania, that this thought is too material; there is more than mere materialism here. The thought that this being is *wholly* mine, that she doesn't want to be apart from me and even sleeps in the same bed with me—this thought has a terrific effect. . . . I found your being by my side so pleasant, that naturally this sensation was altogether *new* to me, even though we had slept [together] before—but I had long forgotten that. . . ."

He recalled what had happened before his departure: "But you were so busy that it happened only once, on our returning from dinner just before I left, and besides that the insane [a line has been crossed out by Anna]. I recall now, my angel, that I permitted you [another line crossed out] but now I am afraid. . . . You may laugh at the word 'permitted.'" (The reference, probably, is to her having wanted to prevent another pregnancy.) And several days later there sounds in his letters that frenzy which had been his in his youth: "I kiss the five tiny toes on your little foot, I kiss the little foot and the darling heel, I kiss and cannot get my fill of kissing, I am imagining this all the time. . . . And, finally, how can you wonder that I love you as a husband and a man? Come, who delights me as you do, who have blended into one body and one soul with me? Yes, all our secrets *in this matter* are mutual ones! And after that I'm not supposed to deify your every atom and not to kiss *all* of you insatiably—as is the case? For even you yourself cannot comprehend what an angel of a little wife you are in this matter! However, I'll convince you of all this on my return. Let's say I am a man of passion, but is it possible you actually doubt (even in the case of a man of passion) that one can love a woman with such insatiability as I have shown in your case?"

Several letters are obviously written in a state of acute erotic excitement: "My priceless one, my wife and mistress, you promise to put on weight—there, that's enchanting. If there is more health there will be more of *everything* . . . may God grant you health, not for *that* alone; it goes without saying we won't let up on that . . . *in that respect* it is time we got together (ooh, it's high time!). Your husband who is infatuated with you; I kiss your toe . . ."

In the summer of 1879 he was again in Ems; his health was very bad, his pulmonary emphysema (inflammation of the respiratory tract and atrophy of the blood vessels) was practically impervious to treatment, he was fifty-eight—but the letters to his wife still breathe the same passion, jealousy, desire: "You come to me in my dreams every night . . . I kiss all of you, I clasp your little hands, your little feet . . .

take care of yourself . . . take care of yourself for *me*—do
you hear, Anka: for me and for me alone . . . how I'd like
to take you around as soon as possible—not in that sense only,
but in that sense as well, until there's a conflagration [passage
crossed out by Anna]."

The possibility of imminent death merely intensified his
love. Yet at the same time her name-day slipped his mind.
He was absent-minded and forgetful: on one occasion, while
in an official bureau on some business in connection with his
daughter's birth certificate, he could not recall Anna's maiden
name.

Regrettably, most of his letters from Ems to his wife were
mutilated by her since she did not wish to have anybody learn
all the intimate aspects of Fyodor's sexual life, and we can
only guess what he meant to say. "Now about something very
intimate," he wrote in August, 1879. "You write, my queen
and clever girl, that you see the most seductive dreams [two
lines expunged]. This threw me into rapture and delighted
me, since I myself think here not only at night but during
the day of my queen and sovereign, inordinately, unto madness. Don't think it's that aspect alone—oh, no, no—but then
I frankly confess that as far as that aspect is concerned I think
until I am all inflamed. You write me rather dry letters, and
suddenly this phrase pops up [ten and a half lines expunged]
. . . which she failed to grasp instantly, remaining quite the
clever girl and angel, and therefore everything came about
only for the sake of the joy and delight of her hubby, since
her hubby is particularly pleased when she is quite frank. That's
the very thing he appreciates, that's the very thing that he
was captivated by. And suddenly the phrase: the most seductive dreams, [six lines expunged]. Allow me, Madam [six lines
expunged]. I kiss you, awfully, this minute. But in order to
decide about the dream [two lines expunged] . . . what the
darling heart of my adored wife [a line and a half expunged].

Anka, by this page alone you can see what's come over me. I am as if in a delirium; I am afraid of a seizure. I kiss your hands, both back and palm, and your little feet and all of you."

Three days later he reverted to the same theme: "And so I have become convinced, Ania, that I not only love you but am also infatuated with you, that you are my sole sovereign —and this after twelve years! Yes, and speaking even in the most earthly sense, that is also so, despite your having changed, of course, and having grown older since the time I first knew you, when you weren't nineteen yet. But now, would you believe it, I find you to my liking, and in this sense immeasurably more than at that time. This may sound improbable, but that's how things are. True, you're still only thirty-two, and that's the very time when a woman is in full bloom [five lines expunged] . . . that, now, attracts a fellow like me irresistibly. If only you were altogether frank—it would be perfection. I kiss you every minute in my reveries, all of you, every minute, succulently. I especially love that of which it has been said: 'And with this resplendent object / he enraptured is and tipsy.' This object I kiss at every minute in all its aspects and intend to kiss all my life. Annichka, darling, I never, under any circumstances whatever, can lag behind you in this sense —lag behind my entrancing pamperer, inasmuch as it is not merely a matter of this pampering—there are also that readiness, that charm and that intimacy of frankness which are extended to me along with all your pampering. Goodbye; I have talked myself silly; I embrace you and kiss you succulently."

Occasionally this erotic patter of his is reminiscent of the babblings of old Karamazov and his unrestrained, sticky voluptuousness. Certain passages are especially revealing: "In my thoughts I kiss you every minute; I kiss, as well, that with which 'I am enraptured and tipsy.' Ah, how I kiss, how I kiss! Annka, don't say this is coarse—for what am I to do:

that's how I am, I'm not to be condemned. You yourself [a word expunged], my light and all my hope . . . you will understand this down to the last refinement. . . . Goodbye, my angel (ah, if only our meeting would come as soon as possible! I kiss your tiny toes, then your little lips, then the [one word expunged] again."

Repetitions, postscripts, exclamations and coy hints not infrequently add an unwholesome, almost pathological tone to these effusions. Their torrent does not abate even during the most notable days of his life when, in 1880, on the occasion of the unveiling of a monument to Pushkin in Moscow, he delivered a speech that brought forth stormy ovations and became the blueprint for a whole generation of latter-day Slavophiles and journalists with Native Soil leanings.

For it was in Moscow that he voiced his cherished hopes for Russia's mission: "Yes, the Russian is indubitably chosen to be all-European and universal. To become an authentic Russian, to become fully Russian . . . means merely to become brother to all men, an *all-man*. . . . This means: to bring reconcilement to European contradictions, to point out to Europe that the way out of its melancholy is to be found in its Russian soul, the all-human and the all-unifying . . . and at the very last to speak, it may be, the final word in the great general harmony, in the final fraternal concord of all tribes in keeping with the evangelical law of Christ."

Yet in the middle of all the excitement and the raptures evoked by his speech, after the celebrations and banquets where, as an acknowledged genius and the exponent of the national idea, he was the object of universal atttention and admiration, he was thinking of his Ania and writing her: "But I am still having the most abominable dreams, having nightmares every night about your betraying me with other men. Really, by God. Am tormented dreadfully."

With age he had become so accustomed to Anna and his

family that he simply could not get along without them. In the domestic circle the volcano of his spirit quieted down somewhat, his inner turmoil lessened. But no sooner did he find himself alone than all sorts of doubts and fears arose within him with new force. He went off to Ems for the cure, after several months of peaceful existence in Staraya Russa and without any need of anticipating anything unpleasant. Yet the parting with his family crushed him. He arrived in Ems nervous, tired out, "all broken up," as he himself put it, sat down in an armchair, closed his eyes—and dozed off for an hour and a half in utter exhaustion. "I've grown horribly womanish sitting at home during these eight years, Ania," he wrote in 1875. "I can't be apart from all of you for even a short while—that's the pass things have come to."

He had to go abroad every summer, since his asthmatic condition was growing worse and the doctors prescribed the medicinal waters at Ems. During the journeys to the spa and his stays there he suffered from acute boredom, feared that his epileptic attacks would return, exaggerated his financial difficulties beyond all belief, and saw the most insignificant trifles of everyday life in some sort of feverish, fantastic light. His irascibility remained at just as high a pitch as it had been during his youth and, by comparison with those about him, he still experienced everything with tenfold intensity. He read the Book of Job and all but wept with rapture. When, during a walk in Ems, he came across a child whose eyes were infected, but whose father, a cobbler, would not take him to a doctor for reasons of economy, the incident was enough to upset him for the whole day. Anna wrote him that she had seen a certain man who had behaved rather sentimentally toward her—and Fyodor was convinced that she had been unfaithful to him and raged like a madman in his despair, horror, jealousy and love.

His character had really undergone little change with the

years—except, perhaps, that he prayed more often, quietly and alone, and reverted more and more eagerly to thoughts of his childhood. Toward the end of his life recollections of times long past inspired many passages in his works. The muzhik Marei, the proponent of Christian love and truth, whose story he told in his *Diary of a Writer* (February 1876), is undoubtedly Mark, a serf who had struck his imagination as a nine-year-old boy in Darovoye, in 1831. The episode with Elizabeth the Malodorous in *The Brothers Karamazov* is the story of Agraphena, an idiot girl on the same country estate.

But, as always, he was drawing on his immediate experiences as well. In *The Brothers Karamazov*, written between 1878 and 1880, there is a great number of autobiographical details related to the last period of Dostoevsky's life, including the peasant woman's story of the death of her child —an echo of Anna's grief on the loss of their son Alexis. There is also the description of Zossima the Holy Ancient, so reminiscent of Father Ambrosius. Dostoevsky had seen him in the Optina Desert monastery when he had visited the place in June, 1878, with Vladimir Soloviev, the young philosopher who, in the opinion of certain critics, served as the prototype of Alësha Karamazov.

During 1879 and the beginning of 1880, Dostoevsky's health became much worse. His speech at the unveiling of the monument to Pushkin was not only his last public appearance but his literary and social testament as well. By January, 1881, after he had prepared for print a new issue of *The Diary of a Writer*, containing the famous speech on Pushkin and a reply to its critics and commentators, he was already hopelessly ill. Only his wife and friends knew of this. "He was unusually thin and wasted," wrote Strakhov, who saw him during these days, "he tired easily and his emphysema made him suffer. He was, obviously, living only on his nerves, and all the rest of his body had reached such a state of frailness that it could have been laid low by the first jolt, even a slight one."

Alexis Suvorin has told of a tragic conflict which hastened the great writer's death. While in the Summer Garden, Dostoevsky had happened to overhear two revolutionaries talking. It became clear they were Terrorists (the Party of the People's Will was at that time preparing an attempt on the life of Alexander III). Dostoevsky grasped what the talk was about and listened as if spellbound. He did not move, or call out, or summon help, and his first step was to go not to the Secret Police but to Suvorin, one of his friends. Could Fyodor, once a member of the Petrashevsky circle who had suffered in Siberia, turn informer? As a citizen he was obliged to act "patriotically," but as a man, concerned with the highest moral problems, he simply could not do it. Yet the very fact that he was incapable of action, that he had felt a certain closeness, almost a kinship, to these two men who were opposing both the Czar and the Czar's political views, horrified him. Could a natural struggle against the enemies of society be considered a betrayal? But again, were they really enemies? Was it possible he had never lost his old tendency to rebellion? Apparently it had survived somehow. Doubts, questions, repentance over his own confusion tormented him, and he punished himself with self-accusations and self-justifications. His inner contradictions were so harrowing that he did not know what to do with himself.

Toward the end of January all this disturbance led to a ruptured lung artery and hemorrhages. They grew worse, the doctors could not stop them, and he lost consciousness time and again.

On the twenty-eighth of January he asked that the New Testament he had brought back with him from penal servitude be opened at random, and that the lines at the top of one of the open pages be read aloud: this variety of fortunetelling was something he always resorted to in times of difficulty. Anna obeyed and read aloud from St. Matthew, III: 15: "And Jesus answering said unto him, *Suffer it to be so now*: for thus it becometh us to fulfil all righteousness."

"There, you hear that," said Dostoevsky. " 'Suffer it to be so now'—that means I am going to die."

Then he called Anna to him, took her hand and whispered, "Remember, Ania, I always loved you with all my heart and have never been unfaithful to you, even in thought."

Toward evening he was no more.

BARON WRANGEL WAS NOT LIVING IN ST. PETERSBURG at the time and learned about the death of his friend only from the newspapers. He recalled the frosty morning on Semenovski Place—the first time he had seen Dostoevsky. He recalled their talks in Semipalatinsk and Maria's departure from his villa; he reread Fyodor's spluttering letters concerning Apollinaria, his tender ones about Anna; he pictured to himself all the extraordinary passions whose flame had consumed this magnificent and frightful, this frenzied and enigmatic man. At the thought that he was now lying still in his grave, that his battles, his torments and loves were over and done with forever, he broke into painful sobs.

Anna's faithfulness remained unchanged after her husband's death. In the year he died she became thirty-five, but she considered her life as a woman at an end and dedicated herself to serving his name. She published his complete works, compiled a bibliography of them in 1906 in an edition of five thousand copies, organized a division devoted to his manuscripts, mementoes and portraits at the Moscow Historical Museum, founded the Dostoevsky School in Staraya Russa, gathered together his letters and notes, made his friends write biographies of him and wrote her own recollections. She gave all the time at her disposal to organizing his rich literary legacy, and her services in this respect are undeniably great. But another factor is also undeniable: she tried to pass on to posterity only a painted-saint image of the great writer and left in the shadows everything that in her opinion might perhaps detract from his memory.

However, it must be admitted that she was not simply trying to whitewash his reputation and conceal his vices, perversions and turbulent deviations from the norm. For her he remained that endearing and good husband, simple and passionate, tender and considerate, he had so often been, and her all-forgiving, never-shaken love transformed and softened her darkest recollections. He lived in her memory as a great man who had loved only her, faithful and devoted to her heart and soul, and this was the image of him which gleamed in her waning consciousness during her last hour.

She died in the Crimea, all alone, far from her family and friends, in June, 1918—and thus went to the grave the last of the three women whom Dostoevsky had loved above all others.

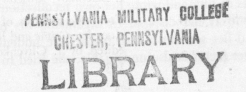

BIBLIOGRAPHY

IN RUSSIAN:

DOSTOEVSKY, F. M.   Collected Works, 12 Vols., St. Petersburg, 1894

DOSTOEVSKY, F. M.   Collected Works, 13 Vols., Moscow, 1926–1930

DOSTOEVSKY, F. M.   Letters to his wife, Moscow, 1926

DOSTOEVSKY, F. M.   Letters, Vols. 1, 2, & 3, Moscow, 1928–1934

DOSTOEVSKY, F. M.   Correspondence with Turgenev, Moscow, 1936

DOSTOEVSKY, F. M.   Notebooks, Moscow-Leningrad, 1935

DOSTOEVSKY, F. M.   Biography, letters and notes from a memorandum book, Moscow, 1883

DOSTOEVSKY, F. M.   An unpublished chapter from *The Possessed*, edited by V. L. Komarovich, *The Past*, No. 18, 1922

DOSTOEVSKY, F. M.   From the archives of F. M. Dostoevsky: *The Idiot*, unpublished material edited by P. Sakulin and I. Belchikov, Moscow, 1931

DOSTOEVSKY, F. M.   From the archives of F. M. Dostoevsky: *Crime and Punishment*, edited by I. Glivenko, Moscow, 1932

ALEXEIEV, M. P.	An Early Friend of Dostoevsky, Odessa, 1921
ALTMAN, A.	Pryzhov and Dostoevsky, *Penal Servitude and Transportation*, Nos. 81–82, 1932
ANTHONY, Most Rev.	Dictionary of Dostoevsky's Works, Sofia, 1921
ARSENIEV, K.	The Genealogy of the Dostoevskys, *Novik*, No. 2, Athens, 1934
BOEHM, A. L.	Dostoevsky, Berlin, 1938
BERDYAEV, N. A.	Dostoevsky, Berlin, 1926
BOTZYANOVSKY, V.	An Aspersion on Dostoevsky, Photostat, New York Public Library
CHIZH, V.	Dostoevsky as a Psychotic, Moscow, 1885
DOLININ, A. S.	Articles and Materials, Petrograd, 1922–1924
DOLININ, A. S.	Collection of Essays on Dostoevsky, Leningrad, 1925
DOLININ, A. S.	Studies and Documents on Dostoevsky, Leningrad, 1935
DOLININ, A. S.	Dostoevsky and Strakhov, *Literary Archives*, No. 2, Leningrad, 1939
DOLININ, A. S.	In the Creative Laboratory of a Writer, Leningrad, 1947
DOSTOEVSKAYA, A. G.	Diary, Moscow, 1923
DOSTOEVSKAYA, A. G.	Recollections, Moscow, 1925
DOSTOEVSKY, A. M.	Recollections, Leningrad, 1930
FIRSOV, N.	From the Reminiscences of a Man of the '60's. *Historical Messenger*, June 1914

G——V, B.	Dostoevsky in Semipalatinsk, *Siberian Lights*, Nos. 3 and 4, 1924, 1926.
GARSHIN, V. M.	A Ruined Life, *Historical Messenger*, February 1884
GRIGOROVICH, D. V.	Literary Reminiscences, Collected Works, Vol. 12, St. Petersburg, 1896
GROSSMAN, L.	One of Dostoevsky's Feminine Companions, *Russian Contemporary*, No. 3, 1924
GROSSMAN, L.	Bakunin in *The Possessed*, *Press And Revolution*, No. 4 & 5, 1924, No. 2, 1925
GROSSMAN, L.	Dostoevsky Seminar, Leningrad, 1923
GROSSMAN, L.	The Life and Works of Dostoevsky, Moscow, 1935
GROSSMAN, L.	Dostoevsky's Path, Leningrad, 1928
HERZEN, A. I.	Collected Works, 22 Vols., Petrograd, 1922
HIPPIUS, Z. N.	Living Faces, Vol. 2, Prague, 1922
HIPPIUS, Z. N.	Fragrance of White Hair, *Contemporary Notes*, No. 21, Paris, 1924
KNIZHNIK-VETROV, A.	A. Korvin Krukovskaya, Moscow, 1931
KONI, A. F.	Personal Recollections of Nekrassov and Dostoevsky, Petrograd, 1921
KOVALEVSKAYA, S.	Recollections, Moscow, 1945

KULIKOV, S. N. — Contributions to Dostoevsky's Biography from unpublished material, Central Historical-Military Archives, *Penal Servitude and Transportation*, No. 3, 1934

LAPSHIN, I. I. — The Aesthetics of Dostoevsky, Berlin, 1923

MEREZHKOVSKY, D. S. — Tolstoy and Dostoevsky, St. Petersburg, 1902

MILLER, O. F. — Material for a Life of Dostoevsky, Moscow, 1883

MILLER, O. F. — The Home and Study of Dostoevsky, *Historical Messenger*, No. 27, 1887

MIKULICH, V. — Meetings with Writers, Leningrad, 1929

MOCHULSKY, K. — Dostoevsky, Paris, 1947

NECHAEVA, V. S. — The Dostoevskys' Family and Their Estate, Moscow, 1939

NEKRASSOV, N. A. — Letters, edited by V. Evgeniev-Maximov, Moscow, 1930

OPOCHININ, O. — Conversations with Dostoevsky, *Links*, No. 6, 1936

PANAEVA, A. — Reminiscences, Leningrad, 1927

POCHINKOVSKAYA, O. — Record of a Visit to Dostoevsky, *The Voice of the Past*, No. 3, 1923

POLIVANOVA, M. — Working with a Famous Writer, *Historical Messenger*, February 1904

PROKHOROV, G. — Letters of Martha Brown to Dostoevsky, *Links*, No. 6, 1936

SKANDIN, A. V. — Dostoevsky in Semipalatinsk, *Historical Messenger*, No. 91, 1903

SKOBTZOVA, E.   Dostoevsky and Our Time, Paris, 1929

SOLOVYEV, V. S.   Works, Vol. 5, Moscow, 1903

SOLOVYEV, V. S.   Recollections of Dostoevsky, *Historical Messenger*, March 1881

SHTAKENSCHNEIDER, E.   Some Reminiscences of Dostoevsky, *The Voice of the Past*, February 1916

STEINBERG, Z.   Dostoevsky in London, Paris, 1932

STRAKHOV, N. N.   Recollections of Dostoevsky, St. Petersburg, 1883

STREICH, S.   The Korvin Krukovski Sisters, Moscow, 1934

STREICH, S.   Dostoevsky and Korvin Krukovskaya, *Red Virgin Soil*, No. 7, 1931

SUSLOVA, A. P.   Diary, Moscow, 1928

THEOKTISTOV, N.   The Lost Letters of Dostoevsky, *Siberian Lights*, No. 2, 1928

TOLSTOY, L. N.   Correspondence with Strakhov, Petrograd, 1924

TRUTOVSKY, K.   Recollections of Dostoevsky, *Russian Survey*, 1893

VERESSAEV, V. V.   The Living Life, Moscow, 1911

VETRINSKY, C.   Dostoevsky in the Reminiscences, Letters and Notes of His Contemporaries, Moscow, 1912

VOLOTZKOY, M. V.   Chronicle of the Dostoevsky Lineage, Leningrad, 1933

Von VOGT, N. N.   A Contribution to the Biography of Dostoevsky, *Historical Messenger*, No. 12, 1914

WRANGEL, A. K. Recollections of Dostoevsky in Siberia, St. Petersburg, 1912

YAKUSHKIN, E. A. Letter to His Son, *The Little Light*, No. 46, 1946

  Also articles and notes *passim* in various issues of *Literary Heritage*, Moscow, 1934–1955, of *Press and Revolution*, Moscow 1924–1926, of *Bulletins of Literature and Life*, St. Petersburg, 1910–1915, and in *The Creative Path of Dostoevsky*, a collection of essays edited by M. Brodsky, Leningrad, 1924.

IN VARIOUS LANGUAGES:

ABRAHAM, G. Dostoevsky, London, 1936

CARR, E. H. Dostoevsky, Boston, 1931

MEIER-GRAEFE, J. Dostoevsky, the Man and His Work, New York, 1928

RAE, I. The Breath of Corruption, London, n.d.

SIMMONS, E. J. Dostoevsky, the Making of a Novelist, New York, 1940

TROYAT, H. The Firebrand; the Life of Dostoevsky, New York, 1946

YARMOLINSKY, A. Dostoevsky, a Life, New York, 1934

ZWEIG, S. Three Masters, New York, 1930

BERCOVICI, L. Dostoievski, Etude de psychopathologie, Paris, 1933

GIDE, A. Dostoievski, Paris, 1925

LOYGUES, P. G. La Maladie de Dostoievski, Lyon, 1913

DONNINI, D. Dostojevski Vivente, Firenze, 1936

MOSCARDELLI, N.   Dostojevski, Modena, 1941

DOSTOEVSKAYA, A.   Dostojewski Geschildert von
                                Seiner Tochter, Muenchen, 1920

FREUD, S.   Dostojewski und die Vatertoe-
                                tung (in *Die Urgestalt der Bruder
                                Karamazoff*, Muenchen, 1928)

MUELLER, Rene Fuelop,   Der Unbekannte Dostojewski,
und ECKSTEIN, F.   Muenchen, 1926

NEUFELD, J.   Dostojewski, Skizze zu einer
                                Psychoanalyse, Wien-Zuerich-
                                Leipzig, 1925

NOETZEL, K.   Das Leben Dostojewski's, Leipzig,
                                1925

Articles and notes in various French, German, Italian, British and
American periodicals, as well as introductions to Dostoevsky's
works, are not listed in this Bibliography.